Reported Missing
in the Great War

Other books by John Broom

Faithful in Adversity: The Royal Army Medical Corps in the Second World War (Pen & Sword Military, 2019)

Opposition to the Second World War: Conscience, Resistance & Service in Britain 1933–45 (Pen & Sword Military, 2018)

A History of Cigarette and Trade Cards: The Magic Inside the Packet (Pen & Sword History, 2018)

Fight the Good Fight: Voices of Faith from the Second World War (Pen & Sword Military, 2016)

Fight the Good Fight: Voices of Faith from the First World War (Pen & Sword Military, 2015)

Reported Missing in the Great War

100 Years of Searching for the Truth

John Broom

Pen & Sword
MILITARY

First published in Great Britain in 2020 and reprinted in 2021 by
Pen & Sword Military
An imprint of
Pen & Sword Books Ltd
Yorkshire – Philadelphia

Copyright © John Broom 2020, 2021

ISBN 978 1 52674 951 2

Typeset by Mac Style
Printed and bound in the UK by CPI Group (UK) Ltd, Croydon, CR0
4YY

FSC
www.fsc.org
MIX
Paper from
responsible sources
FSC® C013604

Pen & Sword Books Limited incorporates the imprints of Atlas,
Archaeology, Aviation, Discovery, Family History, Fiction, History,
Maritime, Military, Military Classics, Politics, Select, Transport,
True Crime, Air World, Frontline Publishing, Leo Cooper, Remember
When, Seaforth Publishing, The Praetorian Press, Wharncliffe
Local History, Wharncliffe Transport, Wharncliffe True Crime
and White Owl.

For a complete list of Pen & Sword titles please contact

PEN & SWORD BOOKS LIMITED
47 Church Street, Barnsley, South Yorkshire, S70 2AS, England
E-mail: enquiries@pen-and-sword.co.uk
Website: www.pen-and-sword.co.uk

Or

PEN AND SWORD BOOKS
1950 Lawrence Rd, Havertown, PA 19083, USA
E-mail: Uspen-and-sword@casematepublishers.com
Website: www.penandswordbooks.com

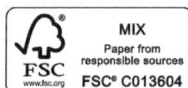

Contents

Acknowledgements

The following experts on aspects of family, local, regional and military history were generous with their advice: Alison Crampin, Linda Parker, James Uzzell, Peter Bayliss, Barry Blades, Paul Bishop, David Blanchard, Peter Bennett, Dan Hill (www.danhillmilitaryhistory.com), and Paul Reed. Staff at the West Yorkshire Archive and University of Leeds Special Collections provided a swift, friendly and efficient service.

Relatives of First World War soldiers granted me the privilege of viewing precious family archives in order to honour the sacrifices of their ancestors: Dan Donnelly, Philip Donnelly, Mark Doherty, Mark Gallagher, Steve Storey, Matthew Pawson, Peter Simpson, Mike Irwin, Melanie Baldry, Rosemary Gregory, Rosemary Phillips, Nick Previté, Oliver Pope, Chris Mead, Steve Storey, Jacqueline Wadsworth, and Robin Williams.

To the memory of Maurice Stokes, whose final major contribution to public life was the co-ordination of the campaign to restore the memorial of Private George Wallace Jackson.

Dedication

In gratitude to William Broom and John Broom, my grandfather and father, whose lives were mercifully spared in twentieth-century warfare. In hope that Rosa, Sophia and David never experience the sadness of total warfare. And to Dawn for her support and presence throughout all this.

Foreword

In the 1990s I lived in a small village in the heart of the old Somme battlefields. A former front-line trench ran through my garden, and in the fields within just a mile from my front door, more than 6,000 soldiers had gone missing in 1916 alone. As I spent the years walking that ground, even just working in my garden, the evidence of those missing men would frequently surface; everything from a tiny fragment of human bone to the complete remains of soldiers. The Commonwealth War Graves Commission treated all of these with rightful reverence, and I found myself attending the funerals of soldiers who had died half a century before I was born. It was clear, the history of the Great War was far from a closed book.

These experiences more than anything demonstrated to me how the cruel hand of war between 1914 and 1918 robbed soldiers of a decent burial and created a new and terrible consequence on such a vast scale for the families of those who had 'no known grave'. It brought to mind the Great War veterans I had interviewed who recalled how men had sunk in the mud, hung on the wire for months, and when attempts were made to reclaim and rebury them, the task was all but impossible. Reg Glenn, a veteran of the Sheffield City Battalion – the Sheffield Pals – saw his mates die on 1 July 1916 and helped the padre finally bury them in the spring of 1917. In finding them he later remarked, 'I don't fear death, as I have seen Hell.'

This extraordinary book by John Broom transports us into the dark heart of the grief and the torment experienced by the families of these missing soldiers. We learn of the famous who had missing sons; Rudyard Kipling feeling that he had somehow betrayed his son, missing at the Battle of Loos, by sending him so easily to war. We hear of those who turned to the supernatural, like Sir Arthur Conan Doyle, in a hope to reconnect with that lost life. Others never stopped searching, and one of the most tragic photographs in the book is that of Amy Lott, sitting in a shattered Delville Wood, while trying to make sense of what had happened to her brother, missing in October 1916. The uncertainty haunted them all their lives, and women like Amy were as much casualties of the Great War as those they lost.

For many the cruellest stroke in the story of the missing was Hope: hope that somehow, these men were still alive and might return. The parents of Lieutenant John Butt clung on to fragments of words that might indicate he was a prisoner in Germany, when instead he lay in a shallow, unmarked grave at Ypres. The sister of Arthur Greensmith, whose stories weave throughout this book, even wrote him a letter after the attack in which he had been posted missing, but it was returned unopened by the War Office. Hope beyond hope, which extended into the post-war world when the names of men like Arthur were added to the great Memorials to the Missing.

The stories of how the battlefields were cleared, and the extraordinary lengths the Graves Registration Units and the Imperial War Graves Commission went to in an attempt to recover unidentified bodies discovered on the battlefields, is both spine-chilling and deeply moving. And we learn that it is work that continues to this day.

More and more as I continue to walk the battlefields of the Great War, I find myself drawn to the graves of those 'Known Unto God'. Who were they, what were their hopes and fears, dreams and desires? This book brings them alive again, they live once more in John Broom's words, and I recall that time in the 1980s in a cemetery on the Somme when I saw a veteran kneel at the grave of an Unknown Soldier and whisper softly to him, 'Son, we owe you a lot.'

Paul Reed
Elsecar, South Yorkshire

Glossary

AIF	Australian Imperial Force
AOC	Army Ordnance Corps
ARCS	Australian Red Cross Society
BEF	British Expeditionary Force
CCS	Casualty Clearing Station
CEF	Canadian Expeditionary Force
CRS	Camp Reception Station
CWGC	Commonwealth War Graves Commission
DGR&E	Directorate of Graves Registration and Enquiries
EFC	Expeditionary Force Canteen
FA	Field Ambulance
GOC	General Officer Commanding
GRC	Graves Registration Commission
GRU	Graves Registration Unit
HMAT	His Majesty's Australian Transport
IWGC	Imperial War Graves Commission
JCCC	Joint Casualty and Compassionate Centre
KRRC	King's Royal Rifle Corps
MO	Medical Officer
MOD	Ministry of Defence
OTC	Officers' Training Corps
QAIMNS	Queen Alexandra's Imperial Military Nursing Service
QUB	Queen's University Belfast
RAMC	Royal Army Medical Corps
RAP	Regimental Aid Post
RMF	Royal Munster Fusiliers
RMFA	Royal Munster Fusiliers Association
RMO	Regimental Medical Officer
SLI	Somerset Light Infantry
VAD	Voluntary Aid Detachment
WDRC	Wolverhampton and District Recruiting Committee

Prologue

'It is not the length of existence that counts, but what is achieved during that existence, however short.'

On Friday, 23 April 1915, almost 5,000 mourners thronged the narrow streets of the small Flintshire town of Hawarden to pay their respects as the bier carrying the coffin containing the body of Lieutenant William Glynne Charles Gladstone MP made its way down from Hawarden Castle to the parish church of St Deiniol. Twenty-nine-year-old Lieutenant Gladstone, grandson of the eminent Victorian Prime Minister, was the second Member of Parliament to have been killed in action during the war. When Britain entered the war in August 1914, Will, as Lord Lieutenant of Flintshire, was active in the county's recruitment campaign. Despite admitting 'far from having the least inclination for military service, I dread and dislike it intensely', he set an example by enlisting, and was commissioned as a second lieutenant in the 3rd Battalion of the Royal Welch Fusiliers. Will left for France on 15 March 1915, joining his battalion on the Ypres Salient six days later. His first experience of front-line service came on 11 April. He was concerned his inexperience would endanger the lives of his men, writing to his mother, 'I rather dread the work, because I am so unfamiliar with it, and one will omit things through innocence which are essential to the safety of one's men.'

Will's war service would be short-lived. On 13 April he was shot in the forehead by a rifle bullet near Laventie, France, while trying to locate a German sniper. He lived for two hours after receiving the mortal wound. Second Lieutenant Lynch of 1st Battalion Royal Welch Fusiliers,

Lieutenant William Glynne Charles Gladstone MP. (*Author's collection*)

Lieutenant William Kelsey Fry RAMC and Corporal Welsh evacuated the injured Will from the front-line trench and strove in vain to save his life. Initially, Will's body was buried close to where he had fallen but nine days later, by special permission of King George V, it was disinterred and brought by Lieutenant Fry to Boulogne. Here Fry was met by Mr Henry Neville Gladstone, Will's uncle, who accompanied the body to Southampton, thence via Chester to Hawarden Castle.

For four days the corpse lay on a small platform in the former study of W.E. Gladstone, a room known as the 'Temple of Peace'. At the head of the coffin a cross was placed and the same pall that had covered the late Prime Minister's coffin was draped across. On Thursday, 22 April, a short family service was held in the 'Temple'. This was followed by a procession of family, friends and parishioners who had been granted permission to file past the coffin.

The following day's proceedings commenced with an early morning Eucharist in St Deiniol's. The rector, the Reverend F.S.M. Bennett, paid tribute to the young squire, quoting a letter written by Will to his mother just a week before his death: 'Really, you will be wrong if you regret my going, for I am very glad and proud to have got to the front. It is not the length of existence that counts, but what is achieved during that existence, however short.'

The rector went on to pay his own tribute:

> We who knew him, knew that he wrote the words quite simply and meaning exactly what he said. His life and his death alike expressed the power of his conviction. Pure in heart and single-eyed to duty, just and tenacious of his purpose, charming in his manner and sound in his judgement, he combined wonderfully a delightful modesty and gentleness of youth with the wisdom and firmness of much mature years. In his presence no one spoke a wrong word or spoke evil of his neighbour, or told a lie. … He was a power for good.

Bennett noted the heavy death toll among junior officers and that Gladstone had been killed while reconnoitring on behalf of his men. Drawing from John's gospel a phrase that would be used in countless epitaphs, he proclaimed that Will's life was 'less than thirty years, but sealed with the love than which no man hath greater, he laid down his life for his friends'.

In the afternoon an imposing foot procession accompanied the body from Hawarden Castle to its final resting place at St Deiniol's. It included members of the Gladstone family, military officers including Second Lieutenant Lynch and Lieutenant Fry, who had been with Gladstone when he died, magistrates, police, county and parish councillors, churchwardens, political and religious leaders, estate workers and teachers from the parish school. Once it reached the town's main street it was met by a large assembly of people. Blinds were drawn across Hawarden windows as flags flew at half mast.

On reaching the church, about 100 members of the Royal Welch Fusiliers stood on either side of the road, with arms reversed and heads bowed. The bier carrying the coffin, draped in the Union flag, was wheeled into the church. Inside, the mourners were met by many local clergy, including the Bishop of St Asaph, A.G. Edwards. As the procession moved up the aisle, Psalm 39 was chanted. The church was packed with 500 mourners who had each been issued a ticket by the Hawarden Estate Office. The lesson from 1 Corinthians 15:20 was read before the choir gave a rendition of 'Blest are the departed'. Following prayers and the singing of 'For all the saints, who from their labours rest', the organist played the 'Dead March' from *Saul* as the coffin was removed to the graveside.

Further litanies and prayers were said before the coffin was lowered into a grave lined with evergreens from Hawarden Park. A firing party sounded off a volley and a bugler played the 'Last Post' before the mourners withdrew.

As Lieutenant Gladstone had held the position of Lord Lieutenant of Flintshire, King George V, as the *Flintshire Observer* reported, 'showed his kindliness by giving sanction for the body to be brought home'. Whilst carrying the heavy burden of mourning the loss of Will, the Gladstone family were privileged in ways that were to be denied to hundreds of thousands of other families during the war: firstly, they had a definitive eyewitness account of the circumstances of his death; secondly, there was a body to bury in a grave at which they could continue to mourn his passing; finally, that grave was close to the family home.

But what of those families who were to receive the dreaded telegram that their loved one was 'missing'? Families for whom there was no body to be buried, much less brought back home. Where would they mourn? Even when a man had been buried in a marked grave by his comrades, there was a high risk that it could be obliterated by shelling, or its location ceded to the enemy in the ebb and flow of war.

Will Gladstone's return to Hawarden, although providing some form of closure for his family, caused disquiet amongst the wider British public. The previous month, Marshal Joffre, Commander of French forces on the Western Front, had prohibited battlefield exhumations. Part of his rationale was that such disinterments, which had amounted to a few dozen in the war's early months, produced a health hazard. For Fabian Ware, who would later form and lead the Imperial War Graves Commission, such ad hoc repatriations of the deceased created the impression at home that officers and men were unequal in death. Ware would secure, the following year, an order from the Adjutant

General banning future repatriations, to ensure equality in death as in sacrifice. The ban was needed 'on account of the difficulties of treating impartially the claims advanced by persons of different social standing'. This decision applied the principle that was to become the very core of the Imperial War Graves Commission: parity of memorialisation.

This book tells the story of families thrown into paroxysms of anxiety at the news their loved one had gone missing. Families for whom equality of sacrifice could never be realised as there would be no post-war grave at which to mourn their loss. It relates the work of the searching agencies who strove to bring news, good or bad, that would allow this anxiety to transition into relief or mourning. But most of all, it tells of the lengths that households would go to in order to feel at one with their men's final moments, and the days, months, years and decades over which precious memories of the lost would be curated and commemorated.

Chapter 1

Searching for the Missing

'It is depressing in a way, for if one does get news about the missing it is generally bad news.'

Bereavement was a near-universal phenomenon in wartime Britain. Virtually every street, workplace, church, chapel and sporting club lost a friend or colleague. For the first time, the British Army was mostly composed of volunteers and conscripts rather than professional soldiers. No longer could death be treated as an incidental loss. The public demanded individual recognition of the worth of each human life, thus a soldier could not be merely written off as 'missing', his family left in extended limbo as to his fate. An attempt had to be made to trace his whereabouts, dead or alive.

Around half the men killed in action serving in the British and Commonwealth armies were to remain unidentified or unidentifiable, either being laid to rest in graves under the inscription 'Known unto God', or their bodies being destroyed to the extent that no remains were ever recovered. The maelstrom of battle frequently obviated against a sustained attempt to relate the mass of body parts to an individual identity tag. Burial parties often had to work quickly, and under the cover of darkness. For many bereaved families this left an aching hole, craving precise knowledge of the circumstances of death and a desire to have an identified resting place where respects might be paid by family members at a future date. The word 'presumed' also allowed space for hope. Perhaps the man had been taken prisoner? Or lost behind enemy lines? Or wounded and in the care of a civilian?

All belligerent countries had organisations that sought to provide answers to these questions by attempting to trace soldiers who had been reported as missing. For the British and Commonwealth armies, the Joint War Committee of the British Red Cross and Order of St John's Wounded and Missing Enquiry Bureau was the most prominent. The Bureau had been established in the autumn of 1914 by a group of Paris-based British Red Cross volunteers. Its leader was 50-year-old Lord Robert Cecil, the deeply devout Vicar-General to the Archbishop of York.

Initially, the Bureau restricted itself to providing information to the families of missing officers. However, news of the service soon spread, and the Paris office became inundated with requests from families of soldiers of all ranks. Therefore, organisation was expanded and by the end of the war, the Bureau had establishments spread across the European mainland and the Middle East, with a London central office, established in April 1915, co-ordinating the work. Three months later, in July, the War Office designated the Red Cross the single officially sanctioned search organisation in Britain.

Often a search would begin by a volunteer visiting one of the hundreds of convalescent hospitals spread across Britain, armed with lists of the missing issued by the War Office, to ascertain if any of the patients could shed light on the fate of those men. Occasionally, volunteers struck lucky, and a man declared missing would be reported to be in an Allied or enemy military hospital. Often, a missing man might be found to have been taken as a prisoner of war. Notwithstanding these successes, most findings reported by the Bureau to anxious families were melancholy. As the novelist E.M. Forster, working as a volunteer for the British Red Cross in Alexandria, Egypt, recorded, 'It is depressing in a way, for if one does get news about the missing it is generally bad news.'

In such cases the findings served to end the anxiety of those whose menfolk had disappeared, enabling the family to move on to the next stage of their grieving process. Tracing the fate of a missing man was a complex and frustrating process. Searchers would tour hospital wards and convalescent homes, speaking to patients who may have been serving alongside the missing. The task was frequently frustrating. Frank Pulsford, an Australian searcher, estimated that only five patients out of a hundred approached in this manner provided useful information. Bureau members would also write to prisoners of war asking for similar intelligence. The War Office provided questionnaires that could be despatched to prison camps then returned via neutral intermediaries. Finally, Red Cross searchers conducted interviews at base camps and depots and would write to men on active service to mine the seams of their first-hand knowledge.

Once the information collected by the searchers had been recorded, their reports were submitted to the London headquarters, where staff would analyse each contribution for its veracity and worth. In the confusion and terror of battle, men often had partial and conflicting memories, leaving Bureau volunteers to assemble the inconsistent available information into a best fit picture of a man's final moments. Therefore, searchers would often ask questions about a missing man's appearance and request as detailed a narrative as possible about the circumstances of disappearance, in order to be able to corroborate varying testimonies. A post-war report by the Joint War Committee emphasised the level of detail that searchers had to elicit:

It should be remembered that the searcher's report may be the only news ever received by the family. It is therefore necessary to get from the informant all the circumstances as far as they affect the missing man. Moreover, these details are very important tests of the accuracy of the informant's story. The report has to be read in London and its value decided upon by someone who has not had the advantage of seeing [the] informant. A report which only says, 'I saw X killed in the attack at Messines Ridge in June' is a bad one, for it follows that [the] informant could have told more if had been asked. He should have been asked how far he was away, in what part of the body X was hit, how he fell, if he moved or spoke after he fell, if [the] informant saw him dead, if they were progressing or retiring at the time, who held the ground, and what became of the body.

Despite the assiduousness with which many enquiries were undertaken, testimony often proved ambiguous and inconsistent. The time that had to be spent by the volunteers in London reconciling this conflicting evidence would lead to a hold-up in reporting back to families desperate for information. The view was rightly taken than delayed information was better than incorrect intelligence. One volunteer, Granville Barker, wrote, 'little by little the contradictions are sifted down and good evidence built up. The stark facts will appear quite suddenly sometimes.' Only when volunteers were satisfied that the best possible account had been formulated, would details be forwarded to next of kin.

Sometimes, the reports were so contradictory they proved impossible to reconcile and both were sent to the family. Private Herbert Cochrane of the 10th Battalion AIF had been reported missing at Gallipoli in May 1915. One report stated he had been cut in half by a shell while standing upright in a trench sending semaphore signals on 2 May, whilst another said he had been seen lying ill, vomiting in a trench, in September 1915. Similarly, the family of Corporal Kenton Moore of the 52nd Battalion of the AIF, deemed to have been killed on 11 April 1917 on the Somme, was sent, in December that year, the full text of conflicting reports with an accompanying letter stating, 'We regret that the foregoing reports are contradictory and that no definite tidings have been obtained. However, we thought you would be anxious to have every particular which comes to hand.'

Sometimes, no report on a man's death could be elicited. In such instances, Bureau staff would compile a general account of the action in which he had disappeared. Such reports had to emphasise the ferocity of the fighting so that families would be left in no doubt that their loved one was dead. Before being issued, reports were subject to army censors attached to the British Red

Cross Society, although *The Times* reported that the Bureau was 'unfettered by official restrictions' and that 'Direct communication between the Department and inquirers remains undisturbed'. A memorandum issued to Australian Red Cross Society Bureau staff advised on the semantics of reporting in a sensitive manner. A report from the field that stated a man had been 'blown to bits' should be translated to 'killed by a shell', and 'buried in a trench by a shell' should be given as 'killed by shell fire'.

Despite this advice, the occasional insensitive phrase managed to slip through the net. In early January 1917, ARCS volunteers in Queensland responded to an enquiry from Annie Winifred Black about the fate of her son, Sergeant John Victor Black of 26th Battalion AIF. Nothing had been heard of him since his disappearance at Pozières in August 1916. Mrs Black learned that her son had been killed by a shell explosion in no man's land during a charge against German defences. The report stated he had been 'blown to pieces … J.V. Black's head [was] blown off by a shell'.

Furious at the candour with which the Queensland Red Cross had relayed the news about her son, Annie Black complained to the Department of Defence in Melbourne, stating that such a 'brutal copy' of a volunteer's report ought not to have been sent to her: 'For the benefit of the poor mothers, I tell you this in order to try and impose on you that many women would die of shock or go insane when such frightening news arrived.' Annie's complaint was escalated, and after months of robust correspondence between the Defence Department, the Australian Red Cross Society and the Queensland Red Cross, a letter was circulated to individual Australian state bureaux advising that 'greater care might be exercised in sending out reports to relatives in crude form'. However, this remained a suggestion rather than an instruction, and individual bureaux continued to have the jurisdiction to edit or retain information gathered in the field as they saw fit.

Indeed, subsequent communications continued to contain phrases of a graphic nature. One enquirer was told his friend had been killed when a shell penetrated his back and went right through his body. The mother of Private Charles Baker was told that her son had been killed when working on a wiring fatigue in no man's land, having been 'riddled with bullets'. Although such terminology might have appeared harsh, it served to convey the reality of modern warfare, and the absolute certainty of the soldier's death.

For some families, the absence of a known grave gave a faint hope that their relative might somehow have survived. This scope for doubt had to be shut down as far as possible by written communications issued by the Bureau, even if this meant conveying the stark truths of war to wartime civilians. Granville Barker wrote:

We want to know that a shell 'blew this man to pieces so that burial was impossible', that this other man 'was hit in the stomach on May 9 and he crawled into a shell hole and has never been seen since'. We want to understand that 'the pond was in some places quite deep up to our necks. Many men were wounded and went under and were drowned.'

In contrast to Annie Black, many relatives were grateful to have been provided the most horrendous of details, to be able to share in some way their man's final moments.

Family searches
Some families were fortunate enough to be able to venture close to the front line to search for clues as to the fate of their loved one. Sir Lionel Earle, a senior civil servant, crossed the English Channel in the autumn of 1914 searching for news of his brother, Lieutenant Colonel Maxwell Earle, commanding officer 1st Battalion Grenadier Guards, who had been wounded at Gheluvelt during the First Battle of Ypres on 29 October 1914. It had been reported that Maxwell had last been seen on the Menin Road lying on the ground with a bullet in his head and a human eye resting on his cheek.

Lionel heard many rumours of his brother's fate; variously that he was dead in Frankfurt, having been captured by the Germans, or that he had been taken with a mass of German wounded to the Town Hall at Courtrai, where he had been spotted lying on a bed of straw. After many fruitless weeks, Maxwell's wife, Edith, received an unsigned letter requesting that she attend a chapel in London's East End at a certain time and date, where she would receive news of her husband. On Lionel's advice, she went to what she thought was the empty tabernacle, where she spied a man whom she thought resembled a clergyman, who handed her a note. Lionel recalled:

> This was a line from my brother, saying he was in hospital and suffering terribly in his head. This clergyman was a Swiss and was walking one day in Brussels with a small grip in his hand, when a girl came up to him and asked if he was going home on a journey. 'Yes,' he replied, 'to England.' Upon which she slipped a note into his hand, addressed to my sister-in-law.

From the note, Earle's family were able to learn not only that he was alive, if not particularly well, but something of the circumstances regarding his wounding and capture.

> My brother's wounds were more severe, even than we had thought, as after the bullet had gone clean through his head, the regimental doctor

was binding up his head, when the Germans surrounded them, blew the brains of the doctor, although unarmed and covered with the Red Cross, all over my brother's face, and the [medical] orderly was killed at close range by a rifle bullet, which after passing through the poor man's stomach, passed all down the leg of my brother, infecting the whole leg with Bacillus coli.

Lionel reckoned that Maxwell had been spared as his rank meant that he might prove a valuable asset to the Germans in any future prisoner exchange. Having managed to get news of his survival to his family, Maxwell Earle was subsequently able to provide details to the family of Lieutenant John Butt RAMC, the medical officer killed while dressing his wounds, of the circumstances of his death.

Whilst Maxwell Earle's brother and wife had received news directly from him via a surreptitious route, other families received news from a decidedly unexpected source. Bertha Buck, wife of Private Percy Buck of 1st Hertfordshire Regiment, was shocked to receive a letter from a German soldier in October 1917. After a year and a half of home service training new recruits in rifle skills, Percy had volunteered for overseas service on 10 January 1916, landing in Boulogne on 25 November that year. On 7 December, Percy joined the battalion at Ypres. Known affectionately as the 'Herts Guards', the 1st Battalion was involved in minor skirmishes until July 1917, when they were assigned, along with the rest of 118th Brigade, to the front line as the Third Battle of Ypres began.

Percy was killed a little before 12.30 pm on 31 July 1917 as the remnants of the 1st Herts fell back in the face of a German counter-attack. Of the 620 officers and men who had begun an attack at 10.00 am, no officer and only 130 other ranks returned. The scale of destruction was summed up in a conversation between battalion Quartermaster Sergeant Gordon Fisher, who had arrived with rations for 620 men, and the brigadier general commanding 118th Brigade: 'I said to the general "excuse me Sir, I can't seem to find the Hertfordshire Regiment". He looked at me for a while and then said "I'm sorry Quarters, there is no Hertfordshire Regiment."'

On 10 August, Mrs Bertha Buck received the dreaded telegram informing her that Percy was missing. Two months of anxiety was ended when a letter, dated 8 October 1917, was delivered to Bertha via the British Section of the International Red Cross in Geneva. Enclosed was a photograph of her and her child. How had the Red Cross managed to come across this picture? The letter explained that the photograph had been forwarded to them by a Josef Wilczek, a German soldier, along with an account of how he had acquired it:

I beg to enclose a Post Card, which I took from a British soldier in Flandres. He was holding the card in his hand, and, as I learnt later on, that the finder was asked to forward it to his wife. I wishing to fulfil the last will of the dead comrade, send it to you with the request to forward it to his wife. The address is written on it. He fell on 31st July or 1st Aug near St. Julien in Flandres.

May he rest in peace. I should be very pleased to hear whether the wife has received the card.

Bertha was not yet ready to accept the finality of her husband's demise. Supported by Percy's parents, John and Elizabeth, she sought further information. Official notification from the War Office on 5 December 1917 that they considered Percy as having been killed in action on 31 July did not satiate her thirst for further news. On 11 March 1918, John Buck received a letter from the man who had served as the 1st Herts's chaplain during Passchendaele, Captain Alfred Edgar Popham, MC and Bar. Recalling that Percy had been reported missing, Popham informed John:

He was a great friend of mine. ... I can remember him so well: he was in 15 Platoon. Time after time he would be the first in church and would give me a hand. ... He gave me the impression of being a reliable man. Dear fellow I am sorry he has been officially returned as killed, as he was a good soldier and I am sure a good son to you.

The Buck family also sought the support of the Joint War Committee Bureau. One of its volunteers had interviewed a Private Ramsell, at the time convalescing in a hospital in France. Ramsell was able to provide a definitive account of Percy's final moments:

He was in my platoon and we went over the top together soon after dawn – about 5.30 on July 31st. It was the St Julien front.

We advanced too far and as it was against machine gun fire aimed low, we had a lot of casualties and had to retire. Our men were falling all round and had no time to pick our wounded. I did not see him [Percy] hit, but several other fellows did. He was hit in the side and fell into a shell hole. He was too severely wounded to move.

He showed me a photo of his wife and child the night before. On the back of it he had written his wife's address, and the words – 'Whoever finds this please forward' – or words like it. We never saw him again and his body was never found. ... Whether he was taken prisoner or died where he fell, and a German found the photograph, we never heard. Our belief was that he was too badly wounded to live.

Sadly, Josef Wilczek, the German soldier who had showed so much compassion in ensuring Percy's postcard had reached Bertha, missed surviving the war and returning to his own family by a mere twelve days, being killed in action on 31 October 1918.

In the case of Lieutenant James 'Jack' Brewster, communication from an enemy soldier brought joyous news. Jack had been fighting with the 3rd Battalion Royal Fusiliers during the First Battle of Ypres in the spring of 1915 when he was reported as 'missing'. Captain James Laird, a fellow officer of Jack's, wrote to James and Eliza Brewster, explaining he was attempting to ascertain the fate of their son. Laird described the circumstances in which Jack had gone missing. The regiment to the right of the 3rd Royal Fusiliers had been attacked and one of their men, seeing his own bad plight, had yelled out 'Fusiliers, attack'. Jack heard this cry and assumed it had come via his own battalion commanders. He therefore rushed forward before his own men were ready to support him. Laird reported, 'He consequently got no support and was last seen rushing towards the German trenches.' In a reversal of the usual channels of enquiry, Laird asked Mr and Mrs Brewster if they had received any news of his 'greatest friend' as he was 'desperately anxious to know something definite about him'.

As Captain Laird and Brewster's parents began to give up hope of ever seeing Jack alive, a surprise letter arrived at the latter's Regent's Park abode from Sergeant Egbert Wagner, a German soldier of the 25th Jaeger Regiment. Wagner, writing on 20 May, nine days after the attack that had led to Jack's disappearance, was able to give a detailed account of his fate. Jack had got to within 15 yards of the enemy trench when a bullet had splintered his femur. He had managed to pull himself into a small pond to avoid enemy fire, binding his broken leg to his good one with bayonets taken from the dead who surrounded him to act as splints.

Showing tremendous pluck, Jack had then dragged himself back across the shell holes that pockmarked no man's land, bypassing the wounded and dead. He managed to make 200 yards of ground before falling into a narrow ditch, and thence into an exhausted deep sleep. As he slumbered, the Germans passed over him and took the British trenches, so Jack awoke to find himself behind the German lines and in enemy hands.

Christian faith was a leitmotif that had sent men to war with the righteous anger of the Old Testament blood coursing through their veins, but it had also influenced men and women to follow the teaching of Jesus found in Matthew 5:44 to 'Love thine enemy'. Fortunately for James and Eliza Brewster, Sergeant Wagner's faith was of the latter strain. He wrote:

On 11th of this month, through God's gracious guiding hand, I was led to discover your son, Lieutenant JA Brender [*sic*], 3rd Royal Fusiliers, in a shell hole, where he had been lying for two days with a gun shot wound in the upper part of his thigh. Acting on the command of our Lord Jesus 'Love your Enemies' I bandaged him with the permission of our officer, and provided him with bread and wine. I had a lot of conversation with your dear son, whose condition visibly improved by evening. With eight of our brave Riflemen I arranged to get him conveyed, with the assistance of some medical staff, back from our front line position to the collecting centre for the wounded. There I handed over your dear son to the care of [the] best and competent hands, and now carry out my promise give to your son, when we were lying so happily together in the shell-hole, in spite of the rain of bullets, that I would communicate his deliverance to his dear father. I offer you my earnest wish for peace and await your reply via Denmark.

Sergeant Egbert Wagner

Wagner had sent the letter to a friend, Axel Backhausen, for him to forward it to England with the request that any reply be relayed back to Wagner's battalion. Mr James Brewster did write a reply, confirming their 'great relief' at the news, thinking that Sergeant Wagner 'must be a very good man. …We trust he may live to do other good work in the world for such men are badly needed in these terrible times.' Indeed, Mr Brewster went so far as to extend the impact of Wagner's Christian charity by forwarding his letter to friends: 'I hope you will forgive me for granting their requests. I believe, in some cases, it will be used as a text for sermons next Sunday.' Lieutenant Jack Brewster was taken into captivity, but due to the severity of his wounds, was sent to internment in Switzerland before being repatriated in September 1917.

A belated merciful deliverance from the belief of death was provided to a Sunderland family. Bombardier George H. Hope of the Royal Garrison Artillery's 120 Siege Battery was taken prisoner at Essigny on 21 March 1918. His disappearance was reported to his mother-in-law, Mrs M. Robinson of Ashbrook, Sunderland. George was eventually registered to Stendal PoW camp, but many captured soldiers registered to that camp, 460 miles away, were actually kept in France due to the logistical difficulties of taking such a large number of new prisoners across to Germany. He later told his granddaughter that he was the only man left in a trench, where he stayed down for an extended period of time. He heard someone calling 'George, George are you there?' so came up from the trench to be faced by German soldiers.

As George probably never arrived at Stendal, the Red Cross was initially not informed of his capture. Therefore, his wife Nellie assumed that his missing status, allied to the lack of news, meant he was dead. She gave up the family home to move in with relatives, anticipating a life of penurious struggle. George recounted that he supplemented his sustenance by exchanging his cigarette allowance from Red Cross parcels for the black bread that was supplied. He later told his granddaughter that he managed to escape from captivity, surviving for a week by plucking apples from trees until his recapture. Eventually, word reached the family that George was alive and would be returning home. Upon his release, his family, including his 4-year-old daughter, also named Nellie, had gone to Sunderland railway station to meet him, only to discover that he had caught an earlier train and was waiting for them at home. George was slowly nursed back to full strength by Nellie, apart from the loss of his hearing, destroyed by the constant boom of his siege battery guns.

For some families, the status of 'missing' regarding a loved one was a mercifully short-lived phenomenon. Private George Pittaway, a native of the Yorkshire maritime port of Kingston upon Hull, had previously been badly wounded at the Second Battle of Ypres in April 1915 while serving in the 4th Battalion of the East Yorkshire Regiment. George's younger brother Alfred had perished in late April as the battalion came under heavy gas and shellfire, his official date of death being recorded as 30 April. George was with Alfred when he died, but his body was never recovered. After a period of convalescence, George was transferred to the 2nd Northumberland Fusiliers, complete with his brass wound stripe on his left cuff.

Having lost one son in action, George (senior) and Ada Pittaway were to be subjected to the intense anxiety of having another son reported missing. Living in the tightly knit community of Sharp Street in the Newland Avenue area of Hull, the Pittaways shared the sense of loss with their neighbours. On 8 May 1917, a street shrine was erected containing the names of twenty-one men who had already perished and 121 others serving in the forces. It was in the form a carved timber wall plaque, with

George Pittaway (right), formerly of the 4th Battalion East Yorkshire Regiment, with wound stripe on cuff. (*Courtesy Mike Irwin*)

Sharp Street War Memorial Hull. (*Courtesy Paul Bishop*)

integral framed photographs. Such shrines formed the earliest form of war memorial in the city, erected to commemorate the endeavour of local men serving in the armed forces.

Street or community committees were established, with ladies collecting the names and information to be included while gathering subscriptions towards the cost. Frequently, flowers and flags would adorn a memorial, the unveiling of which was usually accompanied by well-attended opening ceremonies. The unveiling of the Sharp Street shrine was accompanied by music from the choir of St Augustine's parish church and a Salvation Army band. Sadly, as enthusiasm for the war waned as casualties mounted, many such shrines fell into disrepair, with others being destroyed in the Second World War blitz, during which Hull was one of the worst-affected cities in the country. Today, the Sharp Street shrine remains in situ, having been restored and then rededicated by the Bishop of Hull in 2014.

As his community kept in mind his continuing war service and that of his contemporaries, with the Sharp Street committee also raising over £60 to send parcels and other comforts to its men on active service, George Pittaway was sent to the front once more. During the German Spring Offensive of 1918 he was recorded as missing as from 31 March, but his parents only received official notification from the Army Records Office in York some five weeks later, on 7 May. In the meantime, the International Red Cross had provided a swifter service, issuing confirmation on 7 April that George had once again

Private William Waller. (*Courtesy Peter Simpson*)

Sarah 'Lal' Waller. (*Courtesy Peter Simpson*)

been wounded and was being cared for in a base hospital. His parents were not to suffer the agony of two sons lost to the world.

For all too many families, their beloved husband, son or father simply disappeared from the face of the earth. One such family was the Wallers of London. William Waller was a 34-year-old printer on the outbreak of war, having served an apprenticeship from 1897 to 1903 under Friars Printing Association Limited of Blackfriars. He had married Sarah, known affectionately as 'Lal', on Christmas Eve 1905. Two sons arrived, William in 1909 and George in 1912. It appears that William senior was swept up in the initial enthusiasm of army recruitment, the *Middlesex Chronicle* of 19 September 1914 headlining the 'Brave Men of Bedfont' and listing him amongst the 'brave lads of Bedfont, who have rallied to their country's call'. The newspaper had assumed Waller was a local man, despite him having initially enlisted at Camberwell, Surrey.

By January 1917, William was a seasoned veteran who was reflecting on a welcome period of leave at home with his young family. However, danger loomed as he was one of 3,000 men earmarked for transfer for France in early spring. He wrote home on 23 January from a Church Army recreation hut situated at the Eastern Command Depot at Shoreham:

Dear Lal

I received your welcomed [*sic*] letter alright and was glad to hear from you and that you and the children are quite well as it leaves me at present.

I was a bit surprised to hear about Albert, but there, he has had a good innings in England and when you write tell him I wish him good luck and when gets out there to keep a good look out for your HUMBLE who will not be long after him as there is 3,000 of us got to leave here before the end of February so that we shall be able to take part in the big push on 1st March and I shall be one of them.

I am sorry to hear that Annie cannot go to work but you know what these young married couples are they are not like us old birds are they? They are so headstrong. You know the old saying 'If you can't be good, be careful'… putting joking aside I would like to soon get a Blighty one like I had and to return home soon Lal dear. I am glad to hear that you are going to get that extra money as it will come in handy for you now you have not got much work. Dear Lal I wish you many happy returns of the day, and although I shall not be with you in body my mind and thoughts are always for you, so I wish you all the good things of life and I hope that on your next birthday I shall be with you and the war all over. I think I must now close with kind regards to all and my very best love and kisses to yourself and the children and I must tell you that I am in the pink of condition as soldiering again has put new life into me.

I am,

Your loving husband. Will

From the sentiments expressed in the letter, Will and Lal appeared to share a strong marriage bond. Will was neither a starry-eyed nor startled youth but a family man keenly aware of his dual responsibilities to loved ones and country. On 28 April 1917, during the Battle of Arras, Will was relieved of the obligations of this world, never to be seen or heard of again.

It was not until 26 June that Lal received official news that her husband was missing. The letter from the Army Record Office in Hounslow stated: 'The report that he is missing does not necessarily mean that he has been killed, as he may be a prisoner of war or temporarily separated from his regiment.' As official reports that men were prisoners of war would 'take some time' to reach Britain, Lal was asked to forward any 'unofficial news' she might receive.

Like many anxious wives and mothers, Lal established contact with comrades of her missing man. On 7 September, she received a letter from a Mrs Howard of 41 Cavendish Dwellings, London EC1, who had just received official notification that 'my dear boy' was a prisoner of war held at Dülmen in Germany. Mrs Howard was 'very sorry to hear about your dear husband'

and promised to send William's name and service number in a letter she was sending to her son that very day. This held out the hope for Lal that 'it may be the means of your hearing the good news that he is alive and well. There will be the hopes of seeing him again, as I pray to God we shall.' Mrs Howard had lost one son the previous year, but felt herself blessed that she had received news not just of one, but of two of her other offsprings' safekeeping:

> I must tell you I had more good news the same post as your letter came to tell me my youngest boy who was reported missing on the 19th April but was found after lying five days in the front of the Turks lines wounded in four places. He had just arrived at the Military Hospital Hammersmith. It came as a joyful surprise.

Mrs Howard knew only too well of Lal's predicament, 'what a terrible suspense it is'. The news her son had been reported alive had caused further contact from his erstwhile comrades:

> I had a gentleman call on me this evening about the same thing. His son an officer of the 4th. Name Hooke. Reported missing the same as my Ted. They must have all gone over together. Thanking you for your kind wish. I trust that your dear husband may be spared to come back to you safe and well.

Sadly, the parents of Second Lieutenant Alfred Douglas Hooke would never receive the glad tidings they yearned to hear. He was subsequently recorded as having been killed on 28 April 1917, the same day as Will Waller, his name being one of nearly 35,000 recorded on the Arras Memorial.

William's picture appeared in the *Daily Sketch* of 5 November, along with those of nine other missing men, each with the name and address of a relative ready to receive information as to their fate. Lal also explored quasi-official channels in her search for news. In early December 1917, she received a letter from the British section of the International Prisoners of War Agency, part of the International Red Cross based in Geneva. Sadly:

> We very much regret we are unable to give the desired information respecting Pte. W. Waller G.7921 / late 13211 Middlesex Regt.
>
> We have not come across his name on the German lists up to now and fear that, for the present, we can do nothing more than to carefully examine the future lists as they reach us, in the hope that we may find it.
>
> Should you in the meantime obtain a clue of any importance we shall gladly follow it up, and always be ready to do our utmost to help you, should it be in our power to do so.

Sec.-Lt. Lawrence, Yorks Regt. Write Miss Lawrence, 71, Manor - rd., Scarborough.

Private Edwards (53695), Welsh Fus. Write Mrs. Edwards, Church - st., Conway.

Private Edmunds (48232), Ryl. Scots. Write Mrs. Edmunds, 24, Abbotts-rd., Southall.

Pte. Sawyer (204080), Royal Fus. Write Mrs. Sawyer, 16, Raymond-st., Wapping.

Private Aughton (42739), Royal Irish R. Write Mr. Aughton, Friendly Society - cottages, Glasgow-rd., Milton.

Pte. Brown (25352f), Royal Fus. Write Mrs. Brown, 3, Clayton-rd., Hayes, Middlesex.

Corpl. Tett (2,2,92), Middx. Write Mr. Tett, 26, Victoria-st., Exeter.

Pte. Chittleburgh (43468), Write Mrs. Chittleburgh, 204, Victoria-rd., Aberdeen.

Pte. Pearce (13420), East Kents. Write Miss Pearce, 21, Jerdau-place, Walham Green.

Pte. Waller (7091), Middx. Write Mrs. Waller, 53, Elizabeth-st., Walworth.

William Waller in a *Daily Sketch* appeal for the missing.

As no specific information about William could be gleaned from any source, Lal received an amalgam of statements that men from his battalion had given to Wounded and Missing Bureau volunteers regarding the day he disappeared:

4th Middlesex Regt. April 28 1917

Our reports show that this 4th Middlesex were in a big attack on Greenland Hill in the Arras district near Oppy Wood, on April 28 1917. Two Companies advanced too far and were cut off and the greater part taken prisoners. The names of these have since been reported from Germany. Other Companies came up in the afternoon of the same day and after two repulses were able to dig themselves in. The objective was not gained. It appears that those of the wounded who were able to walk had some way to go back the Dressing Station and would have come under heavy fire. Many seem to have failed to reach safety. Men of the Battalion who took part in the advance have given the following short accounts of it:

'A & B Companies got too far beyond their objective at Greenland Hill and the greater part of them were cut off.'

'We went over at 4 a.m. at Greenland Hill. We did not get our objective but were held up by machine gun fire. The Battalion advanced for about 1,500 yards.'

'We did not gain our objective as we were held up, but we dug ourselves in and held the ground.'

'The attack was made from Arras. We came up in the afternoon and carried on till next morning. We were repulsed and had to leave twice. The third time we hung on to it.'

'We had advanced a good way, across three lines and a sunken road so he (a wounded comrade) would have a good way to go.'

During 1918, there was further dismal news for Lal, struggling as she was to bring up two young sons with the family's main breadwinner having been lost for eight months. On 12 January, the Ministry of Pensions informed her that, as from the 27th of that month, her separation allowance would cease and a pension of thirteen shillings and ninepence per week for her and nine shillings and twopence per week for her two children would be paid. 'The change of payment must not be taken as indicating that there is any proof of the death of your husband,' the letter curtly apprised her.

In March 1918, Lal received final confirmation from No. 1 Army Record Office in Hounslow that her husband was officially considered dead:

Madam
It is my painful duty to inform you that no further news having been received relative to (No.) G. 7921 (Rank) Private (Name) William Henry Waller (Regiment) 4th Battalion Middlesex, who has been missing since 29th April 1917, the Army Council have been regretfully constrained to conclude that he is dead, and that his death took place on the 28th April 1917 (or since).

William's remains would never be identified, and his death on active service is recorded on the Arras Memorial.

The shattering impact, not just emotionally, but financially, on a wife whose husband was recorded as missing and then confirmed as killed was felt by Lucy Longden. Her husband, James William Longden, was a 34-year-old coal miner living in the Attercliffe district of Sheffield when, on 10 June 1915, he heeded the call to volunteer. Known in the family as William, he and Lucy had been married for a fortnight under ten years on his enlistment, with a daughter, Elizabeth Mary, born in 1906. Initially assigned to 3rd Battalion York and Lancaster Regiment, William was then transferred to the regiment's 2nd Battalion and sailed for France on 22 February 1916, disembarking at Rouen two days later. He was reported killed in action near Ypres on 21 April, after less than two months of active service. On 17 July that year, Lucy received her husband's effects from the Infantry Records Office at York, although it is not known what items were sent back from Belgium. On 4 November, she was informed that she would receive a pension of fifteen shillings per week for her and Elizabeth. Although the family was spared the weeks or months of agony that could follow the uncertainty of a 'missing' notification, Lucy keenly felt the emotional and financial loss that had befallen her and her daughter. On 11 July 1919, she wrote to the Army Record Office in York:

> Dear Sir
>
> I am writing on behalf of my Late Husband Private J.W. Longden No 21562 Y&L Regt killed in 1916 if I am not entitled to a gratuity of some kind for myself & my girl just 13 years of age.
>
> I am in need of it as I cannot follow work on account of varicose veins in my legs trusting you will do the best you can for me.
>
> I Remain Yours Sincerely
>
> Mrs L. Longden

After providing details of all of William's living relatives, which amounted to three brothers and four sisters, Lucy's allowance was raised to twenty-five shillings per week. Whatever paltry financial recompense was made for the loss of William's life, his wife, child and descendants would forever lack a grave at which to commemorate his sacrifice. Elizabeth rarely mentioned the father she had last seen when she was ten but would avidly watch each year's armistice day ceremony, frequently wiping away a tear as she did so. Ninety-nine years later, her grandson, Steve Storey, visited the area where William had been killed to bring some degree of closure to his family's loss. To further consolidate the memory of the man with no known resting place, he crafted, along with his son and grandchildren, a lasting personal memorial to his great-grandfather.

Private J.W. Longden and family. (*Courtesy Steve Storey*)

Certain unscrupulous individuals sought to profit from the desperate appetite for news of missing loved ones. One such charlatan was an American, Edward

Page Gaston. As a citizen of a neutral country, Gaston claimed to have access to German prisons and other institutions that were beyond the reach of British officials. He encouraged the circulation of reports that he was opening a relief base close to the Rhine, and that he would be able to distribute money and parcels to British prisoners of war held in Germany. In addition, he claimed the ability to locate soldiers who had been reported missing. Maintaining that he had the backing of the American Embassy in Berlin, Gaston was pictured standing by the grave of a British soldier, and in another photograph he was surrounded by the property of missing British soldiers. One of the earliest reports concerning his influence appeared in *The Sphere* on 3 October 1914 under the heading 'How I Rescued Lost Luggage from Germany':

> Mr Edward Page Gaston is an American citizen, born in the state of Illinois, who has been attached to American diplomatic and government services for many years. With great pluck and enterprise he undertook to visit the various cities of Germany and to rescue the lost luggage of his compatriots which they had left behind them in their hasty flight from the Continent after the declaration of war. Mr Gaston has favoured us with the following account of his experiences.

Gaston claimed to have met Americans who had fled from Germany and were being cared for at the Savoy Hotel in London, hearing their stories of personal suffering and loss of baggage. He then decided to undertake a 'special baggage rescue expedition to the Continent' and asserted that he found German military and civil authorities responsive to his appeal as the USA was at that stage a neutral nation.

Some large trunks had been used by the Belgians to erect barricades. Gaston declared: 'As a military necessity this was perhaps all right, but it was hard on the pretty Parisian dresses.' He claimed that he was granted special favours from the German authorities to inspect baggage in German harbours. 'As this depot occupied a strategical position in a most important prohibited naval war area the premises had been closed by Government order a few days before, and not even the proprietary officials of the [shipping] company were permitted on their own property.' Yet, for Gaston, apparently, 'the naval authorities promptly and cheerfully opened up the premises'.

Later that month, Gaston was offering to ensure safe passage of parcels to British prisoners of war in Germany. An insertion in the *Birmingham Daily Gazette* of 22 October 1914 stated:

> As an American citizen, Mr Gaston has paid several visits to Germany on Anglo-American relief work and is continuing his work in this direction.

All correspondence regarding special supplies for distribution should be addressed to Mr Gaston direct. It is essential that parcels should not contain letters.

The *Nottingham Journal* of 16 December 1914 reported on further aggrandisement of Gaston's claims of access to British prisoners of war:

Since the middle of August I have undertaken three relief expeditions. ... From missing baggage to providing British prisoners of war with necessary clothing was a natural step, and the succeeding expeditions have been undertaken mainly with the object of supplying winter comforts to those British subjects interned either in German fortresses or camps.

In view of the immense amount of work which the German authorities have had to do in putting millions of men in the field and providing them with the necessary equipment and munitions of war, they have been unable to supply prisoners of war with the clothing and comforts they require, and owing to the prompt action of Judge Gerard, the American Ambassador in Berlin, I have been enabled to distribute thousands of articles of clothing and other necessitates to those most needing them.

Gaston claimed to have visited several camps holding British PoWs and interned civilians:

The German authorities have asked me whether I would undertake on behalf of the Germans interned in England the same kind work that I am doing for British prisoners in Berlin; and if I am able to act the part of the 'mutual friend' to the prisoners of war on both sides of the North Sea I am sure it will lead to good results.

His claims extended to being able to bring joy to families of missing soldiers who had long presumed their relative to have perished:

It is some comfort for relatives at home to know that even after months have passed by British soldiers who were supposed to be dead are often discovered. It sometimes happens that a man has been seriously wounded in the head, and is consequently unable to give an account of himself, but after treatment in hospital his memory returns and he is able to communicate with his friends in England.

By this statement, Gaston falsely raised the hopes not only of those who parted with their money in order to engage his services, but relatives who were given renewed hope that the man who was lost might still yet be found.

After eight months courting publicity and collecting money and provisions – ostensibly to relay to British prisoners of war in Germany – Gaston's activities came under the scrutiny of the American authorities. In the middle of June 1915, a letter from the American ambassador in Berlin, James W. Gerard, was widely circulated in the national and provincial press:

> My attention has been called to the fact that an alleged American named Edward Page Gaston has issued a circular in which he offers to make arrangements for the supply of food, clothing &c, to prisoners in Germany. I desire to warn friends of British prisoners in Germany against confiding anything to this man – he has no connection with this Embassy, and I will not even permit him to enter it. He has been required to leave Germany and Belgium by the German authorities. I most earnestly beg the British public and friends of prisoners to have nothing to do with him.

Gaston was not to be deterred by such reports, deciding to sue five of the newspapers for libel for printing them. His case eventually reached the Court of Appeal in December 1915, where his counsel stated that Gerard's letter had been 'most injurious'. Their lordships dismissed the appeal but, undeterred, in March 1916 Gaston brought an action against the *Daily Mail*, Business Newspapers Ltd., the *Morning Post*, the *Manchester Guardian*, the *New York Times* and the *Daily Chronicle* in respect of an alleged libel. It was decided to delay the trial until after the war, as it would be impossible to gather witnesses and give it full attention when more important matters were pressing. Gaston, and his promises of being able to trace the missing, faded from the public consciousness.

This was not before he had done irreparable damage in prolonging the false hope that beat in many anxious hearts. One of those who fell victim to his empty promises was Hazel Macnaghten. Her husband of three years, Angus Macnaghten, a 31-year-old lieutenant in the Black Watch, had officially been reported missing on 29 October 1914, during the First Battle of Ypres. Their son, also named Angus, had been born in the spring of 1914. Angus senior, who owned 12,000 acres of 'hill and heather' in Perthshire, had attended Eton College and was a scholar of the Gaelic language. In early October 1914 he had been put in charge of a company of more than 200 men. Angus wrote of the consolations his Christian beliefs brought to him in wartime, 'This life does bring home to one the Power of the High One,' adding that he had faith that he would return home safely to Hazel.

Hazel received her fateful 'missing' telegram on 3 November. Like so many wives, she was thrown into a paroxysm of anxiety, which would last across decades of rumour and speculation. Various outlandish explanations for Angus's disappearance came her way, including one that he had been chosen to stalk his way through German lines during a storm. By the end of 1914, having received no further official communication about her husband's fate, Hazel placed an advertisement in the personal columns of the national press, appealing for information. A Red Cross nurse wrote to her, stating that she had cared for a private who recalled seeing Angus slightly wounded in the leg. A Paris representative of the shipping agency Cox & Co. reported he had heard that Angus had been wounded in a trench. This story was confirmed by the Paris office of the Red Cross.

A press report in December 1914 gave Hazel further grounds for optimism, as it was reported that many PoW lists were being delayed and compiled with incomplete information. She used her widespread network of contacts across the European continent to make extensive enquiries. Sadly, Hazel succumbed to the impostor Edward Page Gaston. She had read in the press of how he had set up his own missing person's bureau for Allied servicemen. Hazel forwarded £50 and a photograph of her husband to Gaston, which the latter promised to circulate via his supposed German contacts. After a few months, Hazel wrote to her sister-in-law, Lettice, concerned at rumours that Gaston was a fraud. Eventually, following Gaston's exposure, Hazel was able to recoup £35 from him.

Both Hazel and Lettice allowed their belief that Angus was still alive to reject reports to the contrary. Angus was automatically promoted to the rank of captain in February 1915, which further fuelled their belief in his survival. This hope was further bolstered by reports that German PoW camp commandants would burn letters that officers had written to be sent home, which would explain why they had not heard from Angus for months.

In June 1915, the War Office passed on two reports that proved that Angus was no longer alive, requesting that Hazel allow his name to be added to the roll of honour. Nevertheless, she stuck to her hope that he would one day be found. Five months later, the War Office insisted that he be assumed dead, as it was by then over a year since his disappearance. Both Hazel and Lettice publicly announced that they would continue searching for Angus. Hazel persisted in her visits to military hospitals, keen to gather news that would affirm her decision to reject the official conclusion. In 1916, condolences were received from Buckingham Palace.

At one stage, Hazel consulted a clairvoyant, sending him one of Angus's letters. As big a fraud as Gaston, this man replied that Angus was in a hospital, unable to walk and unaware that Hazel did not know his whereabouts. The supernatural swindler forwarded to Hazel the names of places where he claimed Angus had been held, further prolonging her search for her husband.

One of the trustees of Angus's will interviewed three men from his platoon who had been released from captivity, who were able to provide a detailed account of his final hours, concluding that 'death was instantaneous'. Yet still Hazel refused to concede. She instigated door-to-door enquiries in Belgium, fuelled by occasional newspaper reports of men regaining their memory after years of mental and physical absence, and returning home to their loved ones. By 1930, she was still writing to survivors of the war, hoping against hope that positive news of Angus might be forthcoming. A report of a man who resembled Angus on board a train in the Balkans in 1931 further invigorated her quest for her husband. As in the cases of the Butt and Pope families featured later in this book, money and connections only served to prolong the agonies of the searching process. Sadly for Hazel, the closest she would come to her husband would be in August 1939, when she took their son to the Menin Gate memorial in Ypres, accompanied by Lieutenant Macnaghten's erstwhile comrades who had previously assured her he had been taken prisoner. Like the Pope family's search for news of their son, a published book tribute to the lives of Angus and Hazel Macnaghten would eventually stand as a permanent memorial of their agonies. It would be written by their son Angus, a mere babe of five months when his father disappeared from the earth.

Hazel Macnaghten was not the only anxious relative to turn to the supernatural. Whilst some spiritualists were unbalanced and others were fakes, many were honest and true believers in their craft. Spiritualism had flourished in Victorian England amongst those who rejected mainstream religious beliefs and practices but still believed in the paranormal. During the Great War, interest in the mystical and afterlife naturally deepened, with a need to communicate with the fallen an irresistible urge for many bereaved families.

Sir Arthur Conan Doyle, creator of Sherlock Holmes and prominent believer in the supernatural, lost his son Kingsley in the war. Through attendance at séances he was able to reach Kingsley, who allegedly asked for forgiveness and offered his parents the consolation that he had been intending to leave England to work abroad in the medical service.

Conan Doyle was not the only prominent literary figure to contend with the loss of a loved one. Rudyard Kipling's 18-year-old son, Lieutenant John Kipling of the Irish Guards, went missing in action on 27 September 1915 while fighting in the Battle of Loos. Kipling mobilised his considerable range of contacts and access to resources to find his beloved 'Jack'. The assistance of the Prince of Wales, the Crown Princess of Sweden and the American ambassador to the United Kingdom was marshalled, and members of the Royal Flying Corps were tasked with dropping mimeographed sheets behind enemy lines requesting information on '*der Sohn des weltberühmten Schriftstellers Rudyard Kipling*'. In doing so, Kipling was hoping that citizens of the nation he had so recently vilified (writing, 'There are only two divisions in the world – human beings and Germans') would treat his son with respect and show Kipling the human decency of informing him of his whereabouts. Kipling and his wife Carrie visited war hospitals in Britain and on the Western Front, interviewing comrades of John's, but found no conclusive information.

Kipling's zealous enthusiasm for drumming up support for the war had led to a degree of unpopularity amongst some, and he was to receive a letter stating that he deserved to lose Jack on account of his fervour in sending other people's sons to their deaths. Finally, the Kiplings were compelled to accept the reality of Jack's death when one of his men reported that he had been shot through the head before his body had been placed in a shell hole, where it had been pulverised by shellfire. Kipling would eventually become instrumental in suggesting and selecting a fitting epitaph to adorn the stones of remembrance on thousands of war memorials: 'Their Name Liveth for Evermore'. In addition, the most inscribed words on British war graves, 'Known unto God', were conceived by Kipling. As a personal act of tribute to his son, Kipling would write the poem 'My Boy Jack', and spent seven years writing his history, *The Irish Guards in the Great War*, published in 1923. However, he could never fully find closure on the imperialist enthusiasm that had led him to bang the recruitment drum so loudly during the war, penning the short poem 'Common Form', which bleakly states:

> If any question why we died,
> Tell them, because our fathers lied.

When Vera Brittain was informed by telegram of the death of her brother Edward, on 22 June 1918, Marie Leighton, the mother of Vera's late fiancé, Roland, queried whether there might have been a mistake. However, letters arriving from Italy from Edward's senior officer, his batman and a Red Cross worker confirmed the facts of how he had died, allegedly shot through the head by a sniper, dying instantly. Vera wished to immerse herself in Edward's final hours, so contacted Colonel Charles Hudson, his commanding officer, whose name she had noticed on a list of the wounded, and, after making enquiries via the Wounded and Missing Bureau, was able to track him down to an officers' hospital in Mayfair. The meeting was not a comfortable one, as Hudson later recalled:

> I tried to give as much comfort as I could to the poor girl by telling her that since he was shot through the head he could have suffered little pain, but at this she flared up and said she was tired of hearing this story. Why was it that all her friends and acquaintances killed in the war had been shot through the head? Did I think that because she was a woman she was too weak-minded to be told the truth, or so gullible that she could not recognise such nonsense?

Vera developed a fixation with Hudson, bombarding him with more enquiries, and wondered whether his refusal to disclose any further information was down to the fact he might have harboured romantic thoughts about her. When Hudson went to Buckingham Palace in September to receive his Victoria Cross for his gallantry in the actions during which Edward Brittain had been killed, Vera went to witness the ceremony, shortly afterwards writing the bitter poem 'To a V.C.', containing the lines:

> 'Tis not your valour's meed alone you bear
> Who stand the hero of a nation's pride;
> For on that humble Cross you live to wear
> Your friends were crucified.

When Vera's searing account of her war experience, *Testament of Youth*, was published in 1933, Hudson was compelled to write to her stating that he had indeed deliberately withheld certain facts concerning the circumstances of Edward's death. A tense meeting was arranged on 9 July, at which, rather than revealing any further evidence about Edward's death, Hudson informed Vera that his caginess at speaking too freely of Edward had been due to the strong suggestion in a censored letter that her brother had been involved in various homosexual relationships. Hudson had alerted Edward to these findings, and the senior officer had harboured a suspicion that his death, rather than being due to a keen-eyed sniper, had actually been a suicide driven by despairing thoughts of potential disgrace. Vera's search had not brought her the closure she had so desperately needed following the wartime deaths of the three men closest to her in life.

Other families sought to memorialise their missing relatives with plaques, memorial windows or gravestones in their local church. One unusual memorial was paid for with the bitter funds of war. Charlotte Padley, a Nottinghamshire housewife and mother, had already lost her first husband, George Jackson, in a mining accident at Wath Main Colliery near Rotherham in 1898. With four children to raise, including 2-year-old George Wallace Jackson, she married William Padley in Doncaster the following year. The family moved to Carlton in Lindrick, 3 miles north of Worksop, where upon leaving school George had found employment as a grocer's assistant with the Worksop Co-operative Society, working alongside two of his siblings.

George enlisted in the Sherwood Foresters, serving in the 5th Battalion. He was reported missing as from 21 March 1918, the first day of the great German Spring Offensive. His battalion had been charged with defending the line near Bullecourt and had been overrun by midday, with 108 men confirmed dead and another 600, including George, recorded as missing. It was a further fruitless

Private George Wallace Jackson. (*Author's collection*)

year before Charlotte received official confirmation of his death. George's body was never identified, with his name being inscribed on the Arras Memorial.

The *Worksop Guardian* of 1 August 1919 reported: 'After many months of suspense, the news has reached Mrs W. Padley, Carlton, that her son, Pte George Wallace Jackson, 2nd/5th Sherwood Foresters, reported missing since March 21st 1918, was killed on that date.' The heart-tugging report continued: 'Pte Jackson was a son any mother might be proud of and he leaves behind a memory which will long be cherished. The Army Council forward a message of sympathy from the King and Queen, and his mother has also the sympathy of all who knew her gallant son in her bereavement.'

Charlotte received the sum of £24 3s 5d upon confirmation of George's death, using the sum to erect her own memorial to her son in the churchyard of St John the Evangelist, Carlton in Lindrick. A plinth was constructed bearing the inscription:

To the glorious memory of Pte George Wallace Jackson, 2/5 Sherwood Foresters, who fell in action in France, March 21st 1918, aged 22 years.

Greater love hath no man than this that a man lay down his life for his friends.

This memorial was erected by his sorrowing mother.

Above the plinth was placed a sculptured soldier in battledress. Charlotte was buried beneath her son's memorial in 1926.

Sadly, the memorial was vandalised at some point in the latter part of the twentieth century, the statue being decapitated. In 2015, a group, including the author, a local councillor and members of George's family, gathered sufficient funds to have the memorial statue resculpted to its original state. A rededication service was held on the hundredth anniversary of his death, with members of his regiment and local dignitaries in attendance, along with hundreds of people from his local community, including Councillor Maurice Stokes, who

Memorial to George Wallace Jackson, before and after restoration. (*Author's collection*)

had worked tirelessly in the quest for restoration. In this case, the whole village of Carlton in Lindrick achieved closure and remembered the loss of one of its sons.

Sometimes a family member on active service was in the best position to make enquiries about a missing loved one, able to utilise contacts across the army to ascertain information that the Red Cross might not be able to elicit. Private Edwin Wood's younger brother Fred had been one of the first to go over the top on 1 July 1916. Fred's unit, 1st Battalion Somerset Light Infantry, suffered losses of 463 men killed, wounded or missing that morning. Fred was one of those who would disappear into the ether of history, his body never being identified. The very morning Fred was killed, Edwin, in reserve with 4th Battalion Gloucestershire Regiment, had received a postcard from him. His diary entry at the conclusion of that terrible day read: 'Fred not retd with batt.' On 6, 7, 9, 10 and 15 July, Edwin poignantly recorded: 'No news of Fred.'

Private Edwin Wood. (*Courtesy Jacqueline Wadsworth*)

Meanwhile, one of Fred's comrades in the SLI wrote to the Wood family in Bristol, stating that Fred had been injured. Edwin subsequently received further inconclusive news from a friend nicknamed 'Booge' who was stationed at No. 55 Infantry Base Depot in Rouen. Addressed to 'Chip', the almost inevitable nickname assigned to Private Wood, it read:

> I have had an answer from my mate in the Som LI, his knowledge of your brothers case will not enlighten you much I'm afraid. I have attached the paragraph in which he speaks of it.
>
> Hope all the boys are alright, give my best respects to Skip and the others.
>
> The sniping down here is awful.

The attachment read:

> Fred Wood's platoon touched out bad, a shell pitching in the centre of them while they were attacking, of course there is every chance of him being in hospital, well I hope he is.

Sadly, no further evidence of Fred's whereabouts would ever be found, and his name is recorded on the Thiepval Memorial, alongside those of 73,000 other missing men whose families remain forever bereft of a final resting place at which to grieve.

In all, the Wounded and Missing Bureau received over 340,000 enquiries and issued 384,759 reports to enquirers. Its director, Lord Lucan, estimated that 4 million servicemen had been interviewed throughout the war. Granville Barker summarised that the 'supreme value of these simple stories is that they sink to the sheer rock bottom of war. We can see in them fighting, as it was to the men who had to

Private Fred Wood. (*Courtesy Jacqueline Wadsworth*)

fight, in all its beastliness, in all its dignity. And finally, that is all there is worth knowing about war.'

Post-war searches

Once the guns had finally fallen silent, the search for the missing continued as families held out hope that perhaps their long-lost loved one would be freed from a prison camp from where they had been unable to send communication. For most though, thoughts turned to locating the missing remains of their dead son or husband. Not knowing the circumstances of their fate would leave a yearning in the lives of millions of people afflicted by the lack of closure from the Great War. The presence of a grave to visit would provide some form of resolution to the terrible set of circumstances that had led to death, and this meant that the British authorities felt morally obliged to continue the search for the missing in the years following the cessation of hostilities.

Whilst most soldiers serving on the Western Front and elsewhere were keen to return to Britain as soon as possible, some stayed on in France and Flanders after the Armistice as members of army exhumation parties, scouring the scorched landscape of sacrifice for the remains of their erstwhile comrades. Already, during the war, men had been buried in unidentified graves, as those who came across their remains had neither the time nor expertise to establish an identity based on the pieces of extinguished life they came across. Lieutenant Francis Mond, whose body would eventually become the subject of a long search following his death in 1918, provided his mother with a sharply observed description of the area around Neuve Chapelle in September 1915: 'particularly pathetic, and only too common when the fighting has been thick, "Here Lies the Body of an Unknown Soldier"'. Mond's mother, Angela, was another, like Rudyard Kipling, whose affluence, available time and access to resources to spend on a relentless search was to cause years of torment. Long quests for information could act as part of the grieving process, whilst delaying the eventual acceptance of a loved one's death and the subsequent need to move on with life. In Angela Mond's case, her unremitting mission yielded a positive outcome, as she was able to establish that her son had been buried under a grave marker bearing another man's name.

The vision and drive to deliver order and rigour into the registration of the dead, thus meaning that hundreds of thousands fewer families would avoid the perpetual loss of the remains of their loved one, had been provided by Fabian Ware. By 1914, the 45-year-old Ware had enjoyed an eclectic career as journalist and educationalist in Britain and South Africa. In the early months of the war, Ware had organised members of London's Royal Automobile Club to support the work of the British Red Cross Society in Amiens and Paris, ferrying wounded soldiers to medical dressing stations. It was while driving through territory that until recently had been battle sites that Ware noted the existence of isolated British war graves. Ware and his staff took it upon themselves to place wooden crosses on the graves, and to paint on them a more durable record of the dead man's details than his comrades had hastily pencilled on.

As the casualties mounted, Ware's unit was issued with a device for manufacturing aluminium tags onto which the man's particulars could be stamped and then attached to each cross. However, as the toll on life escalated, it quickly became clear that such an incidental approach would be insufficient to meet the needs of respectfully burying the dead whilst providing for the prospect of recording and curating their whereabouts. On 9 January 1915, a letter was published in *The Times* that reported the anguish of an anonymous lady who had visited France to pay respects at her brother's grave:

> Comrades in his regiment had given her particulars of the exact locality and even described the temporary wooden cross and its inscription, erected over the grave. She found the places, where quite a number of victims had been interred, but every trace of the identifying crosses or other marks had disappeared. I will not dwell on the distress of our friend.

On 2 March 1915, the Graves Registration Commission (GRC) was established, with Ware appointed as its honorary major. Two Graves Registration Units (GRUs) were set up with a complement of administrative and motorised staff charged with systematically combing former battlefields now in Allied hands. The GRC also contained a photographic branch that could, upon request, provide a photograph of a man's grave to his grieving families.

Whilst the GRC could assuage the demand for burial information to some extent, it had no facility to search for the whereabouts of soldiers reported as missing by their battalion's adjutant. The commission became part of the British Army in October 1915 and in March 1916 was renamed the Directorate of Graves Registration and Enquiries (DGR&E), with full responsibility for recording burial details and locations. The importance of its work in sustaining morale in the army was noted by Douglas Haig, as its officials would be seen by men visiting makeshift cemeteries located close to the front line, fully exposed to shell and rifle fire. It was clear that official importance had been attached to the respectful memorialisation of their recent comrades' – and potentially their own – lives.

Each army division would contain its own burial officers who would liaise with DGR&E staff. These officers would instruct the men under them who prepared the dead for burial to remove pay books and any other personal effects that might be able to identify the individual. Clearance of battlefields and burial of remains were undoubtedly amongst the most unpleasant and unpopular tasks of the war. Private J. McCauley was attached to an exhumation and burial unit from August to November 1918. He noted: 'For the first week or two I could scarcely endure the experiences we met with, but I gradually became hardened.' He described his work:

Often have I picked up the remains of a fine brave man on a shovel. Just a little heap of bones and maggots to be carried to the common burial place. Numerous bodies were found lying submerged in the water in shell holes and mine craters; bodies that seemed quite whole, but which became like huge masses of white, slimy chalk when we handled them. I shuddered as my hands, covered in soft flesh and slime, moved about in search of the disc, and I have had to pull bodies to pieces in order that they should not be buried unknown. It was very painful to have to bury the unknown.

An estimated 160,000 isolated graves were relocated into existing cemeteries and smaller cemeteries were concentrated into larger ones. However, over half a million men remained missing upon the signing of the Armistice on 11 November 1918, and searching and exhumation work began in earnest on 21 November, with men volunteering for this grisly work paid an extra allowance of 2s 6d per day. As well as British troops, Canadian, Australian and French search parties scoured the areas where their armies had sustained heavy losses. Captain J.C. Dunn encountered Australian exhumers at Villers-Bretonneux in April 1919, and recorded: 'Large numbers of troops were engaged in burying or reburying their numerous dead, left where they fell since the historic advance on August 8th 1918. Most of the actual work was done by troops freshly drafted from England, men who had not previously been in France.'

When a body was discovered, each exhumation would require between five and nine men to expedite the digging up of the remains, the transportation to the final resting place and the burial.

Searches were systematic, with a survey officer selecting a 500 square yard piece of ground to be searched by exhumation companies, which contained squads of thirty-two men. Each squad was issued with the mundane items to carry out their macabre commission: 'two pairs of rubber gloves, two shovels, stakes to mark the location of graves found, canvas and rope to tie up remains, stretchers, cresol and wire cutters'. As far as the IWGC was concerned, it was crucial that men who had been previously engaged in such work during the war were retained; otherwise, up to 80 per cent of bodies that remained to be found would be lost forever. Existing parties had become experts at spotting indications of remains from above the ground, stated to be:

i.   Rifles or stakes protruding from the ground, bearing helmets or equipment;
ii.   Partial remains or equipment on the surface or protruding from the ground;
iii. Rat holes – often small bones or pieces of equipment would be brought to the surface by the rats;

iv.   Discolouration of grass, earth or water – grass was often a vivid bluish-green with broader blades where bodies were buried, while earth and water turned a greenish black or grey colour.

Once a dead solider had been found, a careful examination of neck, wrist and braces for the presence of an identification tag was required, although this process was not always as thorough as it might have been due to time pressures. On other occasions, exhumation parties would go to the lengths of examining a dead soldier's boots. One such search revealed the footwear had been manufactured by 'UNITY CO-OP SOCY LTD RINGSTEAD' in 1913. However, no further identification could be made of that individual.

Australian Private W. Macbeath described the psychological effects of exhuming the dead: 'Working in the fields digging up the bodies, a very unpleasant job.' He also had to process the pitiable effects of war on others, recording in his diary: 'Working in cemetery. An English lady came over to see her son's grave, found him lying in a bag and fainted.' Macbeath summarised: 'I cannot say I am exactly in love with the job.'

In addition to the stark reality of daily contact with the dead and the dark humour sometimes needed to endure the strain of the job, the work of exhumation and reburial parties was called into question by the IWGC: 'Exhumation Companies, obsessed with the idea that their reputation depended on their concentrating the highest possible number of bodies in the shortest possible time, have often paid little or no heed to the essential matter of identification.'

Some of those who held specific information that might locate the remains of their missing relative took matters into their own hands. Agnes Littleboy's son, Lieutenant Wilfred Littleboy, had been killed during an attack on Polderhoek Chateau on 9 October 1917 while serving with 16th Battalion Royal Warwickshire Regiment. After the war, Agnes travelled to Gheluvelt, 6 miles east of Ypres, and knocked on the door of Father Delrue, the local priest, explaining that her son had been killed in the area in 1917 and that she had in her possession papers that might, with the assistance of someone with local topographical knowledge, be able to locate the whereabouts of his lost grave.

Wilfred had grown up in the north-eastern holiday resort of Saltburn-by-the-Sea before his Quaker parents sent him to Rugby School in 1909, where he served as a cadet officer in the Officers' Training Corps (OTC). This experience had whetted Wilfred's appetite for military service, and he requested to leave the school two months earlier than intended in order to join the army. Having received his commission in January 1915, and a promotion to the rank of lieutenant in November that year, he had left for France in July 1917.

Father Delrue advised Agnes to return to his house early the following day after he had performed the 7.00 am Mass. The pair, along with two friends of the priest, searched the area around the chateau where Agnes believed Wilfred to have been buried. Miraculously, the search revealed his remains. Overwhelmed with gratitude, Agnes asked Father Delrue how she could repay his kindness. The reply came: 'For me nothing, but for my church ...' On 25 June 1920, the priest received a generous donation for his house of worship and a plaque was erected there in memory of Lieutenant Littleboy. His remains were taken to the Hooge Crater Cemetery and laid to rest amongst other fallen men whose remains had been found on an ad hoc basis. His parents chose the inscription 'ALL YOU HAD HOPED FOR ALL YOU HAD YOU GAVE' for his headstone. In addition, they donated a plot of land in Thornaby-on-Tees for the creation of an open green space, which to this day bears the name of Littleboy Park.

Captain Willie Lott had last been seen in October 1916, attached to the Royal Sussex Regiment from 6th East Kent Regiment. He was shot through the head while jumping into Rainbow trench, just north of Gueudecourt, on

Amy Lott.
(*Courtesy Matthew Pawson*)

Willie Lott. (*Courtesy David Blanchard*)

7 October. One of the most poignant of post-war photographs depicts his desperate sister, Amy, sitting amongst the desolate landscape of the Somme in 1919. Amy would never find her dear brother, his life commemorated on the Thiepval Memorial.

The War Office and Army Record Offices quickly became overwhelmed with the number of queries emanating from the IWGC and the DRG&E requesting assistance in tracing the identity of the bodies they were uncovering, based on scraps of evidence such as a portion of an army number, or the searchers needing to know the precise location of a particular battalion across a number of days. These requests impacted on the everyday work of the military authorities, and in the straitened circumstances of the 1920s, there were no spare funds with which to hire extra administrative staff to deal with a workload outside the organisations' direct remits.

The British Army continued to scour the former battlefields for its fallen comrades for nearly three years following the Armistice, but by the middle of 1921, plans were being made to wind down the searching operations. The cost of maintaining the staff and equipment needed, and the provision of ancillary support services such as hospitals and transport, had, according to the War Office, become 'an unjustifiable expense to the taxpayer to maintain any longer'. The task of identifying, recording and arranging the burial of any further remains found was to be handed over to the IWGC.

Searching and exhumation parties working under the direction of the DGR&E were already operating with a continually reducing capacity. From January 1920 to January 1921, the total number of men employed on exhumation work had fallen from nearly 6,000 to a little over 600. During this period, the proportion of bodies receiving a full identification from discs or other evidence fell from 75 per cent in April 1920 to 20 per cent by May 1921. This was still a sufficient number to make it politically and ethically awkward to scale back on the searches. Furthermore, the ratio of bodies being discovered to the number of men assigned to the task remained stable.

By August 1921, searches across the battlefield areas of France and Belgium had yielded the remains of 204,654 soldiers who had been concentrated into IWGC maintained cemeteries. However, the army could no longer justify the manpower required to systematically scour the battlefields. By October, all military exhumation staff had returned home. If the British public knew that bodies were still being found at the rate of 200 per week whilst search parties were being disbanded, there would be general disquiet. Sir L. Worthington-Evans, Secretary of State for War, issued a response in November 1921 as the second anniversary of the Armistice was to the forefront of public consciousness. He assured the public that 'the whole battlefield area in France and Flanders has been systematically searched at least six times. Some areas in which the fighting had been particularly heavy, were searched as many as 20 times.' Whilst it was 'probable' there were further graves to be found, these would be brought to light by reconstruction work.

It was a certainty that further bodies would continue to be found by farmers bringing their land back into cultivation and civilians re-establishing ditches and hedgerows on their land. A narrative had to be created that made clear to the British public that the army had not abandoned its men yet to be found, but had taken every reasonable measure to find as many of the missing as it could, within a realistic timeframe.

With the army vacating the area, the danger emerged of bodies exhumed by French and Belgian civilians being left unburied, creating the possibility of a market in trafficking bodies and personal effects. Just as Edward Page Gaston had preyed on the anxieties of families desperate for news of their loved ones during the war, so it was feared that some unscrupulous individuals would prey on those desperate to feel close to their loved one's remains and artefacts of their final days.

Despite the concerns of relatives whose men remained lost, in September 1921 the DGR&E's exhumation parties were withdrawn. The public was assured that the IWGC would be on hand to supervise the interment of any further remains found by French or Belgian civilians. The families of missing men would be concerned about what appeared to be a 'permanent breach' with their men. The army within which they had fought and died now appeared to be abandoning them in death. There were still approximately 300,000 dead unaccounted for on the Western Front, and bodies were still regularly being unearthed by French and Belgian landowners. Whilst on some occasions they were keen to assist in the identification of these remains, at other times they showed little interest.

A War Office press release, quoted across the regional press in late September, explained:

> Bodies are becoming more difficult to find. Men who became expert in the work were able for some time to make rapid progress by various signs which showed them where the dead lay. The more bodies that were received the fewer became these signs. If the work had been continued on the old basis it would have meant the retention in France and Belgium of British soldiers for many years to come with comparatively little result.

This statement did little to assuage the feelings of sadness, indignation and anger of those whose loved ones remained unidentified. The hope that one day they would know where their man fell, and where he would rest in perpetuity, seemed to have been extinguished.

In October 1921, the *Daily Mail* sent an investigative journalist to examine what was happening to bodies recovered by civilians now there was no formal process in place for their transportation and reburial. His report revealed that any local workman who discovered a body was paid the sum of two francs by the French or Belgian authorities. The British government, however, paid nothing. Thus, the risk was being run of finds not being reported, as a workman might lose six or seven francs in wages in the time it took him to report them.

The IWGC requested that the British government consider the distasteful matter of paying a bounty for each British body found and reported. It was suggested that dozens of identifiable British soldiers were being abandoned. In addition, the IWGC requested that ex-DGR&E staff be attached to the domestic searching gangs to supervise that due process was being observed. Eventually, a gratuity of two francs per body was agreed.

A further factor that stirred up ill-feeling in Britain was the decision taken by the American government to allow for the repatriation of its war dead. A letter from a Mr H. Francis of Cardiff in the *Western Mail* of 21 January 1920 noted:

> I see by a recent issue of *Western Mail* that the Americans are making arrangements for the removal of their dead soldiers from France and other parts for re-interment in their own country.
>
> Some time ago, if I remember correctly, there was some talk of adopting similar measures with regard to the British soldiers buried in Germany, but one hears nothing of the movement now, and as my own boy lies in a German grave I feel I should like to get in touch with others in a similar position to myself with the object of bringing home to the Government and the public some idea of the fitness of things. To think of them lying in an enemy country only intensifies our loss and grief.
>
> H Francis, 29 Colum-Road, Cardiff

Locally based groups sprung up with the aim of forcing the government to relent on its no repatriation policy, coalescing to form the British War Graves Association in 1919, founded by Sarah Ann Smith of Leeds, whose son Frederick was buried in the Grevillers Cemetery at the Somme. Sarah believed that soldiers killed in action should be brought home for burial. The case of Edith Cavell, the British nurse who had been executed in October 1915 by a German firing squad on suspicion of spying, caused further outcry amongst families whose sons lay still in a foreign field. Nurse Cavell's body was repatriated with some pomp in May 1919 and buried in the grounds of Norwich Cathedral.

An anonymous letter in the *Yorkshire Evening News* of 9 May 1919 articulated this sense of injustice:

> Soldiers and their Graves
>
> Now the government has decided to remove the bodies of the fallen from the scattered cemeteries to large central cemeteries, why cannot they allow relatives who so desire to have them brought home to be placed in the family grave?
>
> Nurse Cavell's body is being brought over to England, and why not others?
>
> I think the feeling is very strong against this attitude of the government, who claimed our boys when living, and now they have sacrificed their lives we are to be robbed of their dear remains, which belong to us and are ours alone.

A grieving mother, Ruth Jervis, wrote to the IWGC asking, 'is it not enough to have our boys dragged from us and butchered (and not allowed to say "nay") without being deprived of their poor remains?' In a second letter, she said, 'the country took him, and the country should bring him back'.

However, the prohibitive financial cost, along with the logistical and emotional energies involved with removing potentially half a million war graves, meant that there was no change in policy. To have relented on its stated sacred desire to have men who died as comrades to forever rest as comrades would have been a breach of trust with those who had already become reconciled that their loved ones would lie close to where

Private Tom Backhouse, whose body was repatriated to the UK on account of him having served in the US Army. (*Author's collection*)

they had fallen. The dead would remain in the sacred landscapes over which they had fought. Furthermore, despite pressure from Sarah Anne Smith and the British War Graves Association, the government resisted calls to provide a free pass for relatives to visit their loved one's grave or collective memorials on the Continent.

One family did manage to circumvent this embargo. Tom Backhouse had been born in Leeds but had emigrated to the USA with his brother, both of them becoming naturalised American citizens in 1913. Tom had been killed in the Argonne on 19 October 1918 while serving with 325 Infantry, 82nd Division of the US Army. His grieving parents placed an insertion in the *Yorkshire Evening Post*'s In Memoriam column of 19 October 1920:

> Years roll on and many tell us
> Wounds are healed by passing time
> But while life and memory lasteth
> Dearest Tom 'twill not heal mine.

When the war had been at its height, Tom's mother Emma had written verse, which she had printed on postcards and sold to passers-by in Leeds city centre. The money she raised was used to fund three spinal chairs and a bed rest in Seacroft Hospital for convalescing soldiers. Her work had won widespread praise, including letters from Princess Mary, the Prince of Wales and Lord Kitchener.

One such poem, written in 1917, was titled 'Lest We Forget':

> This is no time for dreaming,
> No time for idle scorn;
> All should be up and doing,
> To cheer some heart forlorn
> For while our lads are fighting
> On land and sea to-day,
> Our thoughts should all be centred,
> On each one far away
> Dear friends I often wonder
> When you pass through City Square,
> If you notice all the heroes
> That are oft assembled there?
> Have you watched our gallant heroes,
> How they smile and murmur not?
> Tis our duty now to help them,
> They should never be forgot.
> If you read the daily papers,

You will know the City's needs;
Two thousand beds are wanted,
In our own dear City – Leeds.
What a sad and darkened picture,
To imprint upon your mind,
But to each wounded hero,
'Tis our duty to be kind.
Then to each Nurse and Doctor,
May aid and strength be given,
To nurse and tend the wounded,
While some find rest in heaven.
Some sleep upon the battle-field,
And some in a foreign grave;
While some sleep in the ocean
Beneath the angry wave.
To Thee who taught us how to pray.
And say 'Thy will be done'.
We freely give each one we love,
To dwell with Thee at home.
Then may God's blessing from above,
Be showered on those that weep,
The mother, wife and children dear,
Do Thou their foot-steps keep.
Oh! Help them on life's rugged way,
To reach that heavenly shore,
Where loved ones they have only gone
A little while before.
Roll on then day of victory,

When shot and shell shall cease,
When guns shall all be silenced,
And the world be wrapped in peace.
Dear friends, I wish to thank you all,
For help to freely given;
And may our heroes when they fall,
Find rest, sweet rest, in heaven.

Mrs E. Backhouse
1917

Emma, of Altofts Place, Beeston Hill, working with the Leeds War Graves Association, organised for Tom's body to be returned to his home city. The *Leeds*

Mercury of 6 May 1924 reported on a 'Leeds Family's Sacrifice, Recalled by Exhumation of a Soldier'. It was reported that Tom's body was to be exhumed and brought back to England, to be interred at the Holbeck Cemetery. For Emma Backhouse, who had had another son killed in the war and another 'so badly shocked by a bursting shell that he became a mental wreck, and is now being cared for in the Wakefield Asylum', the return of Tom's remains to his boyhood home would provide some closure. Tom was to return on the SS *Hull* via the eponymous Yorkshire port and then be transported by train to Leeds for interment. Sadly, Tom's younger brother, Fred, was not to overcome his mental affliction, residing in the asylum until his early death in 1944. Emma lived to see his tragic decline and demise, herself dying aged 84 in 1946.

By April 1922, the IWGC still had dozens of locally engaged gangs working across the Western Front battlefields. From 1921 to 1928, 28,036 bodies were found, with 25 per cent of these being identified. From 1932 to 1936, 4,079 bodies were recovered, 52 per cent of which had been found by metal searchers, 30 per cent by landowners and 18 per cent by French government search parties. To this day, landowners in France and Flanders continue to turn up remains of soldiers from both sides of the conflict, and the Commonwealth War Graves Commission arranges, in partnership with the Ministry of Defence, for a thorough attempt to be made to trace their identity and for an interment with full military honours. The missing continue to remind us of their presence, and the yearning for closure amongst their families remains unabated.

Chapter 2

Ordinary Lives

Eight young men who went to war and would never return. Eight families who endured decades of inner anguish not knowing the final resting place of their precious relative. The octet includes a barrister, schoolteacher, engineering student, printer, grocer's assistant, medical student, warehouseman and doctor. They had benefitted from a vast array of educational opportunities, from some of the most renowned public schools in England to the council-run establishments set up in the wake of the 1870 and 1902 Education Acts. All eight were young men with drive, ambition and a keenness to experience the joys and challenges of life. They had various talents – artistic, sporting and organisational. They hailed from a variety of Christian denominations; some were Anglicans but there was also a Roman Catholic, a Methodist and a Congregationalist. All had loving families whose agonies at the lack of information as to their fate would haunt them for years, and whose subsequent generations would continue to suffer an aching void caused by the absence of a definitive account of their man's end. To this day, some of them are still seeking a sense of closure from the tragic events of over a century ago.

Percy Pope

'His cheeriness was of a winsome kind, but he had a great strength of will and knew what he wanted.'

The first of these men to arrive for their short existence on earth was Percy Paris Pope. Percy was born on 24 August 1882 at South Walk House, Dorchester. His father, Alfred, was a prominent citizen of Dorset's county town, serving as a Justice of the Peace and President of the Dorset Law Society, and was renowned as one of the region's major industrialists through his part-ownership of the Eldridge Pope brewery. In 1881, along with his brother Edwin, Alfred had purchased 4 acres of land next to the south coast railway which Isambard Kingdom Brunel had brought to the town three decades previously. They commissioned W.R. Crickmay, who had previously mentored Thomas Hardy during the famous Dorset writer's early career in the architectural profession, to design a majestic and exuberant red-brick brewery in which their business could expand.

Alfred Pope. (*Author's collection*)

Elizabeth Pope. (*Author's collection*)

Dorchester is a town steeped in history, with the nearby Iron Age hillfort of Maiden Castle and its Roman walls affirming its status as an important commercial centre in ancient times. In 1685, Judge Jeffries had presided over the series of 'Bloody Assizes' following the defeat of the Monmouth Rebellion,

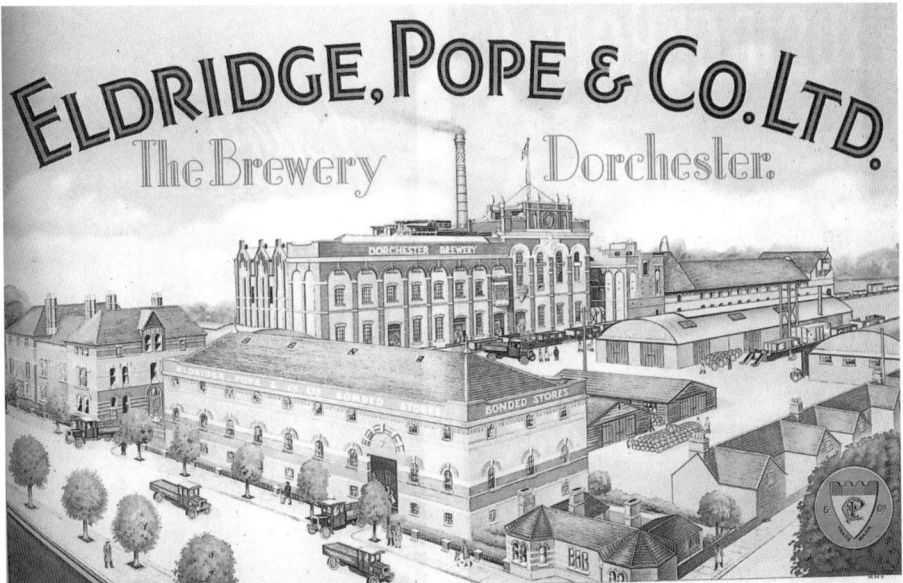

Eldridge Pope Brewery, Dorchester. (*Author's collection*)

ordering the hanging of seventy-four men. The force of the law had also been felt by the Tolpuddle Martyrs, six farm labourers who, in 1834, were sentenced at Dorchester's Courthouse to transportation to Australia for daring to form a trade union. When Percy was a small boy, the town gained further note as the town in which Thomas Hardy's *The Mayor of Casterbridge* was set.

Hardy himself was keenly aware of the town's history and was a frequent visitor to South Walk House, the home of the man who was shaping its future, Alfred Pope. Soon after the building of the new brewery, Eldridge Pope became the biggest employer in Dorchester. Its 'Celebrated Crystal Ale' was sold throughout the south-west of England for one shilling per gallon, being acclaimed as 'So delicately clean and well-tasted'. Alfred, who provided legal services to the Duchy of Cornwall, had also exercised the option to purchase many acres of land from their estates in the area surrounding the old town of Dorchester, and lost little time in developing row after row of town houses and villas for Dorchester's professional classes.

Alfred was abroad in Paris during the high summer of 1882, staying at the imposing Hotel Continental on the Rue de Rivoli when he received a letter informing him that 'You will perhaps be surprised to hear that at 12-30 last night your dear wife presented you with another little son'. Percy was the sixth son of Alfred Pope and the fifth to be born to his second wife, Elizabeth, née Whiting. Part of a large group of siblings that eventually numbered eleven, Percy would pride himself on being the 'central son' of the family.

When Percy was 11, his father commissioned Crickmay & Son to design the splendid South Court, an imposing town mansion of coursed Purbeck limestone with Bath stone dressing, complete with its own billiard room and library. The family's time was divided between South Court and the Wrackleford Estate, a 1,700-acre property encompassing the river Wrackle, feeding into the chalk valley of the river Frome, 3 miles north of Dorchester. Percy, according to his brother-in-law, the Reverend R.G. Bartelot, 'imbibed that admiration for Dorset which is so mysterious to the outsider'. He had a strong love of nature, a keen sporting instinct and a 'lasting interest in the welfare of the worker'.

Percy's brother-in-law reckoned him 'bodily and mentally ... above the average'. Percy possessed a fine profile, and a literary and artistic capacity, whilst his eyes displayed a 'poetic and artistic tendency'. Percy loved books and had a very retentive memory, manifesting 'remarkable quickness and accuracy in the recitation of verses'. His skills also extended to playing the piano and violin.

Percy's first school was Purbeck College, Swanage, under the tutelage of his godfather, the Reverend T. Russell-Wright. An 1891 advertisement in the *Bournemouth Guardian* noted its 'Beautiful Situation. Home Comforts. Sound Education', whilst an 1893 insertion by the school in the *Salisbury and Winchester Journal* boasted of a Mathematical Exhibition that a pupil had gained direct from the school to Emmanuel College, Cambridge. Young boys would be 'carefully prepared for the large public schools' whilst 'Seniors backward or delicate, and others needing help in public Exams, have unusual advantages'. French and German were 'taught conversationally by resident Foreign Masters'.

Russell-Wright, a former scholar of Pembroke College, Cambridge, recalled Percy possessed 'a most interesting personality', being eager to acquire knowledge and persistent in his pursuit of answers. His 'cheeriness was of a winsome kind, but he had a great strength of will and knew what he wanted', he had an excellent memory, 'and for his age an extraordinary insight into character'.

From Purbeck College, Percy passed on to the Twyford Preparatory School in Hampshire, run by the Reverend Charles Townshend Wickham, who considered him 'sensitive and somewhat reserved, but thoroughly keen', setting an excellent example to the other pupils. The historic Winchester College, founded in 1382, was his next school, Percy becoming a boarder in 1896 and excelling at sports and academic work. Headmaster William Fearon made Percy a school prefect. From the sixth form, Percy was one of seven out of thirty scholars who passed a competitive examination to gain admission to New College, Oxford.

In 1901, after leaving Winchester College, Percy travelled to Gersau on Lake Lucerne to stay with his former headmaster, Russell-Wright, who reflected, 'We read together some of his classical work for Oxford.' By this stage of his development Percy was 'always ready for an argument and was full of questions'. He also played the harmonium at Russell-Wright's 'little services'. Making many friends in Switzerland, at one point Percy contemplated taking Holy Orders, but the law held a stronger attraction. One of his close companions was the future Reverend R.A. Courthope, an old school friend from Winchester College who moved to Australia to work with the Anglican Bush Brotherhood, and later recalled Percy supporting him with his work in a London diocese. Percy read for the School of Jurisprudence, graduating with a BA with honours in 1905.

Percy then spent two further years on legal study before being called to the bar by the Inner Temple, paying the sum of £99 10s 'for the use of the Honourable Society of the Inner Temple' on 14 November 1907. That same year, he became a barrister on the Western Circuit and continued to develop his growing legal practice.

Percy enjoyed a final few months of pre-war peace on the Continent. The summer of 1914 found him holidaying in Paris, at the house of M. L'Abbé Bourgeois, on Boulevard Henri IV on the Seine's Île Saint-Louis, where he had gone to immerse himself in the French language. The house afforded a 'splendid view of the river from the windows'. He thus became an eyewitness to the confusion, panic and chaos that beset the city at the news of the German push to take the French capital, with many of its citizens carrying bitter memories of the siege and capture of Paris by Prussian troops during the winter of 1870/71.

Whilst thousands of visitors to the capital left hurriedly during the first day of mobilisation, with the French authorities organising train services to 'friendly frontiers', this facility soon ended as the railway lines were commandeered for the transportation of soldiers. One train leaving the Gare du Nord bound for England was crammed with escapees, with many others being unable to procure seats. For many of those left stranded in Paris, great distress was felt. Percy sent Alfred a cutting from the Continental *Daily Mail* concerning a lady who had applied to the British Chamber of Commerce for advice on her 'pitiable plight'. She had lived in a Paris hotel for years on the income from good securities, but the hotel was to close due to the wartime emergency, and she was unable to cash her security coupons.

For Percy, the crisis afforded some degree of excitement. He decided to stay in Paris to experience the tension of the crucial days when it was thought that the city might fall to the Germans. He wrote home on 5 August, noting with understatement that he was 'afraid our tour in Switzerland is off for the present'. He confirmed that non-military trains had stopped running out of Paris, with 'Messers [Thomas] Cook & Son … issuing no tickets at all'. Percy had attempted to visit the British consulate on 4 August to make enquiries, but 'there was such a crowd waiting with the same object that had I waited till midnight I shouldn't have got in.' He found himself in the same situation as the lady stranded in the imminently closing hotel, with his letters of credit 'so much waste paper just now', with none of the Barclays Bank representatives in Paris able to advance any cash on them.

Paris was, according to Percy, in an *'état de siège'*, being subject to martial law. Rioting and looting had taken place, 'chiefly crowds of hooligans destroying German shops'. Attempts to curtail such outbreaks were hampered by the fact that many police and soldiers had left Paris for the front. Squads of the Republican Guard 'trot about at all hours day and night'. Percy had witnessed a dozen-strong squad patrol pass his room at midnight and 2.00 am the previous night.

It was virtually impossible to take a cab anywhere in the city, with those still running charging exorbitant fares. The Paris Metro continued a very limited service, but no buses were operating. All public buildings were closed, and cafés and restaurants had to finish evening service by 8.00 pm. A de facto curfew was in place, with the few police officers who remained in the city warning people to be in their houses by 11.00 pm. Several hotels had been requisitioned by the government for use as hospitals. Percy had been to the Gare de Lyon, where the large square in front of the station was crowded with relatives bidding soldiers farewell. Civilian travellers were turned back by the military. All foreigners staying in Paris had to present their papers to the police authorities in order to obtain a permit to stay. Due to the near impossibility of obtaining safe passage across the Channel, many English subjects would have a lengthy stay in France.

Although having no experience of military service, Percy was so fired with enthusiasm for the Allied cause that he attempted to join the French Foreign Legion, in order to reach the front line as quickly as possible. Due to the disruption in postal services across the Channel, no news reached Dorset of his whereabouts, causing Alfred and Elizabeth Pope great anxiety as to his safety. Percy's brother Cyril did receive a letter sent by Percy on 24 August. Addressing his reply 'Sur le Continent', Cyril relayed that he had been involved in the Battle of Mons. Serving with the 1st Battalion Bedfordshire Regiment, Cyril hoped to have the opportunity of meeting Percy in Paris, depending on troop movements.

Alfred and Elizabeth's worry was removed in early October 1914, when Percy managed to return to England and joined the Inns of Court Officers' Training Corps. He underwent a private medical assessment by Dr Frederick Stuart of Knightsbridge, who considered Percy 'perfectly fit to go into training'. Nevertheless, Percy suffered from varicose veins, the presence of which led Stuart to assert that he 'might fail to pass into the Army for foreign service'.

Meanwhile, Percy's parents and siblings were all putting their shoulder to the wheel of the war effort, becoming, perhaps, the largest family unit in which all the members were involved in some form of war service. The day following Britain's declaration of war, Alfred Pope was issued with an impressment order under Section 115 of the Army Act, compelling him to take one riding horse to Dorchester Market, where he would be paid market value for the beast. Elizabeth Pope lent her car to the Dorset Section of the National Motor Volunteers for use in ambulance work. The organisation's commandant, Thomas Lynes, reported that the vehicle had proved of great assistance and 'enabled us to move practically all the wounded in closed cars'. The need for motor vehicles for use to transport wounded men returning to the home front was reiterated on 20 March 1916, when Alfred received a letter from the military comptroller of Dorset County Hospital requesting a donation towards the cost of a further motor ambulance to supplement the service of the Red Cross vehicle already in use. Having just had to process the arrival of ninety-eight wounded soldiers, fifty-six of whom were 'cot cases', the existing ambulance's capacity of four stretchers was wholly inadequate. The comptroller excused his begging due to 'the greatness of the cause'.

Percy's nine brothers all gained army commissions whilst his three sisters were involved in hospital work in Dorchester and further afield. Katie Pope had obtained a Voluntary Aid Detachment (VAD) certificate in 1912, and during the war worked at the Dorchester War Hospital depot of bandages, preparing these and other surgical appliances for the wounded, alongside her sister Evelyn. Hilda Pope had raised the Dorset 32 VAD. When war broke out she worked at the Princess Christian Hospital in Weymouth, and in 1916 went to the First London General Hospital in Camberwell. In May of that year, she sailed for France, spending fifteen months at No. 35 General Hospital, experiencing bombardment from the sea and numerous air raids. During her time there she was to meet Captain H.H. Levy, whom she married, and then returned to England to engage in land work for the rest of the war.

Ernest Blackburn

'Happy the lads & lasses who work under his influence & direction.'

Ernest was born of solidly respectable lower-middle class stock in the Yorkshire city of Wakefield on 16 August 1885. His 32-year-old father, James Blackburn, had begun his career as a solicitor's clerk before joining the West Riding Constabulary in September 1881. He had married Eliza Milnes in November 1874 and, in addition to Ernest, the union produced a typically large late Victorian family: three girls – Frances Mary (1875), May (1879) and Lily (1888); and three boys – Albert (1880), Herbert (1883) and Harold (1891). The Blackburns were Nonconformists, attending Congregational churches each Sabbath.

Having completed a stint at the divisional headquarters in Wakefield, James's police service took him to a position in nearby West Morley in late 1886. By the spring of 1891, the family resided in Halifax, with 16-year-old Frances employed in the famous West Riding cloth trade as a stocking knitter. James's career then took his family to the Calderdale town of Todmorden, where the formative years of Ernest's childhood were spent surrounded by steep-sided Pennine valleys and moorlands. Todmorden was a thriving town of 25,000 people and it was here that Ernest Blackburn took the first steps on the long career path into the teaching profession. Having completed his elementary education by the age of 13, James enrolled the academically gifted Ernest in the town's Roomfield School of Science.

On 24 July 1899, James received a postcard from the governors of the Heptonstall Exhibitions charity stating that Ernest had been awarded a £5 elementary scholarship towards the fees at Roomfield. Ernest fully justified the faith placed in him. He had already attained first in his class during the autumn and summer terms of 1898, topping the rankings in English Grammar, History, Geography, Practical Physics, Algebra, Euclid and Theoretical Chemistry.

At the end of the school year 1899–1900, Roomfield School's headmaster, Joshua Holden MA, commented that Ernest had proved himself 'a lad of excellent ability, persevering and painstaking in his work, and pleasant in his disposition'. Holden was 'thoroughly satisfied with his progress & conduct as a student in this school'.

As the new century dawned, so new horizons were opening for Ernest Blackburn. His time at Roomfield was ending. Mr Holden expressed his 'great disappointment' at losing 'one of my most promising pupils'. The Blackburn family relocated to the Dewsbury suburb of Soothill as James Blackburn had secured a position that would enable him to complete the final six years of his police career. He eventually retired in 1906 having received three good conduct awards during his twenty-five years of service.

Holden recommended that Ernest continue his progress towards qualified teacher in a Board School rather than a Voluntary School, due to their superior efficiency: 'it is better for a lad to become a teacher under a Board rather than in a school under private arrangement.' By Holden's estimation, Ernest had already surpassed the standard of work of an Elementary School and hoped that he would be able to find a secondary school where he could continue both his own education and his teacher training. Whilst Ernest's elder siblings were earning their living through manual work – May as a sewing machinist in the town renowned for its manufacture of shoddy cloth, Albert as a moulder's apprentice, and Herbert as a joiner's apprentice – 15-year-old Ernest was a pupil teacher, intent on achieving professional status.

The route into the teaching profession for many people from working and lower-middle class backgrounds was through on-the-job training. From 1846, the monitorial system, in which older pupils assisted teachers in delivering basic literacy and numeracy lessons to their younger peers, had been extended so that the more academically able children in a class could teach their age group peers. At the age of 13, these quasi-teaching pupils could be indentured to serve a five-year apprenticeship in officially approved elementary schools to gain a teaching certificate.

Ernest had chosen a profession that offered great prospects. The 1870 and 1902 Education Acts had allowed for the rapid expansion of state education, increasing the demand for qualified teachers. By October 1903, Ernest had completed a three-year apprenticeship in the boys' department of the Battye Street Provided School in the Pennine town of Heckmondwike, 2 miles to the west of his Dewsbury home. The headmaster, T.W. Crowther, wrote of 18-year-old Ernest that 'He has generally done well at his Examinations. He is punctual and attentive to his duties. I have always found him willing and obliging. I believe he will make a good teacher as well as a good student.' Good teachers needed, as well as the ability to impart subject knowledge to their classes, to be good role models to their pupils. During his apprenticeship Ernest would have had to learn the rudiments of classroom organisation, lesson preparation, assessment of pupils' work and behaviour management and discipline.

In December 1903, Ernest sat the King's Scholarship Examination to gain formal admission into the teaching profession, and in March 1904 his father was informed by postcard from the Board of Education in Whitehall that his 18-year-old son had obtained a place in the First Class. This enabled Ernest to be offered a place at Saltley Training College near Birmingham, which had been founded in 1847. The college stood on top of a hill a couple of miles due east from the middle of the city, a building of compact red sandstone, overlooking the valley of the river Rea. A 1905 feature in *The Schoolmaster* described a hollow square around a grassy quadrangle, and the 'ivied walls suggest the peace and quiet of a monastery rather than the bright and vigorous life of the modern Training College student'.

Saltley College's principal, the Reverend F.W. Burbidge, ran a liberal regime with few rules, as 'each man is trusted to act according to his own judgement'. Days were spent in private study, collective prayers and lectures. On Sundays, students, including the Nonconformist Ernest, were expected to attend St Peter's parish church, Saltley.

Ernest and his fellow students enjoyed the comforts of a recreation room. 'Here one may smoke his pipe over a friendly game of chess, or if disposed for reading take down a volume of Scott or Dickens from the walls or idly turn the leaves of a monthly magazine.' For sporting students, regular cricket and football matches were held against other institutions.

Ernest spent a year at Saltley, benefitting from its excellent academic reputation and the camaraderie amongst his fellow students. 'A capital *esprit de corps* prevails among students and ex-students alike, a spirit so marked as to call forth the hearty commendations of Training College Inspectors.' Ernest acquired the nickname 'Charc', presumably an allusion to charcoal, it being a black, burned substance. In January 1905, Ernest began to collect autographs and ink drawings by his fellow students in a small notebook. On 9 January 1906, Ernest's older brother Harold added a light-hearted comic verse in the book in beautiful copperplate handwriting:

We may live without poetry, music or art;
    We may live without conscience, & live without hearts;
We may live without friends, we may live without books,
    But civilized man cannot live without cooks.
He may live without books: what is knowledge but grieving?
    He may live without hope: what is hope but deceiving?
He may live without love: what is passion but pining?
    But where is the man who can live without dining?

Leaving Saltley, Ernest served as a student teacher at Heckmondwike School, the headmaster, R.S. Cahill, forming 'a very favourable opinion of his capabilities as a teacher … thoughtful, industrious and capable'. In May 1906, Ernest turned to Mr T.W. Crowther for a reference. Crowther affirmed Ernest was 'always punctual and attentive to his duties: obedient, willing and obliging'. He was a 'good disciplinarian' who could 'manage a class very effectively'. His teaching was described as 'creditable and successful'. Ernest was now ready to seek employment as a certified teacher.

Alongside his promising teaching career, Ernest was also active in his local church. Education of the young was no mere Monday to Friday duty for him, as he taught in the Sunday school of the Ebenezer United Congregational Church in Dewsbury. Serving as assistant superintendent of the Boys' Brigade and singing in the church choir, Ernest was also a keen cricketer. His commitment to the church, typical of so many Nonconformists of the era who regarded the institution as a social as well as a religious organisation, saw him become secretary of the church cricket team. Ernest's career at Upper Wortley can be followed in the log book the head teacher was required to complete on a regular basis.

On 27 August 1906, Ernest, Certified Teacher 06/576, took up an appointment at Upper Wortley Council School, which catered for the children of the workers at local brickworks, factories and mills. Containing streets of pavement-fronted back-to-back terraced houses, interspersed with some larger dwellings for factory foremen, clerks and managers, the district was situated 2 miles west of Leeds. Ernest was responsible for the teaching of the higher standard boys' classes. With a complement of staff of around a dozen certified teachers, and a handful of pupil teachers, the 700-strong school roll would have been taught in classes of upwards of fifty pupils. In addition to his teaching load, Ernest contributed to the training of his colleagues.

Mr Howe looked favourably on Ernest, a 1909 testimonial describing him 'a willing, painstaking and conscientious teacher [who] enters into the life of the school and children heartily'. Ernest's classroom management was 'firm, exercising a restraining and beneficial influence over his pupils in the formation

of good and manly habits'. Eli Howe
had led the school for over thirty
years but suffered from increasingly
prolonged absences from duty
caused by bouts of sickness. He
soldiered on into the autumn term
of 1912, but felt compelled to hand
in his resignation on 30 September.
Two weeks later, he was dead, and
the school was closed to teachers
and scholars on 18 October so they
could attend his funeral. Ernest
paid his respects to the man who
had shown faith in him and given
encouragement to his professional
progress.

Ernest was highly regarded in
church circles. The minister of
Ebenezer Congregational Church,
the Reverend Albert T. Hogg, wrote
glowingly that the 27-year-old
Ernest was:

Annie Blackburn and Stanley Blackburn.
(*Courtesy the Blackburn family*)

[A] born Teacher … & as a Friend of boys, who can win them & wield the
forces that make up boyhood, I have never known his superior, young as
he is. It is what every Teacher & Leader should be; manly, straightforward,
courteous, scrupulously conscientious in the performance of his duty,
patient with an unreserved tolerance, full of humour, full of resource &
quietly persistent. … He is a young man with great reserves & bears an
irreproachable character. Happy the lads & lasses who work under his
influence & direction.

On 10 August 1912, Ernest wed Sarah Annie Smith at the Ebenezer
Church. The local press reported that Sarah, known affectionately as 'Annie',
wore 'a gown of ivory crepe-de-chine with a wreath of orange blossom and
an embroidered veil'. Herbert and Harold Blackburn acted as best man and
groomsman respectively, whilst the Ebenezer Company of the Boys' Brigade
provided their former captain with a bugle fanfare as the party left the church.
Annie herself had been pursuing a career as a teacher, serving at Park Road
School, Batley. Her teaching colleagues had bought the couple a set of solid

silver spoons, and Ernest's associates had given a copper kerb. As the newly married couple left for a Belgian honeymoon, Annie faced the end of her teaching career, just as Ernest's was on an upwards trajectory. Until the passing of the Sex Disqualification Removal Act in 1919, no married woman could remain in the teaching profession.

William Grassham, an energetic man of 42 years, replaced Mr Howe as Ernest's headmaster, intent on driving through improvements at Upper Wortley. He set about a transformation of the school, ordering new blackboards, poetry books and dictionaries for the upper classes, which Ernest taught, and meeting frequently with the Leeds Education Authority to request maintenance work to the school buildings and grounds.

This may have been an unsettling time for Ernest, leaving his parents' home for the first time, to set up house with Annie in a modest terraced property at 7 Moorfield Avenue, Armley – a short walk uphill from his workplace. In addition to new domestic routines as a married man, he had to become accustomed to the heightened expectations of Mr Grassham and his new work regime. Head teachers were responsible for the administering of corporal punishment, and Mr Grassham delegated this power to six of his teaching staff. However, Ernest was not one of those authorised to do this, either due to his own personal choice or perhaps an abhorrence of physical chastisement. He was, nevertheless, an extremely reliable member of staff, with not a single absence recorded during his ten years of service at the school.

A local authority inspection report commented on the new headmaster's 'energetic approach', which 'may be expected to make the school a thoroughly good one when his methods and influence have had time to make themselves felt'. Mr Grassham's plans were to be severely curtailed by the advent of war in the summer of 1914. Immediately at the commencement of the new school year in September, the staff agreed to contribute 2½ per cent of their monthly salaries to the War Relief Fund. Despite this act of professional altruism, the loss of European export markets was hitting the Leeds textile industry hard, and Mr Grassham noted the 'growing distress in the neighbourhood on account of unemployment caused by the War; seven families have applied for Free Dinners this week'. A collection was undertaken for the 'amelioration of distress among Belgian Children'.

One teacher, Miss May Thorp, was granted an early finish on 27 October 1914 'to take up ambulance duties at the Railway Station'. As the realisation dawned that the war would not, as some had optimistically expected, be over by Christmas, Mr Grassham noted, on 19 November, 'The roll of "Old Boys" serving their country is steadily growing.' He was also acutely aware of the sacrifices that the fathers of some of his pupils were making, as on 23 December, eight scholars received Christmas gifts from the USA, 'their parents being prisoners in Germany or serving abroad'.

The school performed additional functions as the war progressed. On 15 January 1915, it became a centre for the payment of war allowances to the dependents of local soldiers, with the staff volunteering their services every Friday lunchtime to hand out the imbursements. On 28 April it was agreed that the school would provide a rifle range and purchase a weapon, with the boys encouraged to buy their own ammunition to practise their marksmanship.

It was into this uncertain and dislocated world that Ernest and Annie celebrated the birth of Stanley Blackburn on 22 February 1915. Future hopes must have been severely clouded with anxiety at what the immediate future held for the Blackburns. Colleagues began to disappear. Mr Grassham lost his first member of staff to war duties on 7 June, with May Thorp being granted leave of absence 'with lapse of salary' to train as a Red Cross nurse in Leicester. The school became a focus of frequent collections, with an appeal on behalf of 'Leeds Lads at the front' in September 1915 raising £10 11s 6d. The same month, with the Zeppelin raids which had begun on the Yorkshire coast moving further inland, Mr Grassham arranged for dark blinds to be fixed to one room, enabling evening classes to continue 'without showing a light to the enemy'. Slowly, the secure life based upon family, church and workplace that Ernest had striven to build since his teenage years was being eroded, and by the end of October he could no longer remain personally immune to wartime expectations.

Pupils were dismissed half an hour early on 28 October to enable staff to attend a meeting for teachers at the Albert Hall in Leeds City Square. Men were being strongly encouraged to enlist under the Lord Derby Recruitment Scheme and Ernest duly accepted his fate, signing up that day. Grassham became an important local driver of army recruitment, visiting workplaces in the Armley, Farnley and Upper and Lower Wortley areas, speaking to over 1,000 men. He personally assisted the clerk at the Oxford Place recruiting office, absenting himself from school from 7-10 December to do so. He also

Rifleman Ernest Blackburn. (*Courtesy the Blackburn family*)

organised collections for English prisoners of war in Germany and a flag day for Serbian relief.

On 29 May, five days after the singing of the national anthem and saluting of the Union flag on Empire Day, Mr Grassham recorded in the school log book: 'Mr Ernest Blackburn (TC) absent this morning: he is undergoing medical examination for enlistment into the Army. Result – passed – gone to York.' Two weeks later, another member of staff, Mr George Downend, left to join the Royal Garrison Artillery. Despite being wounded and sent to a military hospital in Boulogne in 1917, George survived the war and was able to resume his teaching duties in early 1919. May Thorp brought credit upon herself and the school, being mentioned in despatches in May 1917. Although there was much relief and rejoicing at the return of George and May following their war service, many tears would be shed at the loss of their longstanding friend and colleague, Mr Ernest Blackburn.

Lieutenant John Gillis Butt RAMC

'a credit to the school and very much liked by all who knew him'

John Gillis 'Jack' Butt was born in Lucknow, Uttar Pradesh, India, on 13 July 1890 and was baptised along with his twin sister, Gladys Gwendoline, at All Saints Garrison Church. The twins' father, Dr Edward Ormiston Butt, a native of County Antrim, was serving on the subcontinent as an army surgeon. He had married Helen Mary Garratt, originally from County Galway, in Dundalk on 17 October 1889. Jack was named after his grandfather, John Gillis Butt, who had enjoyed a successful banking career.

Edward Butt had been educated at Queen's College, Belfast and the school of the Royal College of Surgeons, Ireland, earning an impressive array of medical qualification: LKQCP (Licentiate of the King's and Queen's College of Physicians (Ireland)); LRCSI (Licentiate of the Royal College of Surgeons in Ireland); FRCSI (Fellow of the Royal College of Surgeons of Ireland); and DPH (Dental Public Health). He had joined the British Army as a surgeon in 1881, rising to surgeon major in February 1893 and attaining the rank of lieutenant colonel by February 1901.

Edward was an innovator of military hygiene, serving for several months in Secunderabad before taking up an appointment as Principal Medical Officer in Calcutta. During the former posting he had managed to reduce the hospital cases of enteric fever to only thirty-one out of a garrison of 4,000 troops. According to a local press report, Edward's methods of improving sanitation had proved 'rigorous and decidedly effective' over the years. The presence of enteric fever had 'baffled the skill of many of his clever predecessors'. The remarkable decline in disease was due to Edward's method of 'going to the root of sanitary evils'. Despite initial resistance from the troops to his methods, they produced a 'miraculous effect'. Edward was the recipient of many farewell dinners, his departure being 'much regretted'.

By 1901, the family had returned to Ireland, residing above banking premises at 17 Park Street, Dundalk, in comfortable upper middle-class domesticity. Nine members of the extended Butt and Garratt family made up the household, with the addition of three servants. James Garratt, Jack's maternal grandfather, was an agent of the Bank of Ireland, and the family gave their religion as Church of Ireland.

Edward Butt eventually attained the rank of colonel, retiring in March 1914. This provided the means to send Jack to Marlborough College in Wiltshire from 1904 to 1907. He proved to be a keen sporting competitor as the school sought to develop the physical fitness and character as well as the intellectual capabilities of its pupils. *The Marlburian* magazine of March 1905 mentioned Jack winning a game of Fives against E.W. Evans in an under-15 singles competition. Further entries noted his participation in sprint and hurdle races. Jack was the second-highest scorer as his house, Wall's, finished third in the house gym competition. When Jack left Marlborough, a college master, W.H. Madden, commended his contributions, writing to Edward that his son had 'been a credit to the school and very much liked by all who knew him'.

Lieutenant Colonel Edward Ormiston Butt. (*Courtesy Nick Previté*)

Helen Butt. (*Courtesy Nick Previté*)

Jack's education continued at Trinity College, Dublin, achieving both Bachelor of Arts (BA) and Bachelor of Medicine (MB) in May 1914. His certificate of medical registration was granted on 10 July, and Jack resolved to follow his father into a military medical career, applying for a commission in the Royal Army Medical Corps (RAMC), which was granted four days before Britain entered the war. By this time his parents had moved to mainland Britain, residing at Crumlin Lodge, an extensive red-brick Victorian villa situated in the Berkshire village of Datchet. Jack's hopes that the war would provide him with the opportunity to embark on emulating his father's distinguished military service were to be cruelly extinguished, as he would be cut down before his talents had the opportunity to blossom.

Charles Attwood

'Filling a lucrative position as a printer'

The Somerset town of Somerton boasts an illustrious history. Sitting on a plateau above the deep valley of the river Cary, it was a stronghold of the Saxon kings of Wessex and in 949 was the site of a meeting of the Anglo-Saxon parliament. For a brief period from the late thirteenth century, it was Somerset's county town. A market had been held there for centuries, and a few yards from the 1673 Butter Cross stood the Magistrate's Court and Police Station, a Victorian addition to Somerton. In the years preceding the war,

Henry and Emma Attwood. (*Courtesy Robin Williams*)

Superintendent Henry Mark Attwood was charged with the maintenance of law and order in Somerton and its surrounding villages. It was the fates of his two eldest sons, Charles and James, which were to cause Henry and his wife Emma's deep and long-lasting heartache.

Charles Attwood was born in the Bristol suburb of Bishopsworth on 5 October 1893, the third of Henry and Emma's six children. The couple had married in the summer of 1890 in the seaside resort of Weston-super-Mare, with Edith, the eldest child, being born in 1891 and a second daughter, Ethel, arriving in 1892. However, Ethel was to die of diphtheria in the summer of 1896, having been closely nursed by the family for four years and four months, when Charles was only 2 years old. After a gap of seven years, James was born in 1899, Henry in 1901, and Edward in 1906.

Christianity was an important influence, with a family King James Bible being treasured (in which were recorded births, marriages and deaths) and Emma owning a prayer book embossed with a cross, given to her in 1888. During the first decade of the new century, Henry's career thrived, and by 1909 he had risen to the rank of superintendent and was appointed to ensure that Somerton miscreants were brought to justice.

Superintendent Attwood was a prominent community figure, his role bringing him into contact with many tragic circumstances. On 1 September 1909, the *Taunton Courier and Somerset Advertiser* reported that Kate Lewis, a 26-year-old single woman, had strangled her 18-month-old illegitimate child before attempting to take her own life by cutting her throat with a razor. Henry had collected a suicide note that Lewis had written and would attend the inquest into the death of the strangled child, Winifred Lewis. Henry's duties extended to acting as the local inspector of the Diseases of Animals Act. The *Western Gazette* of 27 October 1911 reported on him supervising the cremation of seventeen milking cows at a farm near Babcary, two of which had died of anthrax.

Meanwhile, young Charles had been apprenticed to Mr J.G. Williams of Somerton to gain grounding in the printing trade. In October 1909, Williams had advertised in the *Western Daily Press* for an 'IMPROVER, young Man, three or four years' experience, case, press, machine', and it is possible that the 16-year-old Charles responded to this opportunity.

However, Charles was eager for adventure, and shortly before his eighteenth birthday, his printing indenture being terminated, he emigrated to Canada, where, according to one obituary, 'he was filling a lucrative position as a printer'. Charles was one of many ambitious Britons who embarked on a new life in the Dominion of Canada. From 1903 to 1913, more than 3 million people emigrated from the mother country, with almost half of these choosing

Canada as their destination. The country, keen to welcome British immigrants, established an emigration office in Trafalgar Square, London, in 1903. The 1910 Immigration Act granted Canadian citizenship to British subjects domiciled in Canada. Charles sailed from Bristol on the Canadian Northern Steamship Ltd. vessel *Royal George*, departing on 2 October 1912 and landing in Quebec harbour a week later to become one of 147,619 Britons to emigrate to the dominion that year. Well over 800 people were on board, and accompanying Charles were a diverse range of prospective settlers: a furnisher, baker, clothier, engineer, painter, carpenter, butler, plumber, mason, and engine driver, as well as domestics and cooks. Most were aged from 17 to 40, with very few children accompanying the passengers, most migrants being unmarried.

On arrival in Canada, Charles moved westwards, to Manitoba province's capital city, Winnipeg. Investment was pouring into the infrastructure of the Dominion's third-largest city, booming businesses offering the opportunity of rapid advancement for the keen and bright. Charles had been well known in Somerton for his athleticism and had been a member of the Somerton Rifle Club. On arrival in his new country, he joined the Winnipeg Rifle Club, under the captaincy of Mr R.J. Wilson. By 1913, Charles was living at 672 Banning Street in the city's West End. The district, with housing for the middle and working classes, had seen large-scale development between 1890 and 1912. It was close to downtown Winnipeg and was served by the city's street railway system. A thriving industrial area provided employment for many West End residents. Less than a mile from Charles's house lay Pine Street, which would later be named Valour Road due to the pre-war residency of three men who would earn the Victoria Cross. By the following year, as a little-known archduke was assassinated in faraway Sarajevo, Charles was employed as a press feeder for Saults & Pollard, a commercial printing company founded in 1907. Charles would have been responsible for the preparation of printing plates and loading paper into the feeding tray of a printing press. He would carefully oversee the running press, adjusting the operation to prevent paper jams. Saults & Pollard took commissions for everything from business cards to vaudeville posters. Charles's fortunes were on the rise, and he had moved a mere 500 yards across the West End's busy Ellice Avenue to take up residence at 835 Lipton Street, a spacious three-bedroomed weatherboard-clad house sitting in its own plot of land.

Charles had reached across the Atlantic Ocean to develop a new life in Canada. Circumstances were to conspire to pull him back across the waters and terminate his ambitious progress.

Arthur Greensmith

'The prosperous state of local industry'

The ambitions of Arthur Clarence Greensmith were set within the Yorkshire and Nottinghamshire coal mining industry, the power behind Britain's enormous nineteenth-century industrial growth. Arthur was born in December 1893, the youngest of five children of Arthur John Greensmith, a Sheffield grocer, and his wife Cecilia. His older siblings were William, Dora, Cecilia and Gwyneth. At the time of Arthur's birth, the family lived in Surbiton Street, Carbrook, in the heart of the industrial Don Valley area to the east of a city famed for its iron and steel production. The Greensmith grocery store was a short walk away on Attercliffe Common, one of the main road arteries that stretched out from Sheffield's city centre.

From the middle of the 1800s, the ancient Sheffield metalworking industry had expanded rapidly, giving rise to large factories and hundreds of small workshops. Many of these factories spread out along the Don Valley, and their workers were serviced by shopkeepers such as Arthur Greensmith senior. New steels were being produced for use on the railways and military and industrial infrastructure, earning huge wealth for the city. The British Association for the Advancement of Science declared in 1910 that Sheffield 'is at the present moment the greatest armoury the world has ever seen'.

Cecilia, Willie, Arthur and Gwyneth Greensmith. (*Courtesy Rosemary Gregory*)

The city's population had trebled between 1851 and 1901. One of those incomers was John Greensmith, a collier from Kimberley in Nottinghamshire, and father of Arthur senior. The Greensmiths had risen up the social ladder, with John owning a small colliery in Killamarsh by 1881 as well as running a grocery shop. Arthur senior had remained in the east end of Sheffield to make his living amidst the smoke and noise of metal manufacturing.

Attercliffe was a bustling hive of industrial and commercial activity and Arthur's business acumen enabled him to advance the opportunities for his family. Bright Street Methodist Chapel stood close to the Greensmiths' home and, like many Edwardian families, they were regular chapelgoers. Arthur's daughter Cecilia sang in a choir, and during a celebration for the Carbook Church Men's Bible Class at which she performed, it was noted that there were 420 students enrolled in the group. The chapel is no longer in existence, the area having been cleared to make way for the palace of purchasing that is the Meadowhall Shopping Centre.

As well as his grocery shop, Arthur senior acted as an agent for J&G Wells Limited, Colliery Proprietors, at the nearby Broughton Lane railway station. These business interests enabled Arthur to accrue sufficient wealth to send his younger son, Arthur Clarence Greensmith, to Ashley House School in Worksop. The school was located on the town's outskirts on one of the highest spots in the northern Sherwood Forest. Surrounded by playing fields, it had a well-endowed library and science laboratories, as well as a gymnasium and arts and crafts rooms. The school offered a full programme of preparation for university scholarships or entry into professional or business careers.

The Greensmiths continued to amass social and financial capital, and by 1911 had taken up residence at Hughenden House on the tree-lined Kenwood Park Road, situated in the fashionable Sharrow area of Sheffield. In contrast to smoky Carbrook, Sharrow had benefitted from the surge in tree-planting in

Albert and Cecilia Spittle's wedding day. (*Courtesy Rosemary Gregory*)

Sheffield's suburbs, with 5,000 saplings planted in the years before 1914. Further municipal improvements had seen 12,000 gas lamps lighting the city's streets, and council-run trams criss-crossing the city's main road arteries.

The large villa housed Arthur senior and Cecilia, with their four youngest adult offspring. Arthur junior had by that time completed his schooling, and become a mining engineering student with J&G Wells. His cousin,John Thomas Greensmith, was General Manager at Brodsworth Main Colliery, near Doncaster, a Wells-owned mine. Arthur could look forward to a successful career in an industry where his skills would be continuously called upon as decades of insatiable demand for coal were to follow.

Arthur and Cecilia Greensmith. (*Courtesy Rosemary Gregory*)

The *Sheffield Yearbook* of 1914 commented on 'a considerable increase in the number of weddings among the Sheffield artisan class as a result of the prosperous state of local industry'. One such ceremony was that of Albert Spittle, a steelworks clerk, to Cecilia Greensmith, daughter of Arthur Greensmith senior. The move to Sharrow meant a change in the family's place of worship, and on 24 September, Cecilia and Albert were married at the Trinity Wesleyan Methodist Church, situated just off the London Road, the ceremony being performed by the Reverend Thomas Miller. Arthur junior acted as best man for his new brother-in-law. A reception was held at Hughenden House before the newly-weds departed for a Torquay honeymoon.

By the time of the wedding, Arthur Greensmith, mining engineering student, had become Private Arthur Greensmith of the 12th Battalion York and Lancaster Regiment. Sheffield in 1914 boasted a population of around 460,000, the sixth-largest city in the United Kingdom. Arthur was one of 52,000 Sheffielders to serve with the armed forces during the war, more than half of available men. Six thousand of them would never return to contribute to the post-war reconstruction, their bodies extinguished of life and laying forever in foreign soil.

Frank Mead

'With you, my friend, with you'

London in 1914 was the centre of Empire, the largest city in the world and the heart of international finance and trade, from which vast fortunes were generated. The desperate poverty and pollution of the city's underclass sat in stark contrast to ostentatious affluence of the its wealthy citizens. Between these two extremes sat families like the Meads: educated, skilled and literate, of comfortable circumstances but needing to exert themselves to maintain and improve their position. Frank Mead was born in 1894 and was baptised in his local parish church, St Saviour's, Brixton, on 13 January 1895. Frank grew up in solid middle-class respectability in Herne Hill. His paternal family had originated in Northampton, a town famed for the production of footwear, where his grandfather and great-uncle had run Mead and Faulkner shoe manufacturers.

Frank's father, Thomas, had moved to London in the early 1880s. Beginning his career as a clerk, he was a man of ambition and inventiveness, using his knowledge of the footwear business to devise an innovation in sporting shoes. On 20 January 1890, Thomas submitted a patent application for 'Improvements in the Construction of Boots and Shoes' and was granted patent No. 994.

Thomas's invention was 'more especially applied to Boots and Shoes for lawn tennis and other athletic purposes' and aimed to reduce the weight of the footwear whilst increasing durability and flexibility by making diagonal grooves in the tread.

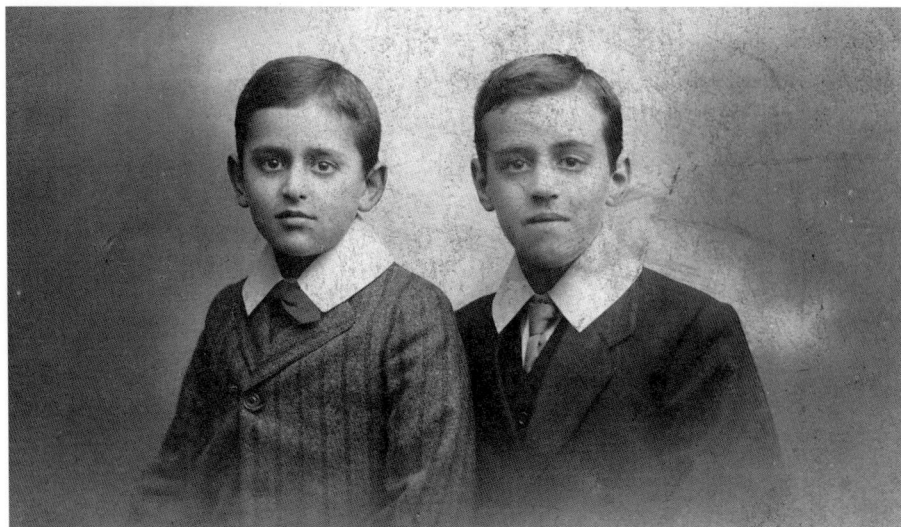

Reggie and Frank Mead as boys. (*Courtesy Chris Mead*)

Ink drawings by Frank Mead featuring current affairs of the time.

By 1901, young Frank and his infant brother Reginald were living in Camberwell, where it is probable that Frank was attending the nearby Wilson's School. The Meads were of affluent enough circumstances to employ a live-in servant.

By 1911, Thomas and his family were living in a large villa on Elfindale Road, Herne Hill, where he was listed as a foreign commercial traveller; indeed, on the date of the national census he was on business abroad, with the family still employing a servant. Reginald attended Bethany House School at Goudhurst in Kent, possibly as a boarder, whilst Frank was still enrolled in school three years past the minimum leaving age. Reginald would continue his studies at the Strand School in Tulse Hill from May 1915 to February 1917. Thomas was clearly minded to invest in the education of his two sons.

Frank was a talented amateur artist, and a series of sketches survive that display both a keen eye for character details and a sharp awareness of the political events of the pre-war era. In one sketch Frank depicted King Edward VII, the 'Peacemaker', looking on somewhat quizzically as Liberal leader H.H. Asquith and Conservative leader Arthur Balfour engaged in a power struggle over the terms of Chancellor David Lloyd George's 'People's Budget' of 1909. In another, Edward's successor, King George V, solemnly gazes at a newspaper detailing the policy headaches that greeted him when he assumed the throne. The constitutional crisis caused by the power struggle between the Lords and the Commons continued, in addition to the looming menace of increasing German naval strength. Furthermore, threats to British foreign trade brought about by the growing might of the industrial powerhouses of the USA and Germany were a concern for the new king. Britain, depicted as John Bull, looks on gravely as the King grapples with those intractable problems.

Frank also kept an autograph book, in which he asked visitors to Elfindale Road to write a few lines of verse or draw a sketch. One visitor, from 'God's own country', emphasised the conviviality of friendship:

> If all the stars were mine
> Do you know what I should do?
> I'd give them all for a glass of wine
> With you, my friend, with you.

Rifleman Alan Stirling

'The baker's dozen'

The marriage of William John Alan Stirling and Emma Craddock was blessed with thirteen children, all of whom grew to be adults. This was a remarkable feat in days of high child mortality, when parents frequently experienced the heartache of burying their young. William, a master baker by trade, certainly produced his baker's dozen. His customers enjoyed a wide range of sweet-tasting treats such as cakes, sweet pastries, tarts, doughnuts, pies, muffins and biscuits. Alan Stirling was the couple's fourth child, born in Cannon Street in the Rycroft area of Walsall, on 7 August 1895. By 1911, William Stirling and his large family were living in a six-roomed house on Station Road, Aldridge, Staffordshire, a row of smart Victorian red-brick terraced houses with compact front yards. Fifteen-year old Alan was a grocer's errand boy, employed by Thomas Potts, a 64-year-old widower, whose High Street business served many locals who were employed in coal mining and brickmaking. Potts had been trading in Aldridge since 1868 and had built up a strong relationship with the town's major employers, who would sometimes pay their workers in tokens that were stamped with Potts's name and only redeemable at his shop.

Emma Stirling. (*Courtesy Rosemary Phillips*)

William Stirling. (*Courtesy Rosemary Phillips*)

In the immediate pre-war years, the Stirling family having moved to 78 Ash Street, Wolverhampton, Alan worked in G.H. Kidson Ltd.'s wholesale grocery warehouse at 34 Wadham's Hill. Kidson's headquarters was an imposing brick building with seven arched windows, a grand entrance doorway and a large opening into which wagons would enter and exit with supplies. A newspaper advertisement from 1892 stated Kidson's was an 'Importer of Irish, American and Danish Produce'.

G.H. Kidson supplied shops within a 25-mile radius of Wolverhampton. Sales representatives would travel the district advising customers on the latest products, special offers, market trends and trading conditions. Alan was at the centre of a substantial international grocery operation that brought foods from Britain and around the world to the Staffordshire town.

The war crept up on Wolverhampton. On 25 July 1914, the *Wolverhampton Express and Star* claimed that Britain and France held no interest in problems in the Balkans, and even as late as 3 August stated that any British involvement in war would be limited to naval engagements. Once war was declared the following day, Alan's workplace was immediately affected. Panic buying began in the shops, and prices rose sharply. In the meantime, the town's German citizens were instructed to report immediately to the Chief Constable's Office in the Town Hall. Ordinary Wolverhampton citizens such as the Stirlings were encouraged to report any knowledge as to 'the residence and whereabouts of all Germans in the Borough of Wolverhampton and neighbourhood'.

By the end of 1914, the Wolverhampton and District Recruiting Committee (WDRC) had been formed, consisting of teachers, clergymen and political agents. They sought to speak to every man from 18 to 40 to explain the necessity of going to war and to encourage enlistment. Young men such as Alan were finding it difficult to resist the calls to join up. Lady members of the WDRC would visit women at home when their menfolk were at work to persuade them to use their influence to have their men enlist. These visits would often be followed up by an evening visit to force home the moral pressure on the man.

Every shopkeeper was encouraged to display a recruitment poster in their window, and posters were also placed on lampposts, giving the address of the recruiting office. Recruiting officers would station themselves in busy streets and market places in the evenings to persuade men coming home from work to enlist. Open-air meetings were held and cinemas showed a recruitment film. Churchgoers such as the Anglican Stirling family were subjected to appeals from their clergy to join the growing number of recruits. For those who had heeded their nation's call, roll of honour cards were issued to houses of those who had enlisted, and these endeavours saw 1,500 new local volunteers joining up by the end of January 1915.

Still more men were needed, so a mass recruitment meeting was held in February 1915, followed by a torchlight procession. A further recruitment week took place in May. The result was that 12,000 Wolverhampton and district men had volunteered before the introduction of the Lord Derby Scheme. Alan Stirling finally succumbed to the emotional, social and moral pressure to which he and his peers were subjected and enlisted in early October 1915. Within a few weeks he was on his way to Dover as Private Alan Stirling 913578 of the Army Ordnance Corps.

Private Alan Stirling. (*Courtesy Rosemary Phillips*)

Gilbert Donnelly

'Glory from Within'

Carl Gilbert Donnelly was the eleventh of thirteen children born to John Donnelly and his wife Jemima (née Doggart). He was born on 25 July 1897 at the family home, 9 Willowbank Gardens, Belfast, a red-brick terraced town house. Gilbert was baptised seven days later at the Holy Family Roman Catholic Church. Disaster befell the Donnelly family in 1901, when Jemima contracted influenza followed by pneumonia after the birth of her thirteenth child, Hugh. After a two-week illness, Jemima passed away on 6 March. The 3½-year-old Gilbert and his siblings were now motherless. John, who was Assistant Superintendent of Post and Telegraphs at Belfast's General Post Office, was left to raise the large brood with the assistance of his eldest daughter, Norah Helen.

At the turn of the century, Belfast was a thriving port city, with linen mills and shipbuilding yards being the main economic drivers. Tens of thousands were employed in the textile industry, and at the time of Gilbert's birth the world-renowned Harland and Wolff shipyard had a workforce of 9,000. It is believed that Gilbert's grandfather, James Donnelly, had migrated to Belfast from the rural parish of Desertmartin in County Derry, Ulster, arriving in the first half of the century. James had begun work as a pavior, laying paving stones on the new streets of the rapidly expanding city. Over the next four decades, he rose through the hierarchy of Belfast's public works department, concluding his career in the position of Superintendent of Works. In doing so he resisted the tides of sectarian prejudice that sought to keep many of the city's Roman Catholic population away from positions of influence and responsibility.

Gilbert's father, John, was baptised in St Patrick's Church, Belfast, on 6 May 1854, the eldest of James Donnelly's offspring. Like his father before him, John was a hard-working and ambitious

Gilbert Donnelly and siblings. Top: Billy, Samuel. Middle: Helen holding Muriel, John, Eugene, Austin. Bottom: Gilbert, Harry. (*Courtesy the Donnelly family*)

Gilbert Donnelly and family. Back: Gilbert, John (father), John (son), Harry. Front: Samuel, Muriel, Helen, Sarah Gibb (wife of Samuel) holding John (grandson). (*Courtesy the Donnelly family*)

man who dedicated his career to public service. John's GPO career had begun in 1870, and he had quickly learned the code invented by Samuel Morse in 1844, becoming adept at the sending and receipt of telegraph messages. His obituary in the *Belfast Telegraph* quoted a work colleague: 'Mr Donnelly was regarded as one of the finest telegraphists we have ever had in the service. He knew his job from A to Z.' Aside from the workplace, John Donnelly was physically active. 'In his young days Mr. Donnelly was an ardent cyclist and was a pioneer in Belfast of the picturesque penny-farthing machine.'

Unusually, as a member of a family that was establishing itself as a stalwart of the Roman Catholic community in Belfast, John Donnelly had married Jemima Doggart, a member of a large and prominent Presbyterian family. Jemima had strong Scottish roots and, like her future husband, had worked as a telegraphist, in the seaside town of Bangor in County Down. In preparation for her marriage, Jemima took instruction in the Roman Catholic faith. Jemima needed a strong mind and force of will to undertake this conversion as she was likely to have been disowned by parts of her strongly Protestant family. She was baptised a Roman Catholic one month before her twenty-first birthday in 1881, marrying John the following year.

The extended Donnelly family lived with Christian principles at its heart. One of Gilbert's uncles, James Joseph Donnelly, served as president of the Belfast branch of the St Vincent de Paul Society, an international charity committed to the relief of the poor. James Joseph's standing in society was confirmed by his appointment, in 1901, as a Justice of the Peace for Belfast. James Joseph's son Charles would go on to serve as a Roman Catholic priest. As a small child, Gilbert was nearly taken in to live with another uncle, William Donnelly, and his wife Julia. Following the death of Jemima Donnelly, it was thought that the ten surviving children would be too many for the industrious John to cope with, but Gilbert and his younger sister Muriel had grown attached to their elder siblings, so in the event, only the youngest child, Hugh, went to live with relatives.

As the century ended, the family moved to a substantial newly built bay-windowed detached home, 'Glastonbury', in a pleasant tree-lined thoroughfare named Glastonbury Avenue, situated in the townland of Lowood overlooking Belfast Lough. Carl Gilbert Donnelly had been named after his godfather, musician Carl Gilbert Hardebeck. Hardebeck, born in Clerkenwell, London, of a German expatriate father and a Welsh mother, had lost his sight aged 3, moving to Belfast aged 24 to establish a music shop and set up as an organ and piano tutor. Hardebeck also served as organist and choirmaster at the church of the Holy Family, then a lowly corrugated iron chapel, where the Donnellys worshipped. Hardebeck's Welsh Gaelic roots inspired his interest in the curation and propagation of the Gaelic language and traditional Irish folk poetry and songs.

Hardebeck's affinity with Gaelic culture would later lead him into association with Padraig Pearse, one of the leaders of the 1916 Easter Rising. Like Pearse, Hardebeck took the view that it was the duty of patriotic Irishmen to unite to throw off the shackles of British rule, rather than to fight in a war engaged by the British state. Hardebeck continued to be held in high esteem in the independent Ireland created after the war, being granted a state funeral in Dublin in 1945, which was attended by government ministers and Dublin's Lord Mayor.

John Donnelly undertook a short-lived marriage to a woman half his age in 1907, but Gilbert grew up in the first decade of the twentieth century under the care of his eldest sister, Norah Helen, and the extended Donnelly family. Gilbert's elder brothers attended the Christian Brothers School in Hardinge Street until they were 16, before entering skilled trade apprenticeships. As John Donnelly's career prospered, Gilbert and his younger brother Hugh were able to earn prizes that enabled them to attend St Malachy's College, a Roman Catholic Grammar school founded in 1833. The school's motto,

Gloria ab Intus (Glory from within) was intended to respect the uniqueness of all individuals, enabling them to reach their full potential. The *Belfast and Irish News* of 2 September 1910 carried an advertisement advising that the college had reopened for the new academic year and that 'Students are prepared for the Examinations of The Intermediate Board, The University and for Civil Service and Commercial Life'. The *Belfast News-Letter* of 13 September 1913 carried extensive lists of Intermediate examination results, showing that Carl G. Donnelly of the Christian Brothers School, Belfast, had been awarded a 3rd class prize of £3 in order to supplement the cost of his time at St Malachy's. The school ranked fifth out of eighteen in the Boys' Schools Order of Merit, one place below St Malachy's, where he would attend for his fifth and sixth year studies.

By 1911, Gilbert's elder brothers were forging promising careers. Samuel was a ships' draughtsman employed by Harland and Wolff, the company commissioned to design and build the ill-fated RMS *Titanic*. A shared endeavour amongst thousands of employees, it is likely that Samuel had a hand in its design as at the time of the ship's commission, he had eight years' experience with the firm. A talented amateur artist, he would create a number of paintings of the vessel, sadly now lost to the family. William, known as 'Billy', practised dentistry whilst supplementing his income as an incognito professional boxer under the pseudonym 'Spencer', talented enough to challenge the Irish bantamweight champion Johnny Curran. The April 1911 bout saw Billy take the champion to twenty rounds before losing on points. Billy's younger brothers John and Eugene followed the path into dentistry. Austin, five years Gilbert's senior, was training to become a ship designer at Harland and Wolff alongside Harry (Henry Edward). Hence, three of Gilbert's brothers were involved in ship design, a respectable and influential position with Belfast's premier employer. The youngest brother, Hugh, a fluent Irish speaker, violinist and pianist, after a brief flirtation with the same firm embarked on a career in education, serving as principal of St Coleman's RC Primary School in Belfast.

They were forging careers in a thriving city of 385,000 inhabitants, 24 per cent of whom were Roman Catholics, with the remainder divided between Protestant Presbyterianism and the Church of Ireland. Most careers of social status and generous remuneration were reserved for Protestants, and children from each side of the sectarian divide were taught in separate faith-based schools. The prospect of Irish Home Rule, for centuries a distant aspiration for Ireland's nationalist community, had become an imminent reality by the early twentieth century. This constitutional upheaval was greeted with alarm by Belfast's Protestant elite, with the unionist leader Sir Edward Carson calling for a separate government in the province of Ulster should an independent Irish state come into being. Political and social tension simmered beneath and would impact on the lives of families like the Donnellys, who sought to steer clear of sectarian strife. The fact that three generations – James, John and Samuel – had all married women from the Protestant tradition helped the family to elide the worlds of Roman Catholic faith and civic respectability.

Gilbert continued to study assiduously and in September 1915 he was accepted into Queen's University Belfast's Medical School. Set amongst the verdant suburbs of south Belfast, the university had been founded in 1849 to provide higher education for Roman Catholics and Presbyterians as a counterpart to the predominantly Anglican Trinity College, Dublin. By the time of Gilbert's admission, a hospital to nurse the mounting casualties returning from war had already been established in the exhibition hall of the Botanic Gardens. The Ulster Volunteer Force had made an offer to the War Office to furnish a complete hospital and the university supported the endeavour by allowing several huts to be built on its land. Many local doctors and nurses volunteered their services and two motor ambulances were sponsored by Belfast firms. Barbers would give up their half-day holidays to cut patients' hair and provide a shave. Thus, the effects of the war were close at hand when Gilbert entered the world of academia. He would not be able to resist the moral pressure to play his part in the conflict for very long.

Chapter 3

In the Service of their Country

Lieutenant John Gillis Butt

'a friend to all his brother officers, and friend and confidant as well as doctor to the rank and file'

Lieutenant John Gillis 'Jack' Butt was the first of our eight young men to join the army, being commissioned three days before Britain entered the war. After a course of training at Aldershot, Jack was assigned to the Grenadier Guards as a regimental medical officer (RMO), one of 5,000 members of the RAMC who were immediately available to provide medical support to the British Expeditionary Force (BEF) – just half the required strength for an army in the field. Numbers were quickly made up by issuing commissions to civilian doctors and enlisting men whose peacetime employment suited them to RAMC service without further medical training. The athletic Jack stood at 5 feet 9 inches tall, weighed 9 stone 3 pounds and had a chest measurement of 33 inches at rest. Jack's battalion, 1st Grenadier Guards, was brigaded with the 2nd Scots Guards, the 2nd Border Regiment and the 2nd Gordon Highlanders to form 20th Brigade, commanded by Major General Ruggles-Brise. The brigade sat within the 7th Division, which was hurriedly dispatched to Belgium at the beginning of October 1914.

Jack's role as a regimental medical officer was to maintain both the health and fighting strength of the forces in the field and ensure that in the event of sickness or wounding men were treated

Lieutenant John Gillis Butt RAMC.
(*Courtesy Nick Previté*)

and evacuated quickly and efficiently. Although a member of the RAMC, an RMO came under the direction of the commanding officer of the unit to which he was attached. In addition to the treatment of the sick and wounded, Jack's responsibilities extended to overseeing hygiene, water supply, food preparation and sanitation. Jack had an excellent role model in his father, whose work in India had seen a drastic reduction in tropical diseases.

When not in the front line, an RMO's daily routine usually began with a sick parade followed by an inspection of the billets and cookhouses. The rest of the day would be spent training stretcher-bearers and water cart orderlies, and overseeing the care of troops in the Camp Reception Station (CRS) who needed treatment or rest, but were not sick enough to be evacuated down the line. The RMO would have a medically trained RAMC sergeant or corporal and a handful of RAMC privates to assist him in his work, as well as a small selection of regular regimental troops trained as stretcher-bearers.

During periods in the front line, the RMO would establish a Regimental Aid Post (RAP) as close as possible to the action. A casualty would receive immediate attention here, before being sent through an evacuation chain via RAMC dressing stations and Casualty Clearing Stations. Stretcher-bearers would move between bearer posts to effect this transfer, all within shelling range of the enemy. Due to frequent proximity to the thick of the fighting, nearly 7,000 RAMC personnel were to lose their lives during the First World War. An RMO such as Jack Butt would find his work to be urgent and vital, an essential cog in the battalion's machinery. Lieutenant Noel Garrod RAMC, the son of one of Alfred Pope's correspondents, wrote: 'I should not advise anyone with any desire to practise their surgical or medical skill to take on the job of medical officer to a battalion, but from the point of view of seeing the war, understanding military methods and the spirit of the men it is the best post open to a medical man.'

Although the medical aspects of an RMO's work were not as varied as he might undertake in civilian service, he would become part of a tight network of army officers, with a keen identification with his battalion and regiment. Captain Philip Gosse recalled:

A good M.O. to a battalion was a privileged and important officer. He was usually on intimate terms with his colonel, a friend to all his brother officers, and friend and confidant as well as doctor to the rank and file. Often and often I noticed that a battalion with a first-class M.O. was always a first-class battalion, had the smallest sick parade, fewer men falling out on a long march and the lowest quota of casualties from trench foot.

Throughout the war, prompt and skilful attention to the sick and wounded by RAMC personnel and nurses of the Queen Alexandra's Imperial Military Nursing Service (QAIMNS), Red Cross, Order of St John and the VAD enabled a manpower saving of 1.6 million, enough to tip the scales in favour of Britain and her allies. Jack was undertaking a role that was crucial in the successful prosecution of front-line fighting by the battalion to which he was attached.

The front that Jack entered in the first week of October 1914 had been fluid since July. Following the stalling of the German advance on Paris at the Battle of the Marne in early September, Sir John French, Commander-in-Chief, BEF, was concerned that the German army would concentrate their forces in Belgium and attempt to break through at weak points in the Allied lines. Although the Germans were in possession of the greater part of Belgium by early October 1914, the Belgian Army had concentrated in Antwerp. Consequently, the German General Staff determined to make good their lines of communication by taking Antwerp and subjugating all of Belgium to their will. As soon as this had been achieved, available troops were to force their way through the Allied line and seize control of the French Channel ports.

Thus the 1st Battalion Grenadier Guards, which 'had settled down to a sort of peace-manoeuvre life at Lyndhurst' in the New Forest, was issued with its marching orders. Sir Frederick Ponsonby's history of the Grenadier Guards recalled:

> It was a quiet, peaceful Sunday when the summons came. There had been so many rumours and alarms that no one took much notice of them, and the idea of departure had faded to a remote possibility. Passes had been given to the men to remain out till 9.30, and a field-day was arranged for the next day. Then came the order to embark at once from Southampton. In an instant there was feverish bustle and energy throughout the camps. The 1st Battalion Grenadiers marched off to Southampton and was joined there by many men who were out on pass.

Jack Butt embarked on the evening of 4 October, leaving the Solent in the dark small hours the following morning, aboard the 'fairly comfortable' SS *Armenian*, and the SS *Turcoman*, 'just a cattle-boat with no accommodation at all'. The vessels managed to avoid the German mines and submarines preying on Allied shipping in the English Channel, arriving in Zeebrugge at 6.00 am on 7 October. Jack was one of thirty officers in the battalion, amongst whom was Captain Lord Richard Wellesley, the great-grandson of the first Duke of Wellington. One eminent person not permitted to make the journey was HRH Edward, Prince of Wales, who had written on 22 September to the battalion's commanding officer, Lieutenant Colonel Maxwell Earle, expressing his disappointment: 'I feel the firing line is the only thing that will satisfy me.' It was felt that the risk of capture of the future king of England by the enemy was too great.

Disembarking was awkward, as the port's jetty was too small to accommodate large vessels, and all equipment, including horses, had to be pushed down gangways. The battalion then entrained to the St André suburb of Bruges, where crowds lined the streets and 'cheered each battalion lustily as it arrived'. Jack Butt may well have witnessed a strange sight in the city that evening, a 'Procession of Humiliation', as priests led a long train of old men and women, with acolytes swinging incense through the streets, chanting a litany. They made an odd contrast with the masses of Seventh Division fighting men in khaki, with their array of weapons.

The battalion undertook a 15-mile march to Ostend, where a brief defensive position was held before a move to Ghent, where German troops posed an acute threat to the port city, forming up 10 miles away. They hoped to encircle and cut off the remnants of the Belgian Army and two British and French naval divisions operating in the area. Streams of civilians were evacuating the city as Jack's battalion dispersed to find rest in an orchard and a timber yard. As the October nights were cold, blankets were requisitioned. These came in the form of huge rolls of expensive velvet from a local dye works. Ponsonby stated, 'The men naturally did not mind what they looked like as long as they kept warm, but as they lay asleep in the yard, with rich velvet such as Velasquez might have painted wrapped round their khaki, they presented a spectacle decidedly incongruous.'

By now the Seventh Division was operating with no base and no available reinforcements, with large bodies of the enemy reported in every direction. Jack's introduction to action had been swift. Trenches were dug and orders received that under no circumstances should a retreat be made in the face of the enemy. But for the primitive flying machines spying on the enemy's movements and providing information, 'such a position would have been impossible'. Having held position for a day, the battalion had to reluctantly abandon Ghent on 11 October, slinking away under the cover of darkness. 'Passing through Ghent at dead of night after the cordial reception they had had from the inhabitants two days before, and with the knowledge that the Belgians were being left to the tender mercies of the Germans, was anything but a pleasant experience for the British Force.' Orders were given to march with haste to Ypres, with few rest intervals. To have tallied would have risked falling into the hands of the advancing Germans.

As the division passed through Belgian villages, civilians emerged from their houses to hand apples and cigarettes to the British troops. By 14 October, rain was falling heavily, causing the roads to turn into a quagmire. Some fatigued men fell behind, to be captured by the Germans, but none of Jack's Grenadier comrades under his medical supervision suffered this fate. Others limped doggedly on in a pitiable plight. Some men removed their boots and tied their puttees round their bruised and blistered feet. Jack, as a medical officer, would have provided what relief he could for these maladies. For those who ploughed on, the knowledge that they were nearly in touch with the British Expeditionary Force raised their spirits.

Jack reached Ypres in the early afternoon of 14 October, when reports were received that a German Army corps was advancing from the direction of Comines. Ponsonby reported that 'most of the men were delighted at the prospect of a fight'. It was at this point that the initial trenches were dug near Ypres, the first drawing of lines that would define the experience of war for hundreds of thousands of British troops. At the time it was thought that temporary shelters providing protection for a couple of nights would be sufficient. Jack's comrades in No. 2 Company of the 1st Grenadiers who dug them little thought that they were laying the foundation of an intricate network of trenches that would see men live, fight and die over the next four years.

Ypres was to be held at all costs, due both to its symbolic importance as the final major Belgian town still in Allied hands and as its possession barred the German Army's access to the French Channel ports. As the Grenadiers marched 6 miles south-eastwards towards Zandvoorde on 16 October, Ponsonby noted the piteous sight of the local civilian population in flight before the advancing enemy:

> Old men and women ran breathless; children trotted by their mothers' sides; some had all their worldly possessions in carts drawn by ponies or dogs; others were pushing wheelbarrows loaded with all the goods they could carry away. All had a look of terror in their eyes, and all hurried madly to safety, spurred on by the thought of the blazing villages that lay behind them.

Two days later, Jack wrote the final letter Helen Butt would ever receive from her son:

> My Dear Mother,
> Just a few lines to let you know that I am free. We have had a lot of marching since we landed here but not much fighting up to the present, only small affairs with outposts.

We have been in billets since we landed so on the whole very comfortable, but sleep is very short as we stand to arms sometimes at 4 in the morning and get to bed at night when we can.

Have had no news of Col. Swanston and have no idea where he is.

When writing to me my address will be:
Lieut. J G Butt RAMC
MD 1st Batt. Grenadier Guards 20th Brigade
7th Division
Expeditionary Force

I am all right for clothing and cigarettes. If you think of it could you get me a map case. I forgot all about it and without it my maps get torn. If you don't know what it is like perhaps father will get it. I wrote to father from Dover when going across on the transport.

The Germans set a village on fire yesterday only 1½ miles from where we are at present and at night we could see several other villages blazing in the far distance.

I'm sorry I can't let you know where we are but things as far as I know are going well.

Write soon to let me know how things are going with you. An occasional paper would be very acceptable as all papers here are in French.

Love to all and to your dear self,
Your Affectionate son,
Jack

Having dug in at Zandvoorde, British troops began to advance towards Menin, but this order was countermanded due to the approach of a potentially overwhelming enemy force. Instead the Grenadiers were tasked with holding a 1-mile line running through Kruiseik to the crossroads on the Ypres-Menin road. Over the next few days the battalion came under heavy attack from waves of German infantry, causing severe casualties. On one occasion the Germans even tried to approach one of the British platoons, shouting out that they were from the South Staffordshire Regiment, but the silhouette of their spiked helmets gave them away. Jack was now on soil that the German Army was determined to take. The scene was set for the final days of his short life.

Arthur Greensmith

'They are proving themselves equal to anything, however, and their record of work and conduct would do credit to any regiment'

Temporary service battalions, or 'Pals' battalions, were raised amongst the towns and cities of the north of England; two students at the University of Sheffield approached the organisation's Vice-Chancellor, H.A.L. Fisher, with the idea that a Sheffield City Battalion could be raised from a core of university students. The War Office quickly approved the idea, and a meeting at Sheffield Town Hall was held, promising municipal recognition and assistance to the raising of the force. In contrast to other Pals battalions, the Sheffield City Battalion was a middle-class milieu, with its original title being the Sheffield University and City Special Battalion of the York and Lancaster Regiment.

The 12th Battalion Yorkshire and Lancaster Regiment (Sheffield City Battalion), as the new formation was eventually named, was formed a little over a month after the outbreak of war, with Arthur Greensmith being amongst the first group of 900 recruits who enlisted during 10-11 September at Sheffield's Corn Exchange on Sheaf Street. Placards at the recruiting office declared 'To Berlin – via Corn Exchange' to encourage the idea that a swift and decisive victory would be the lot of those taking the King's shilling. Sheffield's response to the call to arms was impressive. Forty-five doctors worked in shifts to give medical examinations to the new recruits and forty volunteer clerks worked at a hard pace to process the voluminous paperwork required to turn hundreds of professional men into a formal fighting battalion.

Arthur was assigned to D Company as one of forty members of 14 Platoon. Numbered within his new company comrades was the *Sheffield Daily Telegraph* sports journalist Richard Sparling, who was later to write a gripping account of his service within the battalion. Sparling described the odd assortment of men who would make up the Sheffield Pals: 'Standing there as privates were many men whom no other conceivable circumstances would have brought into the army; £500 a year business men, University and public school men, medical students, journalists, schoolmasters, craftsmen, shop assistants, secretaries and all sorts of clerks.'

Initial drill training took place at Norfolk Barracks on Edmund Road, with Arthur and his new comrades being addressed by various dignitaries, including H.A.L. Fisher, who told the men they were about to 'taste the salt of

Private Arthur Greensmith. (*Courtesy Rosemary Gregory*)

life' and would return home from the war having won honour for city and country. As the barracks did not provide adequate space for the new battalion, on 15 September drill training commenced at Sheffield United FC's famous Bramall Lane ground. Eventually, due to concerns from the club's directors about wear and tear to the pitch's turf, the battalion moved to the 28 hectare Norfolk Park, a mile to the south-east of the city centre, to undertake basic fieldcraft and tactical training. As the recruits gained in fitness, extended route marches were organised, wending their way through the picturesque rolling countryside to the south-west of Sheffield into what would later become the fringes of the Peak District National Park. Until 1946, attendance at church parades was compulsory for men in the British Army, and on 8 November, St Mary's Church on Bramall Lane hosted the first such event for the Sheffield City Battalion, with the first hymn 'Fight the Good Fight With All Thy Might', including the exhortation to 'Faint not nor fear, His arms are near, He changeth not, and thou art dear'.

During these early weeks of army life, most of the men returned home at the end of the day, with those from towns and villages in the surrounding countryside taking up lodgings in the city. However, as autumn turned to winter, the need for premises where the men could live and train together became more urgent. Sheffield boasted the large Hillsborough Barracks, but these were already in use by other battalions, so on 5 December 1914, the 12th Battalion marched to a brand-new camp on high ground to the west of Sheffield. The weather did not smile on the parade, with pouring rain turning to sleety snow as the men snaked their way from city to moorland. Named Redmires Camp, the area soon became a hive of activity, with a trench system being dug beside a disused hillside quarry, in order to prepare the recruits for the Western Front. The camp benefitted from a YMCA hut which variously served as a canteen, church, resting room, post office and concert hall. The *Sheffield Independent* issued a War Album entitled 'Our Boys at the Front' in late 1914, describing the life and work of the camp:

Private Arthur Greensmith in his army greatcoat. (Courtesy Rosemary Gregory)

Redmires Camp is of more than ordinary interest to the people of Sheffield; not merely because it is the headquarters of the 'The Pals' Battalion, but because the bulk of the men in this service battalion of the York and Lancaster Regiment are city men – men from the professional and business classes who, to use a familiar expression, have not been used to 'roughing it'.

They are proving themselves equal to anything, however, and their record of work and conduct would do credit to any regiment.

The camp is built on clayey saturated soil, hence it soon churned to a quagmire. The first roads made needed extending and making more efficient, and the city clerks, chemists, journalists, shopkeepers, draughtsmen, and others who constitute the Battalion were requisitioned to 'make good'. They quarried stone, laid efficient foundations for the new roads, cut trenches for drainage, and finished off the job well. Now the camp is a credit to them.

The winter of 1914/15 was a harsh one, with large snowdrifts frequently blocking the doors of the camp huts and a New Year's Day route march having to be curtailed due to a violent storm blowing up. The sharpness of the weather

Arthur Greensmith (second from left) training with his Sheffield Pals comrades on Redmires Moor above the city. (*Courtesy Rosemary Gregory*)

was relieved somewhat by a period of home leave that Arthur and his comrades were permitted to take.

The Sheffield Pals had developed a reputation for their great sporting prowess, with some of them being noted sportsmen in disciplines as diverse as golf, middle-distance running, association football, boxing, hockey and water polo. A grand sports day was organised for 29 April 1915. Taking advantage of the glorious late spring weather, a huge crowd poured out of the city and up to the camp to watch the competitions. Buses were crammed to capacity, meaning many people had to walk from the centre of Sheffield and beyond, bringing the total number of spectators to an estimated 10,000.

Over 1,000 entrants had signed up to compete in the various events, with contingents taking part from both Barnsley Pals Battalions and the 15th Notts and Derby Battalion. As well as traditional events such as the steeplechase and sprinting races, an Inter-Platoon Mile race took place, with teams of sixteen men, each in full fighting order with their rifles, and carrying 50 pounds in kit, covering the ground. The winning time was an impressive seven minutes and forty-five seconds.

The sports day marked the final occasion at which the residents of Sheffield could see their sons and husbands as one band of brothers. Arthur Greensmith's time at Redmires was about to end. The 12th Sheffield City Battalion had been brigaded, along with 13th and 14th Yorkshire and Lancaster Battalions (1st and 2nd Barnsley Pals) and the 11th East Lancashire Battalion (Accrington Pals) to form 94th Brigade, and it was operationally necessary to have all four battalions training together in one camp in order to practise brigade-level manoeuvres. The area selected for the concentration was the heaths and woodland of Cannock Chase in Staffordshire.

Orders to move were received on Sunday, 9 May, and four days later, having been woken at 4.30 am to take breakfast and then pack, the 12th Battalion began their march into the city centre at 6.15 am. They were met on the Manchester Road by the bands of the Sheffield Engineers and the Hallamshires, who accompanied them all the way down to the town hall. Wives, sweethearts and other family members joined the procession en route and at 7.30 they arrived in Surrey Street to receive a formal send-off. Five thousand people crammed into the area to witness the event. After addresses from local dignitaries, the battalion marched down to the Midland railway station, where the men's families swarmed in to bid farewell. Most relatives believed that this would be the final opportunity to see their loved ones before they went abroad.

Arthur departed at 9.30 am with the rest of D Company, reaching Rugeley Station in the middle of the afternoon. All companies of the battalion then formed and marched up the hill onto Cannock Chase, a vast area of high ground between Stafford and Rugeley, to Penkridge Bank Camp. Eventually, the military camps on the chase would accommodate 35,000 men, but 94th Brigade was the first to move into Penkridge Bank. Four days later, Arthur sent a brief note on a postcard depicting Stafford's Milford station to his sister Cecilia and brother-in-law Albert:

> Dear Sister and Brother,
>   I am quite happy. Just a line to say we are comfortable and I ask you not to let Mother worry.
> Best love to all
> Arthur

The hard yards pounded out on the lanes around Redmires were paying dividends, with the Sheffield Pals' performance on brigade marches being considered outstanding. Arthur sent another postcard, this time of Stafford's picturesque Victoria Park, to his sister and brother-in-law on 22 May:

> In Stafford on parades till Tuesday 10 am. We are getting about somewhat. Thanks for pocket book I have nearly filled it, & memory will soon burst
> Best love, Arthur.

It was a few days until Arthur would hear back from his relatives, as four days later he was about to send a postcard with a cheeky message on the front – 'Say, if you don't write soon I'll enter your name in a correspondence school' – when he hastily scribbled a note at the bottom: 'Sorry have just received yours, Arthur.' Although seemingly inconsequential, Arthur's brief message to Cecilia indicated a longing to feel a greater connection with his loved ones in Sheffield: 'How are you getting on and is your Hubby alright? I am in the pink but I often wonder how you are!!'

It would not be long before Arthur returned to Sheffield to see his family, as each weekend 15 per cent of the battalion was allowed home leave and, from 2-4 June, the entire battalion was given a special break to celebrate the King's birthday. Despite these opportunities, the Sheffield City Battalion's distance from home caused the volume of mail to increase tremendously, with Arthur's postcards being amongst over 1,000 items of post per day being sent home.

On Friday, 30 July 1915, the battalion vacated Cannock Chase to head to the North Riding city of Ripon for further training. The South Camp within the Fourth Army Training Centre, to which the brigade was sent, was located about a mile to the south of Ripon. The focus of training during the sojourn in the area was musketry. Men spent their recreation time variously swimming in the river Ure, walking the Yorkshire Dales, attending organ recitals in Ripon Cathedral and visiting Fountains Abbey. It was from this picturesque ancient monument that Arthur sent a postcard to Cecilia, informing her, 'This is just to show you what the abbey is like 2 miles from here. The place is most interesting and I am enjoying the change. Hoping you are well.'

A further period of four days' leave was granted in the middle of September, before the battalion returned to camp to prepare for a move southwards. Between 24 and 26 September 1915, the Sheffield City Battalion transferred to Hurdcott Camp near to the town of Wilton, Wiltshire. Although set amongst picturesque, wide shallow valleys and rolling downland, Hurdcott was an isolated spot, with little to divert the troops but entertainments provided in the YMCA hut. A bus service ran to Salisbury, which proved a popular leisure destination. Arthur sent a postcard from Hurdcott, depicting the Romanesque interior of the Church of St Mary and St Nicholas in Wilton, anticipating that the battalion would soon be sent overseas in order to play their part in the successful prosecution of the war. Whether Arthur's view of the progress of the war being 'great' and 'grand' was based on the skewed version of events being presented in the press, or from a desire to assuage the feelings of his family is unknown:

Dear Albert and Co
  Just to say I am well and happy. I hope things are doing well at No 8. Don't suppose we shall be long now but the War news is great – there is something grand behind it all.
                        Arthur.

A visit to Salisbury saw Arthur in good spirits, writing to Albert, 'although it is raining I have enjoyed the walk and met the Boys of the A.P.C. [Army Pay Corps] – We are going to have a "Good Meal".'

On Tuesday, 16 November, the battalion, along with the rest of 31st Division, left Hurdcott and moved 10 miles north to Larkhill, on the Salisbury Plain, passing Stonehenge en route. The stay here was short, but Arthur was able to write to his brother-in-law on 20 November. Albert and Cecilia Spittle had welcomed Jeanne, born on 3 September, into the family and Arthur felt himself blessed to have seen her briefly while on leave:

Dear Old Man,
  Thanks so much for the book and letters. I have had not much time for reading and so I was reading 'Cleopatra' at the time of receiving yours. I cannot say whether I like it or not. I [am] confident of us going away either a few days before Christmas or a few days after. But I hope I should have leave – I should like to see the Dear Baby – it seems so strange that I should have another sister as it were and have hardly seen her – Still it

was fortunate I was late in getting my last leave or I might not have seen her at all. We have only come here for a few weeks and these last few days we have spent in some trenches. They are wonderfully constructed, an exact design of some in France you would be surprised if you saw the work in them – dugs outs – machine gun emplacements, listening posts; and tunnels. They are 5′ deep and the communication trenches 2 feet wide. The fire trenches vary from 3 to 5′ foot wide …

Hoping to see you soon
I am your affectionate
Brother Arthur

Further musketry and machine-gun training was carried out, including firing from trenches. The whole of 94th Brigade was now in a state of advanced preparation for transfer to the Western Front, and orders were received for a move to France. Some divisional staff left for the Continent on 29 November, but on 2 December, the order was cancelled. Instead, officers began to receive issues of sola topees, or sun helmets. The 12th Battalion was headed for warmer climes. The failure of the Gallipoli campaign had left the Suez Canal vulnerable to a Turkish counter-attack, and troops, including the whole of the 31st Division, had to be diverted from France to ensure the security of that vital logistical artery.

On 20 December, all four Sheffield Pals companies left Hurdcott in the small hours of the morning to entrain from Salisbury, stopping at Exeter, where the Mayor dispensed cigars and cigarettes and the Lady Mayoress served sandwiches and tea. On reaching Devonport, the men boarded the SS *Nestor*, bound for Egypt. Arthur and his comrades bedded down at 8.00 pm in hammocks, but the men from the steel city were unused to such nautical sleeping arrangements, causing many to fall onto the wooden floor, even before the vessel had left the harbour.

The following morning was spent practising life jacket drills and receiving cholera vaccinations. At 11.15 am, the *Nestor* set sail, escorted by two destroyers. The first two days at sea proved stormy, causing the breakfast of porridge and a protein course of herrings, cheese, tripe, stewed meat, liver or bacon to be of dubious enjoyment. On Christmas Day 1915, longing thoughts of home festivities were tinged with anxiety as the *Nestor* spent the day circling in the Atlantic waiting for darkness to fall before entering the Straits of Gibraltar – a favourite U-boat hunting ground. Some men attended a voluntary church parade on the upper deck. The vessel then hugged tight to the North African coastline for the next few days, affording views of spectacular mountain sunrises, and allowing for belated Christmas celebrations, including a concert on deck. The *Nestor* eventually reached Malta at lunchtime on 29 December, docking at Valetta. Although men were not allowed on shore, the stopover provided an opportunity for letters to be collected and sent to England. Arthur wrote to Albert requesting reading material to occupy the educated minds of the Sheffield City Battalion:

> I am pleased to say that after the first few days we have enjoyed the journey and are all looking better than we ever did, I have made arrangements with the Boys of our hut and each of us are going to have papers sent and we are all sending off for different ones. I wondered if you would ask someone at home to send one. There are only 3 so you will have to get someone reliable to send me every week … Sorry I cannot give you more news but we shall see something soon besides water! So I shall be able to write more descriptive letters. The papers are *Sheffield Weekly News … London Opinion* NOT LONDON LIFE! and *No 3 TIT Bits*! So will you see about this for me -. If 8 or nine do this we shall have plenty to read. Love to you both and Baby. Give her such a Big Kiss for me will you? XX
>   Your affectionate brother Arthur.

The stay in Malta was brief and at 5.00 pm *Nestor* set sail for Alexandria, and Arthur and his pals spent a few days drilling and playing sports on deck. As the ship arrived in port early on New Year's Day 1916, the Sheffield Pals were not entitled to the 1914/15 Star, as they were deemed not to have entered a war zone until the first day of 1916, despite the previous ten days of U-boat threats. In the evening they disembarked and entrained for the twelve-hour journey to Port Said. There the men were served high tea by some English ladies and were allocated tents, with thirteen men sharing each one.

Training began in earnest on 3 January, with rifle inspections, route marches and physical drill, as well as a lecture on appropriate conduct in Egypt. Unused to the climate the men suffered wind-blasted sand by day and below freezing night-time temperatures. The only facilities for bathing were the sea and canal, and much time was spent swimming. On 5 January, in a violent gale, Arthur's D Company left Port Said in open railway trucks bound for outpost duty at Tineh. Lieutenant Geoffrey J.H. Ingold commanded 14 Platoon, including Arthur. Ingold had received his commission due to his experience as a member of the University of Sheffield's OTC. The following day, 14 Platoon disembarked at Ras El Esh, where it stayed for two days before rejoining the rest of the company.

As well as guarding the Suez Canal against potential attack, the men of the Sheffield City Battalion were assigned the arduous job of hauling the chains that propelled the small pontoon ferries across the width of the canal at various intervals. At times men were sent out on 20-mile patrols into the desert in shifting sands. The physical resilience built up during route marches in Yorkshire, Staffordshire and Wiltshire was severely put to the test. Drill parades in full kit were still expected, although Sundays were a day of rest for most men, with many enjoying evenings in Port Said. One of Arthur's D Company comrades, Private J. Dixon, noted the deteriorating quality of rations during the Egyptian adventure. Breakfast and lunch consisted of bully beef and army biscuits, with jam and bread at teatime. Cheese rations had been stopped on the basis that 'there was milk in the tea'!

From late January, the battalion was put to work on improving canal defences. A light railway was constructed to transport materials, barbed wire entanglements were erected, and trenches dug. Each company had, in turn, to sleep fully clothed at three minutes' notice to move. On 14 February, D Company was detailed to repair one of the railway engines. This meant pushing heavy trucks laden with water pipes 4 miles out into the desert, with the transport frequently derailing. Water rations were minimal, with each man initially limited to 2 pints per day for drinking, washing, shaving and cooking. This meagre amount was doubled due to the arduous nature of the work. After a little under two months in Egypt, on 26 February the men were woken by their officers for a kit inspection. The order had just been received to move to France. The next day, the Sheffield City Battalion marched to Kantara.

On 29 February, Arthur wrote to Albert and Cecilia, thanking them for the three books that Albert had sent on. His brother-in-law had included lyrics from John McDermott's folk song 'My Ain Folk' in his previous letter, in which the narrator laments the sadness and longing he feels when he thinks of home. These 'struck me somewhat pensively'. Arthur commented on the 'little sing songs' the men would have by twilight, and the singing of the natives that could be heard, which 'appeals to us'. Even 'God Save the King' could appear to be a song of beauty when far away from home: 'When you are out of England the National Anthem seems lovely and you are apt to believe it is the best you have heard, while in England you are reminded at the theatre, that the show is over by the same thing and you have finished your enjoyment.'

Arthur was also missing seeing his little niece growing up, whilst expressing sorrow for those on the home and fighting fronts:

Now about little Jeanne, do you know every letter I get is full of her ... It is a pity I can not see her for I know how much I should enjoy to see her little smiles and to hear her say Goo Goo! ... You say Cheer up well I think the hardship is harder for them at home than it is for us, but still we have had a rough time lately. Knowing me as you do you will understand that it is pretty bad before I call it rough.

Arthur's own troubles were compounded by the anxiety over the potential for Zeppelin attacks on Sheffield, but reassured both himself and his family that their chances of harm were slim: 'I expect you will be anxious about the Zeppos, but I should not worry for the chance of it being any of you is very remote. We hear rumours but pay no attention to them. If I knew they had been to Sheffield I shouldn't worry much.'

His hint at the imminent move to France managed to avoid Lieutenant Ingold's censor's pen:

> We have been moving all the time since we came here. I think in a day or two we shall make the biggest we have made yet! The weather is very hot but it is not unbearable; personally I think we shall be in a cooler climate in 2 or 3 weeks. How is your John going out in France, I expect the weather is still 'cool' there.

At 6.00 pm on 7 March, the camp was struck and men slept on the ground until the early hours of the morning, then marched to the railhead, boarding the train for Port Said, where they were given the opportunity to spend time at leisure. On the morning of 10 March, the Sheffield City Battalion embarked on the HMT *Briton*, formerly a Union Castle liner converted to a troopship, at 5.00 pm encountering a storm that lasted through to the following day. After stopping at Valetta, the battalion docked at Marseilles on the afternoon of 15 March, where an accumulation of three weeks' mail was waiting.

Disembarking at 7.30 am the following day, the men were marched to a railway siding to join a train consisting of passenger coaches, cattle trucks and horse boxes, with most of the men travelling in the last of these filthy and lousy conveyances bound for French battlefields. Travelling at a sedate pace, the train passed through Arles, Avignon and Lyons, stopping for breakfast the following morning at Macon. During the night the battalion passed Fontainebleau and the outskirts of Paris. There followed a brief stop at Amiens, and at 3.00 pm the journey ended at Pont Remy, after a gruelling, uncomfortable fifty-three-hour passage. There was then an exacting march of 8 miles to billets in Huppy, from where Arthur was able to write to Albert and Cecilia. He thanked them for the 'heaps of papers' they had managed to send to him, 'both for the thoughtfulness of the action and the papers themselves'. The contrast between France and Egypt was great: 'Everything seems so much like England and so much different from the Dessert [*sic*] of Egypt. You could never imagine how pleasing a green field is to look upon after seeing Seas of Sand and no grass at all for 10 weeks which seems like 10 years.'

French cuisine and accommodation were also of superior quality:

The food is wonderful really, we even get butter (and good butter too) now and everything seems like old Redmires. In our Billet there are 10 of us and the Billet is a clean Barn with heaps of room plenty of straw and not too much ventilation holes. We have an extra blanket and so feel like lords in 'My Lord's Bedchamber' at night, (Don't say little boy Blue) ... In the back we have an orchard in which during spare time we play cards read or write and we even like AFTERNOON TEA in the orchard.

The change of atmosphere had instigated an uplift in spirits, with Arthur looking forward to seeing his young extended family grow up, and to the swift and successful conclusion of the war:

You feel awake in a climate like this and fit for anything. In the distance we can hear the big guns go off quite plainly but I suppose we shall not go up just yet. I hope Baby and 'we Two' I often think of you as 'We Two' you seem to be one in two and two in one somehow. Every letter I get is full of Baby and really it makes me feel as if I should just like to come and watch this Gem of a Diamond grow up as I did Mary and Dora.

Well it may not be long. I was thinking of arranging a party for the 12th of June and getting you to come and tell me all you know of the war and why it did not come to an end sooner. Still it may be more like the 12th of May it would be better to wait and see and Cheer up day by day until I am with you and everyone at Dear old Hughenden with Mother.

Training returned to normal with a 10-mile route march, which was followed by an issue of mail. Further exercises occurred on the firing ranges at Poultieres. Drills for gas warfare also began, with masks being issued between 22–24 March. Although formed into a unified fighting formation, a friendly banter took place between the different battalions within 94th Brigade. The largely working-class Barnsley Pals were amused that some of their wealthier Sheffield counterparts had brought their gramophones with them to France, to while away the days of waiting before going into battle. They nicknamed them the 'coffee and buns boys'.

In late March, orders were received to begin the move up to the front, and a gruelling four-day march ensued, via Longpre, Vignacourt, Beauqesne and on to Bertrancourt, with 9 to 14 miles per day being covered, the men carrying heavy loads and suffering from persistently wet feet and painful blisters. The sound of the guns grew ever closer as the march continued and only fitful rest was to be had once they reached Bertrancourt. Men were prepared for front-line service with a hot bath, taken in groups of nine, and the fumigation of their uniforms to minimise the potential for lice. On 3 April, the battalion went into the trenches for the first time, having been issued with gas capes and steel helmets. Ironically, for the men from the steel city, there were not enough helmets for all members of the battalion, so men coming out of the line had to pass them on to their replacements.

Arthur's D Company initially occupied the front-line trenches on the right of a 1,300-yard sector held by the Sheffield Pals, between their own C Company to their left and a battalion of the King's Own Scottish Borderers to their right. During this first spell in the trenches the major alarm came with heavy German shelling of the area held by the battalion on the evening of 6 April; miraculously, no one was killed and only one man was injured. Rain meant that trenches and shell holes soon filled with water, although morale was lifted by a delivery of mail on 9 April. The battalion was relieved on 12 April, after nine days on trench duty, and the men trudged back to Bertrancourt to resume training and working party duty digging trenches around Colincamps. Arthur wrote to Albert and Cecilia on 24 April, declaring, 'you will be pleased to know I am very much alive and I shall be so for many years to come', teasing that he intended to come and live with them once the war was over. He further joked about the new skills he had learned since joining the army: 'I think after this lot I shall be able [to] do anything. From stitching buttons on to washing pots. I am afraid we shall all be too good for husbands.' Referring to the recent long march to the front line, Arthur quipped, 'At one time I did not like the idea of carrying a small parcel, now we carry a pack of 60lbs 50 miles in 4 days – our march here a month ago.' He assured them he was well and happy, 'really I am', as the weather was fine and he had received 'heaps of parcels' over the past week.

Whilst most of the Sheffield Pals began the move back to the front-line trenches on 28 April, Arthur's D Company was assigned to a working party supporting 223rd Field Company of the Royal Engineers until 16 May, remaining at Colincamps and marching to their allotted workplace daily. It was dangerous work, with one man wounded by shellfire on 11 May while working on repairs to Rob Roy trench. The same day, Arthur sent a standard Field Service Postcard to Cecilia and Albert, assuring them he was well and that he had received their parcel.

On the night of 14/15 May, men on trench duty suffered a heavy bombardment by German artillery followed by an enemy raid on their position. This was fought off, but at the cost of fifteen Sheffield Pals killed and forty-five wounded. The death toll would have been higher but for the valour shown by unwounded men in digging out their comrades who had been buried under the earth of the destroyed trenches. The battalion vacated the line on 20 May.

Although the spring had seen the battalion battling against the mud of the trenches, by the summer of 1916 the fine weather had brought out colourful plant life. Richard Sparling noted that through May and June, 'the trenches were outlined with gay flowers – brilliant poppies, charlock, blue cornflowers, and scabious'. June 1916 was spent in preparation for the great offensive, with the battalion out of the line training for their objective: the attack on the village of Serre. Arthur Greensmith was preparing to play his part in an event whose effects would reverberate through subsequent decades.

Charles Attwood

'No more typical army of free men ever marched to meet an enemy.'

It was not only in Britain that the outbreak of war unleashed a patriotic fervour to enlist. The onset of war in August 1914 found the Dominion of Canada ill-prepared to make a significant contribution to the Empire's war effort. There were only 3,110 permanent troops, equipped with a few outdated machine guns and artillery pieces. When Canada's Prime Minister, Sir Robert Borden, asked London what assistance could be given, he was told that Canada should raise a division. Over the next few months, a remarkable demonstration of drive, determination and organisation raised a complete division of over 30,000 men, then trained, equipped and transported them to England.

Like many Canadian citizens in 1914, Charles Attwood had strong familial and cultural allegiances to Britain. Wilfred Laurier, the former Prime Minister, who by 1914 was leader of the opposition, proclaimed: 'It is our duty to let Great Britain know and to let the friends and foes of Great Britain know that there is in Canada but one mind and one heart and that all Canadians are behind the Mother Country.' Besides loyalty to Britain, many Canadians were motivated by a simple sense of duty to share in the hardships of their fellows, still others because army life offered the prospect of meaning and excitement. Whatever Charles's personal admixture of incentives to join up, he was one of many men to readily volunteer his services when the call to war came in the late summer of 1914.

Private Charles Attwood. (*Courtesy Robin Williams*)

The Minister of Militia, Sam Hughes, had contacted all 226 Militia commanding officers across Canada on 6 August 1914, announcing the formation of a Canadian Expeditionary Force (CEF) that would be mobilised at Camp Valcartier, 16 miles north-west of Quebec City. Hughes sent engineers to Valcartier to clear forests, establish tented accommodation, and construct rifle ranges, roads, a waterworks system, a telephone network and an electric light system. Storehouses, offices and a moving picture palace were erected and by the middle of August a huge, functional camp had been constructed, ready to receive its first troops. By the end of the month, over 30,000 volunteers had descended on Valcartier. Two-thirds of them were British-born and they were drawn from all Canadian provinces. The creation of Camp Valcartier was overseen by Sam Hughes himself, who had served in the Canadian contingent during the Second Boer War. Hughes was a man of great resource and energy. Yet this sat alongside obstinacy, impulsivity, overwhelming vanity, heavy-handedness and a tendency to make his own rules as he went along.

Charles received an initial medical examination at Valcartier on 8 September, formally attesting on 22 September his next of kin's address, oddly recorded as 'Police Station, Somerset, Eng'. Charles was measured as a compact 5 feet 5½ inches tall with a girth when fully expanded of 33½ inches. Complexion was medium and Charles had brown eyes and brown hair, declaring his faith as Church of England. He received an inoculation against typhoid and spent his short time stationed at Valcartier practising military manoeuvres and rifle-shooting on the newly constructed ranges.

Charles was given regimental number 26 and assigned to 8th Battalion (90th Winnipeg Rifles), 'The Little Black Devils'. The battalion was raised from men from the Winnipeg area, including men from the existing 90th Winnipeg Rifles and troops from the 96th Lake Superior Regiment. It had been instituted on 6 August 1914, and by the time it left Canada in early October could boast a strength of 1,085 men, being a component of the 2nd Infantry Brigade within the 1st Canadian Division, the Canadian Expeditionary Force. Its commander was Lieutenant Colonel L.J. Lipsett.

Addressing CEF, Sam Hughes asserted:

No more typical army of free men ever marched to meet an enemy. Some of you will not return — and pray God they be few. … For such, not only will their memory be cherished by loved ones near and dear, and by a grateful country … but the soldier going down in the cause of freedom never dies. Immortality is his.

In a prelude of the conditions that would be experienced by many in the fighting in France and Flanders, 2nd Brigade experienced quagmire conditions of Biblical proportions on their march from Valcartier to Quebec:

What a road! Darkness came early that night and with the darkness came the rain. The roads became muskegs, canals. The darkness that covered the Egyptians wrapped itself over the land. The landmarks were blotted out. Men and horses, soaked by the downpour, strained their eyes to see what might be just ahead. But it was useless. The leaders felt about for the road. When they were ankle-deep in mud they thought they were on it. When they were up to their knees they were certain. There was nothing to do but go on. There was no shelter; there was no hope of light for hours. And the rain continued.

As the muddied, tired, soaked, hungry contingent passed through Quebec, people came to their doors and windows to shout words of cheer and hope. On arrival at the docks, the men loaded their equipment onto the ships. Many infantrymen, including Charles, were unable to use the road and were fortunate enough to arrive by train. After the loading of horses and artillery, each ship was then moved down the river to a rendezvous point and on Saturday, 3 October, the first contingent of the CEF sailed from Gaspé Bay Basin.

On 1 October, the Calgary *Morning Albertan* had reported that the troops had embarked to the strains of 'It's a Long Way to Tipperary':

Quietly the transports slip into the docks. Quietly the hawsers are unloosed and the great grey ships get up steam, awaiting the word to weigh anchor and sail toward the sea.

From Valcartier the long troop trains still come hurrying into the city and down to the basin. Up on the terrace, women stand and watch, wondering which ship bears the loved one to whom they have said goodbye. Today the headquarters staff moves on board and the correspondents who are to accompany the Canadian expeditionary force across the water also must find their places in the big transports.

The escort ships were on hand to protect the transport vessels 'from any vagrant German warship that may be pan-handling along the lanes of the North Atlantic'.

A little over a week after attestation, Charles found himself with his new comrades leaving Quebec City port, the same venue that had seen him arrive just under two years earlier with the eager anticipation of a new life. The 8th Battalion, with a strength of forty-seven officers and 1,106 other ranks, set to sea aboard SS *Franconia* on 3 October, disembarking in Plymouth eleven days later. Charles spent his twenty-first birthday, 5 October, speeding across the Atlantic towards his homeland.

The convoy transporting the CEF cut an impressive sight. Comprising a flotilla of thirty-one transport vessels and seven escort ships including the flagship HMS *Charybdis*, Charles would have been familiar with one other ship in the convoy, the *Royal George*, which had brought him, along with many hundreds of other hopeful migrants, to Canada two years previously.

The original intention had been for the CEF to land at Southampton, but the threat of U-boat patrols in the English Channel meant that the convoy was diverted to Plymouth. *The Times* reported on 15 October that 'cheering crowds welcomed the Canadians with the utmost enthusiasm'. The long line of large ships stretched away from the entrance to The Sound as far back as the Eddystone, some 12 miles away, 'and presented a magnificent spectacle'. Decks were crowded with men eager to make shore after ten days at sea. Bands played inspiring patriotic tunes in homage to both Britain and Canada, such as 'The Best Old Flag on Earth' and 'The Maple Leaf'. The unloading took several days to complete, with *The Times* noting, 'The Canadians are splendidly equipped. All are in khaki and on their shoulder straps is the one word "Canada".'

The 1st Canadian Division entrained to Salisbury Plain, making an impressive force in the eyes of the correspondent at *The Times*:

> Nothing like the Canadian Contingent has been landed in this country since the time of William the Conqueror. Friendly forces and hostile forces have reached our shores from time to time; the hostile ones always so badly found that they were quickly extinguished, the friendly ones coming unequipped by reason of their friendliness. But the Canadians come armed cap-a-pie, horse, foot, and artillery. The force has its own engineers, signallers, transport corps, ammunition parks, and field hospitals, and there are 34 chaplains and 105 nursing sisters. It would be a military offence to state the number of million rounds of ammunition brought by the Contingent, so great is it.

Qualities that had led many of the troops to leave Britain seeking a new life in the dominion were reflected in their demeanours: 'Physically, of course, the men are a fine lot, and in intelligence they are up to colonial form, which is usually a trifle ahead of that of the old country.' *The Times* reported that only half of the men of the Canadian Expeditionary Force were Canadian born, with the rest originally hailing from the British Isles and France. The piece continued: 'They are practical as colonials must be practical. And they have courage and character, or they would not be where they are. But the probability is that they will be ready before many others who cherish the same ambition – to strike a blow for their country.'

The hardiness of the colonial troops was put to immediate test by the necessity of sleeping under canvas on Salisbury Plain for six weeks as autumn turned to a harsh winter pending construction of wooden sleeping huts. On 4 November, the King and Queen, accompanied by Lords Kitchener and Roberts, inspected the camp. King George V praised the commitment the Canadians had shown to the mother country: 'Their prompt rally to the Empire's call is of inestimable value, both to the fighting strength of my Army and in the evidence which it gives of the solidarity of the Empire. The general appearance and physical standard of the different units are highly creditable.' On 9 November it was announced three days' leave would be granted.

For many with English roots this afforded an opportunity to visit relatives. Charles Attwood was fortunate in that his family was nearby. He took the train from Amesbury to Castle Cary, before running the final 11 miles of his journey, in full uniform and kit including rifle, to his home town of Somerton. Henry Attwood took the opportunity to have his son photographed in his kit, including his puttees and greatcoat, astride 'Ginger', the family horse. This would be the final time that the Attwood family would see their eldest son. After a few precious days Charles returned to Salisbury to take part in the usual exercises designed to keep the body and soul in fine shape, slogging his way through a cross-country run on 28 November and attending a church parade the following day. On 4 December, the battalion war diary recorded

Charles Attwood during his final visit home. (*Courtesy Robin Williams*)

a 'very stormy day. Orderly room tent blown down.' The following day there was a 'Battalion route march … weather colder with heavy showers. Some snow.' The sodden state of the ground meant that a church parade planned for Sunday, 13 December had to be cancelled. The miserable weather continued into the new year, with the cancellation of a full inspection of the 2nd Infantry Brigade.

The Times continued to show a keen interest in the Canadian Division, not only its physical organisation but in the psychological development of a force fit and honed to face the foe. On 28 November, a correspondent reported:

> For there is no foolish bragging about the way in which the Division is going to acquit itself, any more than there is any real apprehension. The men know that they ought to be able to do whatever the best troops can do. But they know also that even the best troops sometimes have stage fright. 'If we can stick it the first time!' That seems to be the universal prayer. After that they have no doubt. And this sober facing of the seriousness of the job ahead, so vastly finer than any empty vapourings, is in itself a fairly good guarantee that they will 'stick it' grimly and determinedly.

Although thousands of miles away, the welfare of the men of the Canadian Expeditionary Force was deep in the hearts of the Canadian public. Toronto school pupils eagerly compiled fifty books per week packed with news, which were sent to Wiltshire to keep the troops up to speed with news from home. Such remembrances would have meant much to the men engaged in training and drilling through a relentlessly sodden and icy winter which caused the fields and roads of Salisbury Plain to turn into a muddy quagmire. Charles sent home a postcard of members of his unit posing beside the ancient stones of Stonehenge, a testament to ancient times when people lived and worshipped on the plain. Despite the misery of the weather, the Canadians maintained their spirits with games of football and lacrosse whilst some engaged in boxing bouts. A handful of men enjoyed themselves a little too much and were transported back to Canada due to excessive indulgence in cheap British beer. There were complaints about the quality of men's boots, which the extended waiting period before embarkation for France gave the military authorities a chance to rectify. Other military materiel issues were addressed: the Ross rifles that had been distributed were prone to jamming so were replaced by the Lee-Enfield make, although the defective weapons were kept for snipers to use. In addition, the 'Oliver' backpack was prone to ride up and choke the men and was therefore replaced.

On 5 February, Charles and his 8th Battalion comrades packed their kitbags for forwarding on to Tidworth, thence to base camp in France. All rifles and bayonets were inspected too. Practical arrangements completed, spiritual preparation for departure was finalised two days later with a final church parade on English soil as the rain continued to beat down on huts and tents occupied by the Canadian Division. On 9 February 1915, under blue skies, the Canadian 1st Division, under the command of General Edwin A.H. Alderson, started their move to the Western Front, boarding trains at Amesbury bound for embarkation at Avonmouth. However, Charles and his comrades in 8th Battalion had to wait until the dark hour of two-thirty the following morning to begin their journey. They arrived at Avonmouth in the early afternoon and immediately boarded the *City of Benares*, bound for St Nazaire.

The 8th Battalion docked in the early hours of 16 February and was soon met with similar weather conditions to those endured on Salisbury Plain. Company training which had been ordered for 17 February had to be abandoned on account of the 'inclement weather'. Three days later saw brighter conditions, and under blue skies the battalion was inspected by Field Marshal Sir John French, Commander-in-Chief, BEF. The following day, Charles and his comrades moved to Pont Nieppe, with all ranks of sergeant and above dispatched to conduct an inspection of nearby trenches. Time spent in the trenches in late February saw the occasional casualty caused by German shellfire before another move was ordered in early March, this time to base camp at Bac-Saint-Maur near the Franco-Belgian border.

Whilst occupying trenches on 3 March, Private Monahan was killed by shelling. On the evening of 8 March, the 8th Battalion relieved the 10th Battalion in trenches near Fleurbaix. Throughout the next day, 'nothing out of the ordinary' occurred as the enemy was 'unusually quiet' until nightfall, when shelling took place. Private Naylor was killed whilst out in front of the trenches employed on wiring duty. The following morning saw the first significant engagement against the enemy. The Canadian Division was given a 4-mile sector in front of Fleurbaix to occupy. The terrain was sodden, as the water table lay close to the ground's surface, thus the trenches Charles and his colleagues occupied were very shallow, consisting of little more than parapets formed by clumps of grass and sandbags.

On 9 March, a light falling of snow further dampened the ground and a dank mist shrouded the battlefield by the following morning. Night patrols, which had been practised since the Canadians had arrived in France, took place prior to the planned attack. The Canadians were to open fire on the Germans in order to create a diversion, allowing the British First Army to break through weakened enemy lines. A massive bombardment, followed by salvoes of rapid machine-gun fire, began at 7.30 am on 10 March and thirty-five minutes later, the Canadians had created a mile-long breach in the German lines. This enabled British troops to successfully capture Neuve Chapelle without meeting significant resistance, although poor communications precluded further swift, incisive advance.

The following day, the Canadians repeated the action, but the Germans proved better prepared to repulse the attacks. The 8th Battalion's war diary reported that a haze across the battlefield hampered attempts to observe enemy trenches, although three German snipers were reported to have been shot. During the action of 10-11 March, Private Charles Attwood had sustained a minor injury in the back, caused by a splinter of shrapnel, and had had his first taste of combat. He wrote home with defiance and resolution, 'this was not enough to stop me'. Charles was determined to take the battle to the enemy. Unbeknown to him, the Germans were planning to take the battle to him using a new and uniquely indiscriminate weapon.

Frank Mead

'You say that you could hear the roar of the Guns from Westerham Hill, well, how would you like to be out here where you are quite close to them?'

Enthusiasm to join the colours extended through the winter of 1914/15, and it was at this point that Londoner Frank Mead attested. On 18 November 1914 he went to the headquarters of the London Regiment on St John's Hill, Clapham, to take the King's shilling. He was assigned to the 2/23rd Battalion, which was at the time a reserve battalion for 1/23rd. He gave his employment as being a 'warehouseman – draper' and was described of being of 'good physical development', weighing 150 pounds and reaching a tall 6 feet 2 inches. He had four vaccination marks from childhood. Frank was issued with service number 3364 and placed in A Company.

Despite his generally good physique, Frank was initially only considered fit for territorial service, and on 19 June 1915 was transferred to the 108th Provisional Battalion, made up of men from 2nd and 3rd Territorial Battalions of lower

Private Frank Mead. (*Courtesy Chris Mead*)

medical categories. As British casualties mounted through the offensives of 1915, and the number of volunteers waned, efforts to pour more men into the armed forces were intensified. The Derby Scheme mopped up hundreds of thousands more reluctant recruits whilst for those who were inured to those persuasions, the looming threat of conscription awaited from 1 January 1916. Therefore, it made little sense to restrict men such as Frank to territorial service only. On 21 January he signed an Imperial Service Obligation, rendering him liable to go overseas, and six days later he was transferred to 3/23rd Battalion, waiting for three months for drafting into 1/23rd Battalion.

Frank's active overseas service began as one of a draft of seventy-two men joining the battalion at the small village of Ourton, 6 miles south of Béthune. The battalion formed part of 142nd Brigade within the 47th (2nd London) Division. The battalion was refreshed with new recruits throughout April and May of 1916. Training in bombing, helmet drill, target indication and musketry took place as well as ongoing physical fitness and strength training, with church parades arranged every Sunday unless the battalion was in the line. Working parties were assigned to repair trenches damaged in battle. Aside from the grind of training to kill the enemy efficiently, entertainments would

Private Frank Mead (right) with comrades from 1/23rd Battalion London Regiment. (*Courtesy Chris Mead*)

be provided. On 5 June, the battalion was marched to Bruay to attend a performance of the 47th Division Concert Party. Regular bathing parades were organised, to minimise the prevalence of trench foot and lice.

On 11 June, the battalion was inspected by the Lord Mayor of London and 30 June was spent at Bourlon. As tens of thousands of men poured out of the British lines on the Somme from 7.30 am onwards on 1 July 1916, the men of 1/23rd London Regiment spent the day cleaning kit, attending a gas lecture, forming working parties and parading in front of the battalion's commanding officer, Lieutenant Colonel H.H. Kemble. The battalion went into the line at Angres on 3 July, relieving the 20th Battalion London Regiment, sustaining a handful of wounded and killed over the next six days.

Further casualties were sustained on 18 July in the trenches at Vimy. Dozens of reinforcements were sent from a base depot to replace the mounting losses. At the end of July, the battalion was able to have baths, and on 7 August, the band of 1/21st London Regiment began a series of nightly concerts. As a stretcher-bearer, Frank would have transferred battle casualties to the new battalion medical officer, Captain J.H. Jordan RAMC, who arrived in August.

Throughout September 1916, further training was undertaken on bayoneting, the use of gas and trench mortaring. On 10 September, the men marched to Albert, and the following day were put into the line at Mametz Wood in reserve. From 15 to 19 September, the battalion sustained many casualties while under the disposal of 140th Infantry Brigade. At 9.25 am, men left the trenches with the aim of gaining a distance of 1,500 yards, to consolidate a line along a crest with patrols pushing on the Eaucort l'Abbaye.

However, there had not been the opportunity to undertake a preliminary reconnaissance of the ground due to lack of time. At 9.55, the leading platoons extended and moved forward, followed by support platoons and bombers, 'in good order, without casualties', but east of High Wood were subjected to heavy barrage fire. At 10.25 am, reports came back that the attack was going well, but the battalion was subjected to very heavy machine-gun fire on reaching Sunken Road. After dark, patrols were sent out and came across German posts and patrols, and were able to take some prisoners, among them an officer. Frank would have been in the thick of the action, with dozens of casualties stretchered in from the neighbourhood of Sunken Road.

The following morning's attack proceeded in good order until it passed the low ground around Cough Drop trench. Then men were exposed to very heavy enfilade fire from both flanks as well as coming under attack from their own side's shelling. The trenches were obliterated and the ridge was 'far from being a feature of the ground'. Further ground was gained throughout the morning until, at 10.00 am, a strong counter-attack was launched, driving the British troops out of a captured trench. Heavy hand-to-hand fighting took place. The adjutant, Lieutenant W.G. Newton, buried all official records of orders and messages as he saw the attack developing. When the 1/23rd was relieved on 19 September, casualties totalled sixteen officers and 565 other ranks. The unscathed and walking wounded marched back to bivouac at Albert. Frank had tasted the intensity of the war.

On 1 October, having again been placed at the disposal of 141st Infantry Brigade, the battalion moved to Switch Line trench and, after a delay owing to congestion in the trenches, went over the top in four attacking waves beginning at 6.45 am the following day. The firing line, led by Captain A.T. Fearon, was held up by heavy machine-gun fire and had to withdraw and reorganise. On this black day for the battalion, five men were reported killed, eighty-three wounded and seventy-five missing. Whilst German bullets and shells had not inflicted harm on him, in mid-October Frank succumbed to trench fever, a relatively common lice-borne ailment that affected between one-fifth and one-third of British troops who reported ill. Symptoms included relapsing fever, headache, dizziness, lumbago and shin pain, and could require a rest period of up to sixty days. Frank was transferred to No. 12 British General Hospital at Rouen, returning for duty a month later after a short stint at 8th Infantry Base Depot. He had escaped being allocated to a different battalion, rejoining his old comrades.

While Frank had been convalescing, his battalion had entrained to Ypres and marched to the Patricia lines near Poperinghe. Through the winter some time was spent in the trenches. A handful of casualties, a few of them fatal, were sustained in the Canal Subsector at the beginning of December and on 10 December a special church parade was held, during which eleven NCOs were presented with Military Medal ribbons by the GOC of the 47th Division, Major General Sir George F. Gorringe. The new year arrived with the battalion in the thick of the action around Hill 60. Casualties included their commanding officer, Lieutenant Colonel H.H. Kemble, awarded the DSO for his actions. Three other ranks won the Military Medal. In preparation for a series of enormous mine explosions that were planned for the Battle of Messines Ridge in June, a working party was attached to an Australian Tunnelling Company on 17 February. In the dangerous subterranean environment, casualties were sustained.

On 19 April, the battalion went into the front line and five days later, their 300-yard length of trench was attacked unsuccessfully by a fifty-strong enemy raiding party. Unusual light had been fired from the enemy line, alerting the sentries, and at 3.30 am the enemy was detected leaving their trench. There followed an intense barrage of Minenwerfers, a short-range mortar used for clearing barbed wire and bunkers, aimed at the battalion's reserve and support lines. The men on the front line opened fire on the advancing enemy, who managed to get through the barbed wire defences, five of them mounting the trench parapet. Thirteen casualties were sustained by the German bombers, who were eventually driven back to their own trench, leaving men dead and dying in no man's land. Two days later, the battalion retired to Ottawa camp for a rest period.

On 19 May 1917, Frank made his will. Recognised by the War Department as 'constituting a valid will', the brief document read: 'In the event of my death I give the whole of my property & effects to my father, Mr T. Mead. 13 Elfindale Road, Herne Hill, London SE.'

May and June saw further spells in the front line, with Lieutenant Colonel Kemble DSO MC dying of wounds sustained on an attack on the Ypres-Comines Canal on 7 June. At three in the morning, the mines which had been painstakingly dug below the German lines on Hill 60 were detonated, and in the ensuing inferno, little retaliation was apparent from the enemy's guns and Frank's battalion was able to assemble in front of Rennie Street trench in snake formation, in half platoons, without molestation. Kemble insisted on accompanying the four companies in his battalion as far forward as OBI trench, and on his return via Hedgerow trench was mortally wounded by a shrapnel bullet in the chest. Kemble was taken to No. 10 Casualty Clearing Station but died shortly afterwards in the same ward as his friend, Lieutenant Ind.

Meanwhile, several German prisoners had been taken and were interviewed by Lieutenant Colonel Milner of 1/24th Battalion. Valuable information was received regarding the enemy's dispositions and intentions, including the absences of booby traps. Therefore, at 4.35 am on 7 June, the battalion crossed no man's land in waves and, now commanded by Major T.C. Hargreaves DSO, made good progress. At 6.00 am a report was received by wire that the signal officer, Lieutenant W. Lewis, had entered the German trenches and taken officers and men prisoner.

The following day, 8 June, Frank was in action as stretcher parties scoured the north and south banks of the canal, clearing the area of the wounded and dead, assisting in the burials of the latter. Supplies of food, water and ammunition were carried up from support trenches. As the day wore on, the enemy established themselves in the opposite trenches and 'became increasingly difficult' by the use first of snipers then machine guns. At 7.30 pm, an intense barrage rained down on the men of 1/23rd Battalion, inflicting heavy casualties, damaging the trench and putting the remaining Vickers gun out of action.

An intense reciprocal barrage went up, during which No. 6 Platoon, under Sergeant Worsfold made a gallant effort to reinforce Opal reserve trench across the canal, with Worsfold himself being severely wounded. The following day, dugouts and trenches that had been captured were entered and a German telephone disconnected. Some desultory bombardment was encountered but the day passed relatively quietly, before 1/23rd Battalion was relieved early on the morning of 10 June. During the whole operation, the front-line and supporting troops had been constantly supplied with bombs, water, rations and hot tea. In all, 2,320 pints of hot tea were issued and 176 2-gallon tins of water had been sent up.

Two days later, a tally was taken which revealed a heavy toll of nearly forty dead, and 161 wounded and missing. On 24 June, a special parade service took place at St Martin-au-Laert, during which the GOC of 47th (London) Division, Major General Gorringe, presented six Military Crosses, three Distinguished Conduct Medals and nineteen Military Medals for the action of 7–9 June.

On 28 June, Lieutenant Colonel Maxwell DSO joined as commanding officer from 1/8th Battalion. On 1 July, while in the line immediately south of the Ypres Canal, Private E. Marshall chose to take his own life rather than endure war's relentless mental torture, dying of 'self-inflicted wounds'. On 19 July, ten men were wounded by 'a new "mustard-oil" German gas shell'.

The first surviving letter that Frank Mead wrote to his 17-year-old brother Reg came shortly after this intense period of combat and gas attacks. Written on 30 July 1917 on squared file paper in Frank's neatly back-sloping cursive hand, it was penned in a bivouac which was 'by no means very comfortable, I might tell you'. Frank thanked Reg for the receipt of a long letter and some chocolate, but bemoaned the inclement weather, and the fact that he could not be in England accompanying his brother on long bike rides. Reg had noted that the roar of warfare could be heard in London, with the enormous mine blasts during the Battle of Messines in June even being heard in Downing Street by Prime Minister David Lloyd George. Frank commented, 'You say that you could hear the roar of the Guns from Westerham Hill, well, how would you like to be out here where you are quite close to them?'

Having left the Strand School in May, Reg was liking his job as a bank clerk, which pleased Frank. Another pleasure that came his way was a parcel from the firm for whom he had worked before the war, 'with a tinned steak & kidney pudding enclosed. I was absolutely A1 Reg, as you know how awfully fond of pudding I was when in England.' Frank commented that his health had been under strain since the introduction of mustard gas into the German war arsenal:

Old Fritz has got a new kind of gas now, Reg, which he sends over in a shell. It makes you sneeze & also makes your eyes water. He polluted us with them for one & a half hours the other night so you can guess what a state we were all in when he had finished. I nearly sneezed my head off.

The high summer of 1917 saw Frank engaged in further drilling and training at Kempton Park Camp, south of St Julien, before, on 24 August, moving up to the front line at Westhoek, relieving Ernest Blackburn's former comrades of the 9th Battalion King's Royal Rifle Corps (KRRC). The following day a German shell entered and exploded inside the battalion headquarters dugout, killing two and wounding six.

Recreation was provided on 8 September when the battalion sports day was held at Steenvoorde before Frank and his comrades moved to Dickebusch. On 22 September, Frank made what was to be his final relocation, entraining from Bavinchove to Maroeuil near Arras, before travelling by light railway to Wakefield Camp. Frank would have been included in working parties which worked day and night between 25 and 30 September at Oppy, reinforcing the front line and building strongpoints. In early October the battalion entered the front line around Railway Cutting. From here, Frank wrote to Reg while huddled in a funk hole 'with three other fellows … it is a bit of a squash', asking to be excused for his 'scrawl'. He sympathised with Reg over the continuing air raids over London, but reminded him, 'Never mind, old boy, you're much better off in England than out here.' Frank hoped that Reg had been able to enjoy some long cycle rides during the recent fine weather, 'just the time of the year to go for long rides when it's not too hot'. It was a brief letter as Frank could think of 'nothing more to write about at this time'.

Reg heard again from the elder brother he adored on 15 October. On this occasion, Frank wrote from his bed, 'or rather what we have to serve as a bed, which is chicken wire stretched across two bars of wood'. However, he did have some sweets to enjoy, courtesy of Reg. Frank related how he had visited 'a very large town', probably Arras, and 'thoroughly enjoyed myself' in the fine weather. Once again, Frank had read with concern that London was still under aerial attack from the Germans: 'you had had a very rough time of it in London during the air raids but thank goodness they did not go anywhere near Herne Hill.' He still yearned to be able to join Reg on a cycle ride; 'I only wish I had the chance.'

Before Frank's next letter, two companies had raided the German trenches on 4 November, sustaining twenty-one casualties, two of them fatal. The final words that Reg was ever to read of his brother's were written on Saturday, 10 November, from one of the 2,000 recreation facilities run by the Church Army in France during the war. Once again, Frank apologised for having little of note to relay to Reg, although he was able to report 'some very good Cinema shows just lately and a fine concert last night'. Having asked Reg to pass on his thanks to their father for the receipt of a sum of money, ominously, Frank expected to be 'going into the line again in about four days' time'. He signed off from Reg's world:

I remain
Your loving brother
Frank

Percy Pope

'He was one of the best fellows'

It was almost inevitable that Percy Pope would follow his brothers into military service. The sensitive but sharp barrister had already joined the Inns of Court OTC in November 1914, and after five months' training was gazetted, in April 1915, as a second lieutenant in the 3rd Battalion of the Welsh Regiment, under the command of his elder brother, Lieutenant Colonel Alexander Pope, DSO. Proud, and eager to tell his parents the news, he wrote to his father, Alfred:

A line to let you know, in case you didn't notice it, that my name was in the Gazette last Saturday.

2nd Lieut. 3rd Welsh Regt.

I am just now busy getting Kit etc and join at Cardiff next Tuesday.

The welfare of his brothers who were already on active service was prominent in Percy's mind:

Is there any news of Bertie?

I hope the news of Cyril and Decie is satisfactory

Love to Mother and all at home.

Your affectionate Son

Percy

While Percy waited to be sent on overseas service, three of his brothers had already been in action. Albert Victor, 'Bertie', had been an army officer since leaving Winchester College in 1905, serving in India. August 1914 found him serving with the 14th Hussars in Bangalore. Decimus, 'Decie', serving with the 8th Hussars, joined his regiment in France on 16 November 1914, and was later to win the Military Cross for gallantry in the field. Cyril was the first of the Pope brothers to see action. Serving as a lieutenant in the 1st Battalion Bedfordshire Regiment, he was part of the 5th Division

Second Lieutenant Percy Paris Pope. (*Author's collection*)

of the British Expeditionary Force sent to Europe under the command of Sir John French. Arriving at Le Havre on 16 August 1914, Cyril fought at Mons, Le Cateau and the Marne before he was taken captive on 14 November on the Ypres Salient, spending four years as a prisoner of war.

Within two months of obtaining his commission Percy was attached to the 1st Battalion of the Welsh Regiment. The battalion had disembarked at Le Havre on 18 January 1915 and was quickly engaged in heavy fighting around Hill 60 during the Second Battle of Ypres. Reinforcements were added to the ranks in May 1915, although the battalion war diary noted that a draft of three officers and 215 other ranks who principally came from the 3rd South West Borderers had poor military discipline with 'marching bad'.

From May to September 1915, Percy 'saw four months of some of the severest fighting of the war'. On 22 May, the battalion took over trenches near Hooge and on the 24th was involved in heavy fighting near Bellewaarde Farm. During this engagement three officers were killed, eleven were wounded and one was reported missing. In the ranks, a further 266 men were recorded as missing. The diary recorded: 'The missing in all probability are killed as no prisoners were taken as far as is known.' In this case the forlorn expectation was that once a man was reported as missing, the chances of him having survived were slim.

The next week, an inspection by the notoriously short-tempered but incisive-thinking General Allenby, then commander of V Corps, took place. He heaped great praise on the work done by the battalion and the whole of 84th Brigade. To fill the gaps in the ranks, a further ninety-nine men arrived, although they were 'badly trained and show great slackness in discipline'. By the middle of June 1915, the battalion was holding Ridge Wood, an area of high ground between the Kemmel road and Dickebusch Lake, with one officer, Lieutenant Coker, meeting his death from a sniper. The playing of sport, as a boost to morale, an expression of manliness and, in this case, an articulation of national culture, was undertaken on 11 July when, during a rest period away from the trenches, the 1st Welsh Battalion played the 6th Welsh Battalion at a game of rugby football, the former winning by the margin of a try.

The area in front of Locre, 6 miles south-west of Ypres, was then occupied by the battalion. Until 4 August, relative calm prevailed when, at 8.45 pm, German troops exploded a mine they had managed to lay under the British trench, burying seventeen men. Despite the distraction of having to repulse the subsequent enemy attack, ten were eventually dug out alive. The war diary noted: 'Lance Corporal Bancroft, who was buried, as soon as his head was uncovered, began singing and encouraging the digging party near him during the three hours it took to dig him and the others out.'

The remainder of August saw a continuation of mine blowing, with the battalion retaliating with a counter-mine on 18 August, wrecking an enemy gallery. The Germans struck back with a bombardment by a large Minenwerfer. This wounded several men and the trenches had to be restored while under constant fire. Another mine caused further structural damage and human casualties on 3 September.

In addition to the destruction caused by German explosive materiel, one of the battalion, Sergeant Stacey, sustained fatal injuries on 5 August while looking over the parapet. The Germans had indulged in loud cheering across no man's land and the Welshmen were curious as to what was occurring. Stacey had cautioned his men against putting their heads above the parapet, but then did so himself, and was struck by a sniper's bullet. He died of his wounds two days later. During this period, it was customary to have periscopes fixed on bayonets and it was a favourite amusement of both sides to smash them with the accuracy of their sniping.

Further games of rugby took place during August, again against the 6th Welsh and the Monmouth Regiment. By late September, the much-travelled Percy's final journey was to occur. On the 21st, 84th Brigade marched the 10½ miles south from Locre to Pradelles en route to Vermelles. In the four months he had been with 1st Welsh, Percy had created a most favourable impression amongst his comrades, the barrister having made an excellent transition to military life. According to the Pope family historian, the Reverend R.G. Bartelot, 'His men loved him' and he was equally admired by his fellow officers, with Lieutenant Weber later writing, 'he was one of the best fellows'.

Gilbert Donnelly

'Any Unit. Irish Preferred'

Whilst Percy Pope had seized the opportunities provided by a privileged education, establishing a successful legal career, the 18-year-old Gilbert Donnelly enjoyed but a brief professional training. The ambitious young man had determined on a career in medicine, and from St Malachy's College, Gilbert had gained a place at Queen's University, Belfast. There was a significant moral pressure from the university hierarchy for its staff and students to join the war effort. Consisting of fewer than 1,000 students in 1915, QUB was a tightly-knit community. At the spring graduation ceremony held in March 1915, nine medical students were presented with their degrees and one doctor received the diploma in public health. The Vice Chancellor, the Reverend Dr Hamilton, in his address, said the number was small as 'many of the senior students had very properly left the university to attend to what they considered … was the pressing duty of the moment'. Five hundred university men had joined the armed services.

Hamilton also expressed concern that the number of students enrolled on medical courses in 1914 had fallen by 25 per cent since the previous year. With an increasing population and several doctors joining the war effort, 'the attention of all students, of all thinking of becoming students, of fathers and mothers in this North of Ireland of ours ought to be called to the fact … that the prospects of those entering the medical profession were brighter now than they had been for many a long year.' Perhaps these words, recorded in the local press, steered Gilbert towards choosing medicine as his career.

In July 1915, the University Senate made it compulsory for all male students to attend classes for military training for the duration of the war. Thus, when the university's 1915–16 session began on Friday, 1 October, the ambitious Gilbert was in a de facto quasi-military milieu.

On 4 October 1915, Gilbert enlisted in the university's Officers' Training Corps. Three weeks later he applied for a temporary commission in the regular British Army for the duration of the war. In doing so he had volunteered for military service shortly before the pressure to do so would have become almost irresistible. The university's senate urged, a month after Gilbert's application, that all its teachers and students, excepting fourth and fifth-year medical students, should join the forces. This appeal was reinforced with the coercion that the careers of those failing to heed the call would be disadvantaged: 'during the period of the war no person of military age and capacity will be appointed to any position in the University.' Students who enlisted before Christmas 1915, or who had already enlisted, like Gilbert, would have all enrolment and tuition fees refunded. Hugo Bell Fisher, a fellow medical student of Gilbert's from the Protestant tradition, was one who heeded the call, receiving a commission for the Royal Munster Fusiliers (RMF). Hugo was nine months Gilbert's junior and they had been colleagues in the university's OTC. His mother, Dr Elizabeth Fisher, had been the first woman to graduate from QUB with a medical degree and was a prominent campaigner for female suffrage. Hugo, after seeing 'a great deal of active service' during 1916–17, was reported 'missing, believed killed' on 10 November 1917, the final day of the Passchendaele campaign. Cruelly, hope was rekindled for Elizabeth Fisher, whose own war service had seen her on the medical staff of the Military Hospital in Malta, as on 21 November she received a letter from Hugo posted from a German Casualty Clearing Station at Limburg. He reported being feverish and wounded in the left foot. Sadly, this was the final communication she would receive from her son, who died two days later in a German field hospital in Beveren, Belgium, from a shell splinter wound to his left thigh.

Gilbert's preference was for an infantry regiment, his application stating, 'any unit, Irish preferred'. In doing so, he was making a conscious choice to position his war service within a distinctly Irish milieu, making himself available for direction into either the 16th (Irish) or 10th (Irish) Division, which were predominantly composed of Roman Catholic troops, rather than 36th (Ulster) Division, with its broadly Protestant identity. Gilbert's elder brother Eugene had already volunteered for the Royal Inniskilling Fusiliers in August 1915. With older brother William volunteering in 1918, the Donnelly family would supply three of the 210,000 Irishmen who served with British forces during the war, 35,000 of whom would make the ultimate sacrifice.

Gilbert's application was successful, the 'Promotions and Appointments' section of the *Belfast News-Letter* reporting on 25 November:

> The 'Gazette' announces the appointment as temporary second-lieutenant in the Royal Munster Fusiliers of Gilbert Donnelly, of Glastonbury, Ashley Park, Belfast, sixth son of Mr John Donnelly, Assistant Superintendent Class 1, Post Office Telegraphs, Belfast. Mr Gilbert Donnelly was educated at St. Malachy's College and Queen's University, and received his preliminary Army training in the Belfast University contingent of the Officers' Training Corps. He has been instructed to report himself for training at the Palace Barracks, Holywood.

Whether Gilbert's prime motivation was a sense of justice of the cause for which Britain was purportedly fighting, a sense of adventure, peer pressure from fellow students in the university milieu, or a desire to develop leadership qualities, his decision was made in the context of a deeply divided political landscape in Ireland.

John Redmond, leader of the Irish Parliamentary Party, had secured the passing of the Irish Home Rule Act in September 1914, and was keen to demonstrate Irish support for the war effort. The implementation of Home Rule had been suspended by the outbreak of war, but Redmond had received assurances from the British government that limited autonomy for Ireland would be implemented following the conclusion of what was expected to be a short conflict. Furthermore, Redmond wished to demonstrate Irish support for the 'freedom of small nations' on the Continent, particularly Roman Catholic Belgium, arguing the war was being fought in defence of the 'highest principles of religion and morality and right'.

Redmond's added hope was that the common sacrifice of Irish Nationalists and Unionists would bring them closer together, thus increasing the prospect of a relatively peaceful transition to post-war Home Rule. Allowing Ulster Unionists to reap the political and propaganda benefits of being the only section of the Irish public to support the war effort would be catastrophic for the future of Ireland. Redmond urged: 'Let Irishmen come together in the trenches and risk their lives together and spill their blood together, and I say there is no power on earth that when they come home can induce them to turn as enemies upon one another.'

He praised Irish soldiers, 'with their astonishing courage and their beautiful faith, with their natural military genius ... offering up their supreme sacrifice of life with a smile on their lips because it was given for Ireland'.

Gilbert Donnelly's stated preference for an Irish unit would suggest that he saw the volunteering of his services within the scope of Redmond's vision of a distinctively Irish contribution towards an overall British and Empire war effort. The Royal Munster Fusiliers was a largely Roman Catholic regiment that would eventually form part of the 16th (Irish) Division. The RMF had recently suffered severe losses in the Dardanelles and as the war gathered pace, additional recruits were taken from wherever they were available at the time.

By 1916, as Gilbert undertook his officer training, including a period at the RMF's Fermoy Camp in County Cork, his eldest brother, Samuel, had progressed to the position of chief shipyard draughtsman at the Belfast shipbuilding firm of Harland and Wolff Ltd. Whilst shipbuilding continued at a frenetic pace to meet the demands of war, Roman Catholic Samuel found that his career could progress no further in Belfast. Any senior management role would be denied him on account of his faith. Therefore, the firm, respecting his service and ability, offered him an assistant manager's position at Govan on the river Clyde. Samuel migrated with his young family to the outskirts of Glasgow.

It was against this backdrop of continuing discrimination against Irish Catholics despite widespread commitment to the British war effort that the 1916 Easter Rising occurred. Cognisant of the adage 'England's extremity is Ireland's opportunity', some 1,800 volunteers, led by James Connolly and Padraig Pearse, friend of Gilbert's godfather, Carl Gilbert Hardebeck, seized Dublin's General Post Office and proclaimed an Irish republic. Although British forces, including men from the Sherwood Foresters who had joined up with the thought of fighting the German foe rather than extinguishing political opposition within the British Isles, were able to quash the rebellion within a week. The subsequent summary executions of fifteen of the rising's leaders led to widespread public revulsion. Sinn Féin's subsequent success in the 1918 General Election meant that many men who returned from war in Europe found themselves embroiled in a war of independence against their former British comrades.

Second Lieutenant Gilbert Donnelly arrived at Barnafay Wood on 4 September 1916 to join 8th Battalion Royal Munster Fusiliers to commence his active service. His first experience of the trenches came three days later when the battalion occupied the Sunken Road trench, east of Guillemont. British artillery and German snipers exchanged fire before, on 9 September, the men left the trenches to attack the enemy line. The German trench had not been touched by British artillery fire and was held by over 200 men and five machine guns, making a frontal attack impossible. However, the leading companies did manage to penetrate the German line, sustaining seventy-six casualties in the process. Most of these men became numbered amongst the missing of the war, as it was not possible to retrieve their bodies for burial. It would have been a salutary experience of the potential obliteration from the physical realm that could befall any fallen soldier.

On withdrawal from the line, concerts took place and a sports day was held on 16 September. The battalion was then transferred to the Ypres Salient and assigned to rotating trench engagements until 7 November. Gilbert was sent on a week's course on Trench Mortar Work at Terdeghem beginning on 23 October, accompanied by a man from the ranks. Three days later, the commanding officer of 47th Infantry Brigade, Brigadier General Pereira, received a message from John Redmond MP, which was circulated to the troops in recognition of their exploits at Loos and the Somme during 1916:

> Dear General Pereira, will you allow me to send you a few lines of hearty congratulations not only on the magnificent record of the 16th Division, but in a special way the record of the 47th Infantry Brigade. We in Ireland have read with the deepest pride of their gallantry & I only wish it were in my power to tell the men themselves how grateful we are to them for having so worthily maintained the tradition of Irish Valour.

Gilbert Donnelly had joined a brigade with a fine war record, and he was to contribute to the esteem in which Irishmen in the British Army were held during the following year.

Religious observance for the mainly Roman Catholic battalion took place, with a divine service being held at La Clytte on 29 October, the unit war diary recording 'marching to church with the pipes and drums', before Gilbert returned from his Trench Mortar course the following day. On 22 November, the 8th Battalion RMF was disbanded and its personnel, including Gilbert Donnelly, transferred to the 1st Royal Munster Fusiliers.

Gilbert's new battalion was already battle-hardened from action in Gallipoli in 1915. From 16 to 29 May 1917, the 1st Battalion RMF spent time at a specially modelled training ground at Bayengham. From there the companies were moved to Clare Camp, where the men bathed and were fitted with fresh clothes and boots in readiness for the Battle of Messines. Gilbert's next taste of action was to be a successful endeavour. The objective of the battle was to capture the high ground from the neighbourhood of Ploegsteert to Hill 60 and Mount Sorrel to the north. On a ridge south of Ypres stood the villages of Wytschaete and Messines, the ridge forming a salient in the German line. Sir Douglas Haig was determined to capture it prior to launching a further offensive around Ypres.

In preparation, Welsh and Cornish miners had been busily burrowing under the ridge, forming a network of tunnels and shafts, creating twenty large mines packed with 600 tons of explosives. Artillery had been assembled to support the onslaught. The attack was meticulously rehearsed under the direction of General Sir Herbert Plumer, commanding officer of the Second Army.

The 1st Battalion's commanding officer, Lieutenant Colonel R.H. Monck-Mason DSO, issued a proclamation to his men on 6 June 1917, the day before the great offensive:

> I should like all ranks to know that I have absolute confidence both in the officers and men. ... There is not a single blot on the history of the Regiment, and, knowing the Regiment as I have for nearly twenty-five years, I believe it impossible that there should be.
>
> The Battalion is one selected to be the first over the Wytschaete Ridge, and the historic town of Wytschaete is allotted to our share. In a few days Great Britain and Ireland will be ringing with the name of the Munsters, and the Irish Division, and another honour will be added to the long list of the Regiment. Good luck and success to you all. ...
>
> I cannot tell you how proud I am of my Battalion and to be in command at this great moment.

Gilbert was one of four officers commanding sections in Y Company, under the leadership of Second Lieutenant E.T. Hussey.

At 3.10 am on 7 June, the subterranean explosives were detonated, with the eruption being heard in Surrey. Having assumed position at 2.00 am, Gilbert witnessed earth being thrown high into the air. The 1st RMF was in the second wave of attack, advancing at 5.50 am with W and Y companies leading the way. Brigadier General George Pereira recalled, 'This advance across awful country has been reported by all who saw it as a sight never to be forgotten.' A captured German officer stated that the Munsters moved 'as if on parade' whilst another wounded officer recalled that as the men passed him, they were 'full of spirits and some were smoking cigarettes'. Direction and formation remained intact with the intermediate objectives being reached on schedule. Prisoners were captured, although snipers and machine-gun fire sought to hinder their progress. These were summarily dealt with by rapid rifle fire and bombing parties on the flanks.

Despite the overall success of the attack, the leader of Gilbert's company, Second Lieutenant Hussey, was killed when running forward to prevent the overeager advance of one flank in his company. Seeing that his men were in danger from the creeping British barrage, sustaining casualties, he exposed himself to that bombardment and sacrificed his own life. The regimental history recorded: 'He was destined for the Church of England. Both the Army and the Church were losers by his death.'

The third objective was reached at 7.20 am and the fourth at 7.50 am, with the capture of more prisoners and seven machine guns, two light trench mortars and two heavy trench mortars. In total, the British attack of 7 June led to the capture of over 7,000 prisoners, and the failure of a German counter-attack meant that the Messines Ridge remained in British possession. Brigadier General Pereira reported: 'The behaviour of all ranks was splendid, and all displayed the same keenness and eagerness; and, as is usual with the Irish, the difficulty was in restraining the men. The result has filled all ranks with the greatest delight, and has raised the morale of the men to the highest pitch.'

The battalion had advanced over 2 miles in a little over a day with minimal losses, an exceptional feat by Western Front standards. Gilbert Donnelly's first taste of action had gone as well as could be expected, despite the deaths of six of his comrades, with forty-three others reported missing. It is impossible to tell whether the 'greatest delight' described by Brigadier General Pereira was shared by Gilbert, or whether the experience of losing men close to him had produced a more negative psychological effect. Nevertheless, his contribution to the victory is implicit in the words of the battalion's commanding officer, Lieutenant Colonel Monck-Mason:

> The success of the operation was due to the excellent handling of the men by the company and platoon commanders and serjeants, and to the fine discipline, keenness and gallantry displayed by the men themselves. I cannot speak too highly of the conduct of all ranks. I should like to mention the following remarks made by a captured German officer. He stated that he had heard of the fighting capacity of the Irish soldiers, but had never met him personally before. He said that my Battalion advanced to the attack as though they were on parade.

The battle had seen the largest concentration of Irishmen fighting alongside each other to date, the Roman Catholic 16th (Irish) Division serving alongside the Protestant 36th (Ulster) Division. Sadly, this unity of purpose on the battlefield was not to translate to political and social solidarity and harmony on the island of Ireland when the survivors of war returned home.

A well-deserved period of rest followed through June and July of 1917 before the commencement of the Third Battle of Ypres, the objective of which was to take the Passchendaele Ridge. The Germans had created a series of small forts behind their front line, made from reinforced concrete and iron with very thick walls. These would make advancing on the enemy much harder than even attempting to take a trench line.

From 4 to 18 August, the battalion was assigned the grim task of holding the line under heavy bombardments, Gilbert and his comrades cowering in shell holes full of water, with no overhead protection. Losses of men were frequent. As well as the casualties from German shelling, the battalion had dozens of men taken to hospital suffering from trench fever or swollen feet. The rain came down in torrents, making roads impassable. Seventeen RMF men were killed, including Second Lieutenant J.R. Love.

Once again, 47th Brigade came in for praise from its commanding officer:

During the operations extending from 4am on July 31st to the early hours of August 18th you have had by far the hardest time that has fallen to you since you arrived in France. …

Without the glory and excitement of going over the top as you did at Guillemont and Wytschaete you have had the far harder task and drudgery of holding the line under heavy bombardments, lying in shell holes full of water.

You came in for the worst of the weather … and up to your first relief in the early hours of August 6th you have had to stand or lie in the open without overhead protection, with everything soaked, and sore feet, whilst the continuous bombardment banished all chance of sleep for four days.

I cannot tell you how proud I am of you all and the splendid unflinching spirit all ranks have shown during the last eighteen days.

I can never forget what you have done. …

G Pereira, Brigadier General
Commanding 47th Infantry Brigade
18/8/17

On 9 September, Gilbert was subjected to a gas attack unlike the one that would kill Charles Attwood. Rather than the slow spread of the noxious substance across the ground, on this occasion the enemy put over about fifty shells which burst in the air, spreading capsules of gas downwards. The Munsters were able to don their masks, thus avoiding serious casualties. On 17 October, the battalion was relieved by the 6th Royal Irish Regiment and marched to camp at Ervillers. Mud, sweat and blood-encrusted uniforms were refreshed and sports were organised, including cross-country running and boxing.

In the middle of November 1917, the battalion moved to Durrow Camp to undergo special training in preparation for the Battle of Cambrai. The objective of the battle was to break the Hindenburg Line in front of Cambrai and disorganise the whole German scheme of defence on the Western Front, lessening the strength of the forces they could send to Italy. The 16th (Irish) Division was deployed in the neighbourhood of Bullecourt. On advancing, the infantry was to be protected by artillery, machine-gun barrage, smoke screen and 400 tanks.

As at Passchendaele, the Germans had established fortified pillboxes 300 yards behind the front line. In addition, the support trench, known as 'Tunnel Trench', had a tunnel about 30 feet down along its whole length, with staircases leading up every 25 yards. On the right and left of every entrance was a heavy trench mortar shell set into the wall, connected by electric wires, so the whole trench could be detonated from a position to the rear. A German deserter had informed the British that these wires were coloured red, distinguishing them from the telephone system. The Irishmen were able to cut every bit of red wire they came across.

The 1st Battalion RMF was to attack on 20 November, a day that broke with an overcast sky but no rain. It was left to W and X companies to undertake the attack, sustaining heavy losses but taking 167 German prisoners in the process. The battalion was then relieved and was able to spend Christmas Day 1917 attending a church parade and enjoying seasonal festivities. The men in the ranks were given a meal of roast pork, vegetables and pudding, and were issued with beer and other 'comforts'. The Irish Women's Association and the Christmas Comforts Fund of the Royal Munster Fusiliers ensured that men received cigarettes and tobacco, and an evening concert 'finished a very cheerful and successful day'. It was to be Gilbert Donnelly's last Christmas, and he took dinner with his fellow officers in the evening, entertained by a band.

The year 1918 dawned for Gilbert Donnelly with deep snow and bitter wind as the battalion occupied trenches in the Lempire section. He had been granted a temporary promotion to first lieutenant, aged just 20, as the losses of officers led to relatively rapid promotion of so many young men. The 1st RMF had lost its commanding officer, as Lieutenant Colonel Monck-Mason DSO had been refused a pass by the Medical Board to return to his men, damaged by the strain of almost continuous campaign engagement for the past year and a half. His place was taken briefly by Lieutenant Colonel H.T. Goodland, a Canadian officer, before Lieutenant Colonel R.R.G. Kane DSO assumed command. The early part of 1918 was generally quiet, although the occasional skirmish did take place. On 21 February, Father Tom Duggan, the battalion's chaplain, wrote home: 'The Munsters had a famous raid the other night. I have a souvenir for you – a German flash lamp. One of the escorts of an unfortunate prisoner gave it to me. It was most amusing to hear them marching to the starting-off point whistling 'The Rising of the Moon'.'

On 12 March, the battalion moved to St Emilie to prepare for the Battle of St Quentin. It would be the final move that Gilbert Donnelly would make.

Alan Stirling

'I do not mind. I can & will stick it'

Wolverhampton grocer's assistant Alan Stirling seemed ideally suited for service in the Army Ordnance Corps, a supply and repair corps, with responsibility for the efficient provision of weapons, armour, ammunition and clothing, with certain minor functions such as laundry, mobile baths and photography. The scale of the war meant that existing depots at Woolwich, Weedon and Pimlico had to be supplemented by requisitioned warehouses throughout Britain. Alan's experience of warehouse work at the Kidson's warehouse stood him in good stead for AOC service, and he was posted to a base in Dover. Initially he found digs with a Mrs G. Dennis on Clarendon Street. The town was on the front line of the British war organisation, the base of the Dover Patrol, a collection of naval craft, balloons and sea planes tasked with preventing German shipping and submarines from entering the English Channel. The huge Admiralty Harbour supported the patrol in controlling the Straits of Dover and safeguarding troops and supplies moving to and from France. Dover became one huge fortress, with a garrison to hold the port at all costs. Its citizens had been subjected to the first aerial bomb dropped on British soil, which landed close to Dover Castle on Christmas Eve 1914. During subsequent air raids, residents sheltered in local caves.

Alan relayed the circumstances of his arrival in Kent:

Guess what time we got to Dover … @12pm Midnight. We were being marched round the streets & roads of Dover to find our billets. I am pleased to say I have got a good billet & have good food. I am up every morning @6.30 on parade @7 o'clock. My word we do feel the cold, being on the sea coast. Before we came to Dover the officer @ Woolich [sic] told us we would have to work hard & he was not far wrong.

Alan was impressed with the strength of Dover's defences. Enemy aircraft would be due a 'warm reception at Dover for you ought to see the Anti-aircraft guns ready for when they do appear'.

Alan wrote his next letter home on 23 November 1915. Giving thanks for the receipt of a parcel, the former grocer's assistant expressed concern that his family were depriving themselves in order to give him extra provisions: 'I hope I am not robbing any of you by having it off you. I would rather not accept it if I thought I were doing so.' Army life was 'such a change from the Grocery. ... Yes I do like the army very much. I am not sorry that I joined & in fact I am highly delighted. It really is a treat to be amongst a lot of chaps.'

Military aircraft were seen frequently flying over Dover: 'I saw a lovely sight when on the seafront the other Sunday afternoon. A waterplane (the first I have seen) gliding along on the air, then it gradually swooped down on to the water ... I saw the men go into the sea and get out. My word it was a monstrous thing.'

Contact with religious leaders from their native communities helped many men feel part of home. Before leaving, Alan had tried to visit the Reverend Hunt, vicar of St Mark's, Wolverhampton, and asked his family to remember him to the priest. He had also received a letter from the Reverend George Swindells, and in January 1916 expressed that it was 'like old times' to be able to read the parish magazine of St Mark's Church, Chapel Ash, once again. Swindells had trained for the priesthood at St Aiden's College, Birkenhead, and had been ordained by Bishop Kempthorne at Lichfield Cathedral in February 1915.

Alan was pleased with his accommodation, with the caveat of delayed access to his victuals: 'I have a splendid billet, good food, good bed & it is clean. There is only one thing. I always have to wait for my meals ... but there may be worse things than that – although you know how I simply loath to wait.'

Alan's positivity continued throughout December 1915: 'Your letter ... still finds me in good health & strength, & still enjoying myself. It is as the chaps say "We don't get much money, but we do see life".'

However, there was disappointment expressed at the paucity of Christmas leave arrangements, with only twenty-one out of 220 men in 73rd Company being granted a break. The reality of no Christmas with his family hit home with Alan. On 22 December, having received a lavish parcel containing cake, pudding, mince pies, chocolates, bananas, grapes, sweets, dates and some 'very welcome "Turkish Blend"' cigarettes, he bemoaned: 'I should very much have liked to spend Xmas with you, but as you say we cannot have things all our own way (especially in the army). Yes it does seem ages. It seems years since last I was @ home. I should just like to have a peep @ you all.'

As it was, Alan spent Christmas in his Dover billet, which, although a pleasant enough occasion, failed to match up to the warmth and fellowship of a family yuletide. 'It has seemed rather a funny Xmas to me, just like an ordinary Sunday, of course I have enjoyed myself as well as what I could but no matter how good a billet you have it is not like home.' Alan had been sent letters and cards by friends and the Reverend Swindells, who advised him that he intended to visit the Stirling family at their Ash Street home.

A new experience for Alan came in early January 1916, when:

> I had the honour (an honour I say because only a few of us were allowed to go) of attending a military funeral on Thursday, not a Private but one of our Com Officers. First funeral I have ever been to. Strange it should be a military one, that was one of the scenes since being @ Dover I shall never forget as long as I live. All of us were sweating we had to keep our great coats on and our belts over top.

Letters from his family raised Alan's spirits. He wrote, 'you must accept my best thanks for your welcome letter. You do not know one half how I welcome your letters. Or else I feel sure you would write oftener.' Alan yearned for the day when he could visit home, but patience was to be the order of the day in obtaining leave: 'We have chaps here who have been out in the country longer than I have and have not yet had leave. So therefore leave is and must be for some time out of the question.'

Finally, after two months on the south coast, leave was granted, subject to Alan not being drafted at short notice. The train journey from Dover to Wolverhampton was expected to take a little over eight hours. On his return back to the south coast from these precious days spent in the bosom of his family, he was detained for a quarter of an hour on the platform of Dover railway station, as military security arrangements demanded that every individual entering the town possessed a registration card. Officers charged with the enforcement of this measure took some time to check every military travel pass and civilian card belonging to the train's occupants. Returning to his billet, for 'certain reasons' Alan was forced to share a room with his landlord, 'a fat old stogger, but I did not mind. I was too tired to.'

Recent aircraft developments meant that British towns and cities were no longer safe from aerial enemy attack. On 5 February, Alan witnessed a German Taube flying over Dover: 'a few shots were fired & then two of our machines went up after it & gave chase.' This attack came less than a week after Alan's own family had been near a Zeppelin raid over the Midlands. On the night of 31 January, a fleet of airships, destined for an attack on Liverpool, got lost in fog over the Black Country and ended up dropping bombs on Burton-on-Trent, Wednesbury, Walsall, Tipton and Bilston before venturing on to Loughborough, Derby and Scunthorpe. In the attack on Burton, fifteen people were killed inside the Anglican Christ Church, and the total number of fatal casualties across the region reached seventy. Alan was not surprised by this news: 'I hear the Zeps have paid Staffs a visit but it is no more than what I expected – when once they get as far as the coast it does not take them long to get inland & one may depend on it that they would make a raid on unfortified towns.'

Later that month, Alan moved to superior billets in Longfield Road. The young female landlady was childless and could speak French, having crossed the Channel on many occasions. This arrangement, whilst his pals were put up within the Priory Camp barracks, enabled Alan to ensure his hearty appetite was more than satiated:

> Last Sunday my billet lady asked me in to dinner. Of course I accepted. I went [for] a walk with my pals and then they went into barracks for dinner @12.30 I went in with them and had my dinner – roast beef, potatoes, cabbage, gravy, custard. Some hours after that I went to my billet & had another dinner. Roast pork etc. Didn't I just enjoy myself, I could have split my sides @ the table when I thought of it.

Collecting cigarette cards was a popular pastime in the early twentieth century, and Alan sent a selection home to his younger brother Donald on 29 February. On a more sombre note, Alan gave an eyewitness account of the sinking of the P&O liner SS *Maloja* by a mine laid by the German submarine UC-6, causing the loss of 155 lives. Rescue craft were despatched from Dover and the collier *Empress of Fort William*, bound for Dunkirk, diverted to provide assistance. Tragically, this vessel also struck a mine and was sunk.

Alan reported:

> You will have heard of that P&O Liner being mined off Dover Harbour. My pal & I were walking along Folkestone Rd to our billet when suddenly we heard a loud report as if a gun being fired. We smiled & looked at each other & said 'Zepp'. Little did we know what had really happened. After leaving our billet we had a walk to the sea front as we usually do. When we got there we were surprised to hear of the ship-wreck. We saw for ourselves dead being carried on to a station platform. We saw the wounded being carried aboard a hospital ship & we saw some of the survivors. One nasty sight that I saw was of a dead man being carried on a stretcher when suddenly the man carrying the stretcher let go of the handles … the dead man fell to the ground, his head striking hard against the ground they put the stretcher down & rolled him (not picked him up) on to the stretcher. You would hardly believe that a ship striking a mine 2 miles out @ sea should be heard nearly all over Dover but it was so. In fact people that lived near the coast said that it shook their windows.

Following similar incidents, the Admiralty established a convoy system to provide escorts to merchant shipping at risk from U-boat action. Despite these measures, the commander of UC-6, Kapitänleutnant Matthias Graf von Schmettow, became a U-boat 'ace', claiming the sinking of seventy-eight ships, including three warships.

On 20 March, Alan, having been transferred to service in the officers' mess, gave his family some idea of his daily routine: 'I find plenty to do, although of course the work is not so heavy. Starting @ 6.30 in the A.M. & finish @ 10.00 PM Sundays included. Two nights in the week I finish @ 3 o'clock. So I have just snatched a few minutes to answer your letter.'

Zeppelin air raids continued to blight Dover, with Alan at pains to point out that the most recent one was 'worse to me than any'. He claimed that newspapers could not convey the full horror of the experience: 'Picture for yourself having a quiet rest after dinner & suddenly finding the roof fall in or the window blown out. That is just what happens here. Of course there is quite a panic. Women squealing.'

The luxury of Alan's digs was not to last indefinitely, as by the spring of 1916 he was sharing a tent with his comrades. 'Sleeping under canvas is a "bit different" to a sprung mattress. We have 3 blankets & bare board to lie on. It is a bit hard I can tell you but not much to grumble @ after 6 months in billets.' After a month, Alan reported, 'I am getting quite use [sic] to lying on boards.' What was more difficult to reconcile was the disruption to sleep of continued air raid warnings across Dover:

> The worst of it is, is the Zepps. Of course Dover always gets the warning when hostile aircraft is about. 3 nights last week about 12 o'clock midnight the siren went in here … we always get the order to dress and await the next order. Somehow they always forget to get the next order. Result – without knowing we fall off to sleep, only to wake up around 5 and find ourselves dressed.

German two-seater Taubes had been seen over Deal. Their primary role was reconnaissance but they also had the capacity to carry bombs. These would be aimed and dropped by hand but with limited control. On 7 March, 'We had a somewhat exciting time again in the night about 2.30 in the morning. We were awakened by the syren [sic] giving its warning of Zepps. We could distinctly hear them, the searchlights were on, but could not see them.'

Drafts of AOC men continued to be sent to serve in Western Front depots, although Alan managed to avoid this fate through 1916, much to his disappointment. One batch arrived in France in the middle of May, having been bid an enthusiastic farewell by their comrades: 'The 73rd arrived safely in

France last Monday. They had a good hearty send-off from all the "boys" here. It was a lovely sunny morning when they went & the band played some lively tunes for them as they marched to the station. How I wish I had been one of their number.'

He was at pains to point out that he lacked for nothing nourishment wise, getting 'plenty of good food. … I am the youngest of 6 in our two huts and the biggest.' However, other creature comforts his parents might see their way to sending would be welcomed:

As for sending me anything you need not trouble, you see it is like this. I should have to share it with the 6 chaps here (not that I begrudge them having anything) but as you will readily understand it is expense to you all Of course I shall never say 'no' any time the girls like to send me tobacco or cigarettes but you never need send me anything else.

Dover suffered a further air raid in May, 'although it did not suffer much'. One bomb had dropped on a public house, ironically named *The Ordnance*, whilst another had landed in the churchyard of Christ Church. Alan's mess orderly duties continued, with arrangements for those of a different social class having to be exemplary: 'I must have the table set, tea-pots polished, everything spick & span by 4 o'clock. For you know some of these officers are gentlemen from large homes.'

Alan had become accepting of the army's need for conformity:

As you say we have our 'worries' if one may call them so & lots of things we have to do which we don't like to do. You know when we are told to do a thing we have to do it straight away. A great General once said 'A soldier must learn 3 things := 1st Obedience, 2nd Obedience, 3rd Obedience'. & I am quite sure he was right in his remark.

His sleeping arrangements occasioned a bemused acquiescence:

PS. Sleeping in our tent. On one side of me I have a man that often gets drunk. On the other side a man that walks in his sleep. In the night he gets up & starts walking round the tent on the top of the chaps. Then he lies down & pushes his feet in my face & his head by my feet. Such is life.

Alan ended phlegmatically with lyrics from 'It's a Long Way to Tipperary':

> What's the use of worrying?
> it never was worth while.
> SO. Pack up your troubles in your Old Kit Bag
> And Smile, Smile, Smile.

After a period of leave in July 1916, Alan returned to Dover to bid farewell to the men of 50 Company, with a concert and farewell dinner being organised. Alan too was in the final stages of preparation for embarkation for France: 'We are all quite ready to go. Only waiting for the order. Yesterday … we had our photographs taken. I doubt whether you can recognise me on it. … We march to Folkestone tomorrow & there set sail for France. I will write as soon as I get a settled address.'

August 1916 was a momentous month for Alan Stirling. As well as joining the British Expeditionary Force in France and Flanders, being posted to a base depot in Boulogne, he attained manhood, his twenty-first birthday falling on the 7th. He had frugal expectations for any presents: 'You can send me tobacco & cigarettes only. Will you please also send that wristlet watch. Everyone has one except me.'

Alan's first seven months in France passed off relatively uneventfully. Armaments would arrive in bulk by ship to be unloaded, stored and organised into despatches for the divisions on the front line. Technical workshops were also to be found in Boulogne, where equipment would be checked and assembled. In March 1917, having been in France for seven months, Alan was transferred to 'a place we call O.Z.A', possibly a codename for a railhead, a destination he found to be 'much different to Boulogne, Dover or Wolverhampton'. There was a small village situated about a mile from his station, and only twenty Army Ordnance Corps troops at the same depot. Even though far from home, Alan was cognisant of the grim food situation on the home front, as the German U-boat attacks continued to wreak havoc on merchant shipping. Corresponding to his mother while sitting on an ammunition box with a writing pad on his knee, Alan drew reassurance from the fact that many families were in a more precarious financial state than the Stirlings. He also drew familiar solace from his Christian faith:

> I must agree with you that things are serious. I know how hard it must be for you to make ends meet. I have not forgotten what a struggle it was for you in peace time and I can realize how it must be @ the present time. But look around you. One had even only to read the tribunals and see how some people are situated. After that I think we cannot do better than go down on our knees and thank God that we are as we are.

Alan's interest in domestic religious matters was echoed in a separate letter written to his father from his same ammunition box perch: 'I should very much like to hear Rev Thompson's farewell but that is out of the question. However if there is a report of same in the local paper, I shall be much obliged if you will send same to me.'

The awkwardness in composing inconsequential written chit-chat was apparent in Alan's statement that 'You say you are sometimes puzzled to know what to write about, no more than I am I can assure you'. Alan's younger brother Donald was facing conscription. In this eventuality, 'if I were you I would advise him to get into this Corps if possible. I feel sure nothing is more suitable for him.' Alan signed off his letter with reassurance that his family were frequently in his thoughts, and he in theirs:

> Of course leave now is out of question altogether so I shall not see your faces yet awhile, in the meantime I will leave all to think and dream of
> Your loving Son
> Alan
> Xxxxxxxxxxxxxxxx

Alan was soon on the move again, joining a 'small contingent' of AOC men, and by mid-June 1917 was able to report that he was 'Still feeling A1' in the good weather. Domestic chores were irksome, although accepted with stoicism:

> Life @ the present time or rather since I have left has been much harder for instance washing my own clothes doesn't appeal to me somehow. I have no landlady or French woman to do it for me. Still, as we often say to each other 'It's only for the duration' Duration though in this case seems eternal.

Food was wholesome, including portions of salmon, as the men's officers sometimes gave them ten francs 'to get something tasty'.

The following month marked the first anniversary of Alan's arrival in France, but rather than twelve months, 'so it seems to me more like 12 years'. He reckoned he stood 'no earthly chance' of being granted leave in the near future as all the men in his detachment had been in France longer than he had without being able to visit England, 'We have here a chap who came out with ... my old company, and he has not had his leave yet. Our cook who has been out here 2 years is expecting to go on leave any day now.'

Alan was suffering from war fatigue, yearning to return to the familiarity of his pre-war existence as he wrote he 'should just love to see all your faces once more, and return as it were to civilisation'. However, he would just 'have to content myself with writing, after all is done and said. I suppose we must not forget that it is one of the few privileges we are granted. Roll on after the war.' As his twenty-second birthday approached, he was determined that his family should not suffer further privations in order to provide him with unnecessary groceries. He was not in need of a food parcel, as army fare was good, Player's cigarettes could be purchased for half of the price they were sold in England. 'If you do send a parcel I shall not trouble to open it but shall just address it back to W-hampton. Now please read, mark, learn and inwardly digest.'

William and Emma Stirling did accede to their son's request, sending him a letter and 'lovely card' on what would prove to be Alan's final birthday. He heartily wished that his next one would be spent at home. 'Well I have spent my second birthday in France. Let us hope that before another Aug 7 rolls round that I shall once more be in good old Blighty.' Alan was perturbed to learn his father was unwell and that 'circumstances @ home are not as well as you and I would like them to be. Please God father is better by the time you receive this letter.' Despite having

Private Donald Stirling. (*Courtesy Rosemary Phillips*)

only one good eye, his younger brother Donald had been called up. He had been working for William Baker, a boot and shoe manufacturer, an occupation that might have afforded Donald some protection due to the necessity of keeping the army supplied with footwear to withstand the rigours of warfare. The huge casualties meant that even men with a physical disability such as Donald's were now candidates for conscription.

During the high summer of 1917, the Archbishop of York, Cosmo Lang, conducted a tour of the Western Front. The text on which he preached to the troops, 'Keep that which is committed to your trust', was one that resonated with Alan. He resolved to embrace Lang's entreaty to those serving in France and Flanders to be of good cheer, remembering that they were part of a wider continuum of sacrifice, sharing deprivations with their kinsfolk at home. Alan took this advice to heart, reassuring his parents that he acknowledged their forfeit of comforts. Despite the hardships, trust in God would hold people in good stead:

Well dear mother the Archbishop of York as good as told us that the people in the old country were having a much harder time than we were out here, and I know they must be hard times for you, but never mind don't be fainthearted be as cheerful as you can, lastly put all your trust in Him.

Although it was now well over a year since he had been able to see his family in person, Alan, like many men, intensely valued regular written communication with home. He enclosed a handwritten copy of a poem written by 'a Captain in the A.O.D. (Army Ordnance Depot) who was @ my first station in France. ... I would ask you to keep it safe as I have no other copy', advocating that a soldier should eschew the delights of the pictures or concert hall in order to write a long letter to his family.

'The Forgotten Letter'

1. Don't go to the 'Pictures' or 'Concert Hall',
   But stay in your billet tonight,
   Deny yourself to your pals that call,
   And a Good long letter write.
   Write to the Dear ones left at home.
   Who sit when the day is done.
   In the even's twilight cold & grey,
   And dream of the absent one.

2. Don't selfishly scribble 'Excuse my haste',
   I've but little time to write,
   Lest their anxious heart should yearn as they think
   Of many a bygone night;
   When they lost their needed sleep & rest.
   And every breath was a prayer.
   That God should keep their loving son
   Through life in His tender care.

3. Don't let them feel that you have no need
   Of their love and counsel wise.
   For the heart grows very sensitive
   When sorrow has dimmed the eyes.
   Remember comrade your mother's words
   As you entered the ranks with delight,
   'Good-bye' and 'God bless you' my dear brave boy
   And 'Don't forget to write'.

4. Now I wonder if ever you give a thought
   As with comrades you daily unite
   To the anxious suspense you may have caused
   By neglecting that letter to write.
   I know that 'tis well to have comrades true

Who make your pleasures gay
But they have but half the thought for you
That your mother has to-day.

5. So tell them what you intend to do
   Let them and your pleasure wait
   Lest the letter for which your mother has longed
   Be a day or an hour too late
   For with loving heart she waits at home
   With cheeks tear-stained & white
   Longing to hear from her soldier son
   Who perhaps has forgotten to write.

The same letter in which the poem was enclosed assured William and Emma that 'I am getting along A1', although the issue of leave still haunted minds in France and Wolverhampton. Men who had arrived in France eighteen months previously, in March 1916, were only just now preparing to visit England. Any leave would be granted at about four hours' notice, with Alan only able to notify his family once he reached England. The prospect of being able to return to the bosom of his family filled Alan with joyful anticipation: 'Wait until we do get home. We shall make up for lost time.' Alan was making full use of the Expeditionary Force Canteens, reassuring his family he had no need of food parcels. Ecclesiastical matters continued to interest Alan, with him passing comments to his father about sermons he recalled hearing at Christ Church, Wolverhampton, and the installation of a new vicar at St Jude's.

Alan had grown up in Aldridge, Staffordshire, and the town reacted with pride when one of its sons, Lieutenant George Bonner of the Royal Naval Reserve, was awarded the Victoria Cross for his actions on board the HMS *Dunraven*, which had been shelled by a German U-boat. Alan wrote, 'Well done Aldridge V.C I always admire an honoured naval man, as there never seems to be any spare honours flying about for the navy.'

Alan had reverted to smoking the '"Wild Woodbine" of course one can hardly expect to live a gentleman's life all the time with nothing to do but walk about & smoke Tweenies Abdulla' (a brand of small cigar). However, there was one luxury item that he craved – a fountain pen. He joked, 'You see it's like this with Alan, he would rather have the best, no matter what the cost.' He suggested that both he and his parents save their John Bull coupons to buy an expensive pen. During the autumn of 1917, Alan was finally able to return to Wolverhampton for a period of leave, the final time he would be able to spend time with his family. The joy of reunion must have been overshadowed by the cloud of dread at his departure and return to the Western Front.

Upon his return, it was noted that Alan's frugality over the receipt of parcels was not shared by his brother Donald: 'Donald still likes his parcels, ah well when he has been in a bit longer he will perhaps be able to manage the same as I do. I could miss a meal any day & not notice it.' Alan again reassured family he did not need anything sending as he could satisfy his needs from the EFCs. By early December 1917, Alan had received news that would seal his fate.

Private Alan Stirling AOC 913578 would become Rifleman Alan Stirling KRRC 204366, transferred of the 10th Battalion of the King's Royal Rifle Corps. The battalion had suffered recent heavy losses during the Battle of Cambrai and needed reinforcements. Alan would continue to use his AOC address for now but warned there was a high risk that any parcels would take an excessively long time to reach him. William Stirling was concerned for the welfare of his son as a sharp winter approached, offering to send him a waistcoat. Alan replied that it was a 'kind offer … but I am already in possession of a thick jersey which does the necessary first class'. He hoped his brother Donald would be able to 'keep a clean sheet' in his new army life. Alan, too, would face the coming months with grim resolve, now he had been relocated to a fighting regiment:

> Well you will be wondering what I think of it, but you can rest assured that I do not mind. I can & will stick it. I have my own reasons for not transferring previous, although this has been done compulsorily. But you & mother & all @ home can rest content that I am not funking. Well as you can guess I have not much time to spare now. Have commenced training though still in A.O.C. coats.

Alan felt his had been a worthwhile contribution to the war effort, but was ready to stoically embrace the transfer to a fighting regiment:

> Day & night have I toiled hard issuing ammunition to batteries but no matter how much graft or how many hours you put – according to some folks you have not done your bit unless you have been in the line looking @ things all round & taking things on the whole I say that I am ready to do what is required of me.
>
> It is only being popular with the officers & knowing my duties that has kept me so long in the A.O.C. but as you know, there is a power beyond our officers.

He wished his family 'as Bright & Happy a Xmas as circumstances will allow. … I have little to say of Xmas, except that I hope that when next Xmas comes, I shall be back in the homelands, amongst my loved ones.' Christmas 1917 was to be a lonely affair for Alan, and a time of high anxiety for his parents.

The movement occasioned by the transfer resulted in Alan receiving no letters for over a month. He was eventually able to advise his parents that he was in A Company of the 10th Battalion and was now in France. 'Of course you will understand how I felt with not having heard from you. However all's well that ends well and I think now we should be alright.' Constant movement had made it 'a bit awkward' to send individual Christmas cards to all his siblings, for which he apologised. 'All the same I thought a lot about all @ home & wished them from the bottom of my heart A Merry Xmas.'

Despite these adversities, he was 'still going strong', having had a double inoculation. Alan was seeing 'plenty of snow by day & frost @ night. I expect you are getting similar weather.' Optimistically, Alan wished his family a 'bright, happy & prosperous new year'. By late January 1918, Alan could still report that he was 'getting along first class'. His Christmas post had finally arrived. As well as a large haul of letters, he had been remembered by the congregation of his parish church of St Mark, Wolverhampton, receiving a signed card. This meant much to the Christian Alan: 'I know that I am not forgotten by any @ home, & it is vice-versa with me. I always remember each one of you in my prayers & pray for the time when peace shall once more reign over us & that we shall soon return home.'

Alan was adamant, however, that letters and cards were sufficient emotional and spiritual nourishment from his home town, and that he required no physical items to enhance this consignment:

> Now about the parcel, do not think I want to be nasty with you, I know it must be disappointment [sic] to you when you want to do me good, & I turn round & refuse. I can quite understand how you feel, but I know how things must be @ home & the difficulty you must have in obtaining food, but as long as I get some pay I am always able to obtain food … so you will see that I am not being funny but am helping you instead.

He continued in a light-hearted vein, recalling of his boyhood in Pelsall, 'how savage I used to be when I used to come home from school & find no tea ready as Mama had gone to the Mothers Union'. Reference to the Mothers' Union reminded Alan of a prayer that Emma had learned there, which she had passed on to her young son:

> O heavenly Father, bless me, and all I love, forgive my sins & make me sorry for them, help me to love my dear saviour, Jesus Christ & to grow like unto him, fill me with thy Holy Spirit, save me for evermore, for Jesus Christ's sake. Amen.

The deep desire to cling to the fundamentals of faith that had been learned as a child was a feature of many troops' spiritual mediation of their war experience. Alan poignantly explained, 'Please excuse my writing as this is written under firing condition.' Alan's physical condition was robust, despite the psychological exigencies of war. He speculated if he would have a similar appetite once he returned to Wolverhampton: 'You had better look out for yourself. I am bigger now than what I was then.'

In early February, Alan wrote, expressing his sorrow about his grandmother's illness, 'Please give her my very best love, and tell her that there is one out in France who very often thinks of her, and always commits her to the One above.' Sharp frosts were now the norm, and 'Water, here at the present time, is as precious as money, so you can imagine how it is.' A deep snowfall had turned the landscape into a dazzling white. 'Our camp is situated higher above sea level, and as we look down on one side of us we see the sea, on the other side of us we see nothing but snow.' Having seen three Portuguese officers in their sky-blue uniforms, Alan was led to exclaim, 'Of all the active service uniforms I have yet seen, I think the khaki whacks the whole bunch, in style, colour and everything.'

Alan heard representatives of the Church of England's National Mission of Repentance and Hope speak. Launched in the autumn of 1916 by the Archbishops of Canterbury and York, the mission exhorted a reflection on the sins that had led all nations to war, and to division and strife on the home front. It aspired to a renewal of faith in order to build a better post-war world. Fate would conspire to prevent Alan playing any role in that post-war fellowship of faith.

Erenst Blackburn

'Kiss our Stan for me'

The First World War had been dominating British life for fifteen months by the time Ernest Blackburn, with his young son Stanley a mere two months old, volunteered for military service. In November 1915, during the height of a recruitment drive spearheaded by William Grassham, Ernest's head teacher at Upper Wortley Council School, he wrote to the Leeds Education Committee applying for leave of absence, 'in order to join His Majesty's forces under Lord Derby's recruiting scheme of grouping according to age, the said leave to commence at the date when I am called upon to serve in a military capacity'. Lord Derby, Director General of Recruiting, had introduced this system in October 1915 in a final attempt to avoid full conscription. Men aged between 18 and 41 were asked to indicate their willingness to serve, with the understanding that single men would be called up before the married.

It had been arranged that half of a teacher's salary would be paid to his family, and that his position would be kept open at the conclusion of the war. On attesting, Ernest was issued with a khaki cloth armband with a red cloth, embroidered King's crown, with an army stamp confirming his status. This could be worn in public to indicate that a man was not avoiding military service, to prevent the possibility of ridicule or admonition from well-meaning but over-assertive fellow citizens.

The morning of Monday, 29 May 1916 marked the formal beginning of Ernest's military career. Making his way down from his modest terraced house in Armley into Leeds, he presented himself at the recruiting office in City Square and was accepted into the Royal Garrison Artillery. Just before midday he sent a postcard home informing Annie of this fact, and that he would write soon with further news. Later that day, upon reaching York railway station, Ernest wrote with further dramatic news: that he was not in the RGA after all, as only infantry regiments were open to men of his modest height of 5 feet 5 inches. Instead, a sergeant major at the station confirmed he had been posted to the King's Royal Rifle Corps. He was in familiar company as his barber, Jenkinson, had been similarly assigned. Both men were put on a train to Newcastle-upon-Tyne, where they obtained beds for the night at the YMCA for sixpence. The following day, Ernest travelled the 13 miles north to Seaton Delaval, a small Northumberland village. 'I feel very tired, as it is a slow job getting all papers signed etc, standing about & so on.'

Ernest and Jenkinson were instructed to report to a camp near Cambois, an 8-mile walk away. On arrival they were issued with blankets and a waterproof sheet, as they were to sleep under canvas without the luxury of straw. There was a YMCA hut 'for writing, singing etc' and the camp afforded a fine view of the North Sea, over sand dunes. Royal Navy destroyers patrolled just off the coast whilst trenches and dugouts were spread along the coastline as a first line of defence against a German invasion.

Money was a constant concern for Ernest, as was the psychological well-being of his wife and infant son. On 30 May, he wrote to Annie:

Like all lads away from home, I shall want some money, but I will tell you how to send it when I next write. ... I hope you & Stanley have not been too much in the dumps. Doctor's bills lie that way. Keep your pecker up & talk to somebody. ... Kiss our Stan for me. Now chick, I do hope you are taking it like my Annie & I think you will. I am quite all right. You need not worry yet.

By the end of the week, Mr Ernest Blackburn, schoolmaster in the boys' department of Upper Wortley Council School, Leeds, had become:

Rifleman EB
No. 8 tent
B. Co. K.R.R.
North Camp
Cambois
Blyth

The 24th (Reserve) Battalion of the King's Royal Rifle Corps had been formed in April 1916, moving to Cambois on 19 May. Although the Cambois camp was reasonably well-provisioned, and items could be bought in nearby Blyth, Ernest requested that Annie send him various mundane items:

1. A Victory Gum tin box to put my hair blacking brush, mirror, toothbrush etc in.
2. A Small tin tobacco box to keep soap in. If you can't get one buy a tin of tobacco (1 oz) any medium mixture & send the lot.
3. A dish cloth.
4. As many handkerchiefs as you have left & any more (khaki ones if you like) to make to make say ½ doz. I have only one.
5. A very little tin with vim or panshine to clean with.
6. Address of Mr J. Lyon TPS [Teachers' Provident Scheme] Burley Lodge Rd I think.

He also requested that Annie arrange for the heeling of a pair of his boots as his feet had become sore in his new army footwear. Ernest had derived great delight from the scrawl toddler Stanley had put at the end of Annie's letter and he entreated her to 'don't let Stanley forget he has a Dad' and to 'keep your pecker up'. He was impressed by his new comrades, 'very good fellows', amongst whom were 'no beer-swillers', to the approval of the Nonconformist Ernest. Annie sent the requisite items, and on 9 June, Ernest wrote to say he had 'quite recovered from inoculation', from which men were given two days to recuperate. 'All day Tuesday I was starved & couldn't get warm whilst my body ached as if I had rheumatism all over.'

The new recruits were made aware of the KRRC's traditions: 'Our regiment is the 60th Foot & was founded in the year of Quebec. It has more honours than any other regiment & has fought heaps of battles.' Lectures on drill and saluting had taken place, as had physical training. There were regular kit inspections. There was only a distant prospect of securing leave – men had to serve for six weeks before becoming eligible for a thirty-six-hour pass. For Ernest, this would mean a very rushed weekend, travelling down from the north-east to arrive in Leeds by Saturday teatime before returning twenty-four hours later. Leave for other companies was already being stopped as the need to cram preparation for front-line combat into twelve weeks took precedence. Additionally, the east coast had to be guarded, therefore Ernest's commanding officer would not allow too many men to be away at any one time, 'especially during this time of trouble in the North Sea'. Aeroplanes, destroyers and submarines were a common sight off the coast. Ernest was to take his own stint at coastal guard duty 'at No 5 dug-out, by the ferry'.

Ernest had been wagered a cigar that the war would be over by the time of his birthday in August, but he wryly noted, 'In the army, however, rumour reigns supreme.' Despite his cricketing pedigree, Ernest was not adept at army physical training. He was the 'worst jumper in the lot, though I tried till I fell down nearly. What I shall do when it come to frog-leaping etc I don't know.' He complained of being exhausted from constant physical exercise.

The emotional strain, even after less than a fortnight apart, was becoming evident: 'Oh Annie, if you could see me now you wouldn't say a wrong word I'm sure. Never mind. It must be chronic for you. I have plenty to do in the day. It's hard work – real hard work, but in the evening I think of home & wish I was back.'

The leave issue led Ernest to suggest that Annie visit him at Cambois. While it could offer 'lovely clean sands', there were no shops, and it was a 'significant walk' into Blyth, there being no tram service. Ernest could be available for Annie on weekday evenings, earlier on Saturday and nearly all day Sunday. The dearth of Cambois amenities would mean Annie spending the daytime playing on the sands with Stan. A room could be found about ten minutes from camp, affording maximum family time. Annie's reluctance to journey to Cambois was due to her being five months' pregnant. She was due to receive a payment of thirty shillings in October upon the baby's birth under the terms of the Teachers' Provident Scheme, of which Ernest was a member.

Ernest spent his disposable income on fresh daily deliveries of 'little buns & cups of coffee etc at the YMCA tent here', affording better regular fare than relying on parcels from home. However, the sharing of parcel contents provided an opportunity to bond with his fellow recruits. Ernest requested 'Some fairy buns, say, & then some of your best biscuits & perhaps a little cake. But be sure to pack well.' He would be able to 'act as host' in his tent, repaying the generosity previously displayed by his comrades.

Separation caused anxiety. Annie had visited a house in Birstall, possibly to earn some extra money as a cleaner, and relayed information about the family's domestic life to Ernest: 'Believe me love, I realise now a thousand ways in which you did your best to make me happy & I believe you will have felt the same. Our happiness when the war is over will be great I'm sure.'

Parading and road-marching with a full kit took place, 'belt, pouches &
braces on every parade. After a while, the haversack, water-bottle, trenching
tool … etc will be added.' The teacher was becoming accustomed to new and
mundane tasks: 'Yesterday afternoon I was put on fatigue – can you imagine me
wheeling a barrow load of old bricks on a main road?' As the physical strength
and endurance demanded of the recruits intensified, so did the quality of the
nutrition provided to them. 'We have had the best meals to-day that have been
served since I came. Porridge, bacon (boiled), bread & tea for breakfast. Stewed
meat, potatoes & beans for dinner. Bread, butter, marmalade or jam or rhubarb
for tea.'

Through the drudgeries, Ernest was developing a new military self-identity.
He observed a draft of West Yorkshire Regiment troops, the 'Bantams' leave
camp, expressing a collective affinity: 'I couldn't help but march with them. It's
a curious sight & you have curious feelings yourself when you wear a khaki
suit.' Military ambition was rebuffed when Ernest applied for NCO's training.
Despite his undoubted peacetime intelligence and leadership qualities, he was
rejected due to the number of applicants. 'The Army knows no fair play – only
luck'.

Annie yielded to Ernest's entreaties to spend a short time at Cambois, and he
eagerly set arrangements in place. Annie's stay would begin on 3 July, lodging at
the house of 'Mrs C … and she is looking forward to seeing you'. He requested
that she bring a knife with a pricker for him to clean out his pipe with, a
writing pad from Woolworth's and some khaki thread for clothes alterations.
Separation had opened cracks on the domestic front, with Annie not taking
kindly to inferred criticism of her culinary skills:

> Please, please Annie don't let some little matter stand in your way. I am still
> in love. There is a chap in our tent who is always talking about his wife's
> dinners, bread etc etc. I can't. I just think it & make fun of something else.
> Besides I want to see my little cake-spoiler. Thanks for that little incident.
> It made me laugh out loud.

Jane Cuthbertson, 'Mrs C', was given two shillings and sixpence rail fare to
Newcastle to meet Annie and escort her back to Cambois. Jane already had a
room let out to a guest, and there was a suggestion that this lady stay in Armley
for a week as a reciprocal arrangement. Ernest was keen that Stanley be allowed
to stay up later than normal, so that he would have time to play with him.

Ernest was becoming wise to the ruses of military life. He was given the
choice of being allocated to a squad run by a 'bully' or a different squad under a
'nice' NCO. He chose the former, as the squad was deemed to have undertaken

two weeks' less training than Ernest had already completed: 'It means doing all over again what I was doing over a fortnight since – form fours, right turn etc – over & over & over again till today I am tired to death, but I don't mind that if it keeps me this side of the Channel.'

Annie's welfare was frequently at the front of Ernest's mind, as he encouraged her to 'travel about a bit' to keep occupied. He strove to paint a positive picture of their future life together, assuring her of the happy marriage they had shared and would share once the war was over:

> [K]eep a good heart. I've made up my mind that if I do get to France I shall look out for myself – no French peeping for me. I don't intend going if I can help it but it's surprising what luck there is in the army. ... And when the war is over, well we _will_ have a time. Don't think of all the things you didn't do for my pleasure, but think of the many many happy times we have had & the absence of friction. Oh Annie, don't blame yourself too much I love you yet as much as ever, & we shall be all right some day.

Ernest informed Annie that Mrs Cuthbertson had five children and would be willing to look after Stanley if Annie wished to visit Blyth. Whether Annie was keen on leaving her son in the care of a stranger while already suffering separation anxiety from her husband is questionable. Ernest suggested he and Annie spend an afternoon in the Victorian seaside resort of Whitley Bay. He hoped for fine weather as it had been 'like December' since he had arrived.

More prosaically, Ernest advised Annie to arrange a money transfer to Cambois Post Office recommending her not to bring too many clothes as Mrs Cuthbertson would wash as often as Annie wished. Ernest was assiduous in preparations for Annie's stay: 'I keep calling in there, & seem quite at home already, so if you want to know anything just ask.'

Ernest's physical resilience and appetite were growing:

> I am getting hardened to it by degrees, but the doubling & jumping etc take it out of me. As for food, you would laugh to see me grabbing for a spoonful of dirty bacon dip to help the dry bread down. I eat all that comes along & hardly miss a day without buying extra at the YMCA tent.

After ten weeks at Cambois, men went on a firing course at Whitley Bay, a sign that posting overseas was imminent. Rumours continued to abound 'in number and diversity'. The prospect of relocation to France had put officers into a 'fearful rage, as it possibly means a loss of rank for most of them'. One man, Clarkson, had his finger cut with another man's rifle while training. An adjutant, who had previously cut down Ernest's leave pass, ordered Clarkson to do an extra hour's drill for moving while trying to shake off the blood, a punishment to be doubled if he talked back during treatment.

Following Annie's visit to Cambois, in late August Ernest was granted a period of embarkation leave to spend in Leeds. This did little to ease Annie's tension, as the arrival of their second child drew ever closer. On his return to camp 'safe enough', he wrote, 'They all say that I look much better than I did & I certainly feel it. I only hope that you will try to look at the thing in the same light & you will feel much better. Spilt milk etc can't be picked up again with crying.'

By now men were leaving the camp in droves, bound either for France or Mesopotamia. Heavy rain meant a sodden night for Ernest, sleeping with eleven other men in a tent, waking up with his feet outside and his blankets wet through. Ernest had been told that his name was on the next draft, due to leave England on 28 August, arriving at Le Havre the following day. He was medically assessed as 'Very good'. Most personal items had to be sent home by parcel: 'I have had to give in my brushes etc. I shall send home the things I don't need, as we have only to carry out (on our backs) the regulation things. We aren't allowed even a hair brush.'

Despite the intense anxiety he must have felt, Ernest avoided the temptation and shame visited upon a man named Hardy from Wakefield, who had failed to report back from leave and was being hunted by the police as a deserter. Blyth was placed out of bounds for the final weekend in camp, but the draft was treated to a final 'splendid' concert party and a farewell 'capital dinner' of fresh peas, potatoes & mutton, then 'jam roly'.

Ernest entreated Annie to 'keep up a good heart. If writing get it off on Sunday to catch me before I leave England. I should like a last encouragement from you – the real you I mean.' This duly arrived, as in the last letter he wrote on English soil, Ernest thanked Annie for: '[Y]our splendid letter. Although it filled my eyes I am glad of the strength of it. I never remember you writing anything like it. It is quite equal to the occasion & I shall keep it with me.'

Annie's words soothed Ernest, despite her own emotional strain, with a small child to care for, another due within weeks and her husband about to go to war. She felt isolated and insecure about the future of their marriage. Ernest wrote, 'As regards being a single man, I understand your meaning & thank you for it, but I shall always dream of my return to you.'

Ernest felt sympathy for some 'hard cases', including five sergeants who had expected to remain in England as army instructors but faced immediate draft, without the right of embarkation leave that Ernest had been granted. Other men, who had only had nine or ten weeks' training, were being drafted without leave. One ray of hope for Ernest was that he was going out to France as an 'A2' man, partly trained, so would have a fortnight in base camp in Le Havre to be skilled up to full fighting fitness to attain eligibility for firing line duty.

It was important for Ernest, a man of immense organisational ability, to ensure that all his affairs were in order. He made a will in his army pay book and advised Annie to keep the address of 'that Winchester man' who oversaw financial arrangements for KRRC troops. He promised to write as soon as he reached France to check the financial arrangements that Leeds Education Authority would enact should the worst happen. Ernest provided Annie with detailed instructions on registering the forthcoming arrival. She was to go to the 'insurance office past Strawberry Lane Co-op', having ensured to have previously noted the opening hours, within six weeks of the child's birth. If unable to attend in person, she should send a relative, and obtain two copies of a birth certificate, one to send to the KRRC pay and allowances department at Winchester with a covering note, requesting return by post. A vaccination form should also be procured from the registrar, signed by Annie '& put in pillar-box'. Annie was instructed to enquire about separation and childbirth allowances and, should Ernest still be in England, to get her doctor to wire the Officer Commanding A Company 24th KRRC, requesting his presence on the grounds of her health.

In the event of him being listed as 'missing', Ernest instructed Annie to 'buy one or two daily papers – e.g. *Yorkshire Post* morning *Daily Mail*, *Daily Dispatch* – see how to address enquiries & write one letter of particulars. Send a copy of the same letter to each & order a copy of each daily until answers appear.' He was well versed in the procedure for tracing missing soldiers, having read of hundreds of cases in the press. Ernest also provided two work contacts, including his head teacher Mr Grassham, who were in touch with 'people who are appointed to deal with such cases'.

On arrival in France Ernest was sent to No. 1 Infantry Base Depot. He tried to sound upbeat: 'As the final weeks of army life gave me beans, so this final training does here.' The early autumn weather was 'delightful' in the morning and later in the evening but extremely hot in the day. He anticipated that his next move would be 'up the line' and asked to be remembered to 'all enquirers & to those at school'. Ernest requested 'some mints to suck' but commented that tobacco could be had cheaply. *Sunday Pictorial* newspapers were available, complete with positively spun war news, including recent anti-German political moves in Greece.

News from home had not yet been forthcoming, and Ernest entreated Annie to 'Let me know how you go on as often as you can, as perhaps there may be a delay in the arrival here. A short note is better than nothing & I shall always write to you. … Kiss Stanley for me.' A short note the following evening advised Annie to refrain from writing until he knew of any transfers of battalion, but repeated his request for mints, as well as 'some Gillette safety blades (4/-a doz I think) – at Taylor Drug Stores or Central Stores, & half a doz safety pins'. He had enjoyed a bath that afternoon, and read news about the 'Somme & the Zepp [which] is very good'.

Three days later he sent a standard army postcard stating he was 'quite well' but had not received a letter 'for a long time'. On the same day, 7 September, he wrote a letter announcing that his draft had been split up, amongst various battalions of the KRRC, he and 'sixty' others being attached to the 9th Battalion, with Ernest in No. 12 Platoon, C Company. The battalion formed part of the 42nd Infantry Brigade, operating within the 14th (Light) Division, which consisted of 41st, 42nd and 43rd brigades.

The beginning of September found the battalion enjoying a well-earned rest in the picturesque village of St Maulvis. Here, out of sound of the guns and under 'the pleasantest of conditions', it was possible to reorganise after the heavy losses sustained in the strenuous fighting around Delville Wood in late August. In early September, a draft of seventy-four men, including Rifleman Ernest Blackburn, arrived to join the battalion. Major H.C.M. Porter, who recorded the battalion's escapades in the unit war diary with some degree of colour, judged that the new additions 'were not as good a lot as usual, and needed much drill and discipline to smarten them up'.

A scheme of training was drawn up for the fortnight ahead, and companies were kept hard at work with drilling and physical exercises. A further draft of 200 men, arriving the following day, evinced a greater degree of approval from Major Porter, being 'a much better lot than the last draft, most of them coming from the 5th and 6th Battalions, and there being many old soldiers among them'. Following strengthening of 9th KRRC, parties of NCOs and men were sent on forty-eight hours' leave to the seaside town of Ault, 'where they all seemed to enjoy themselves thoroughly'. Officers, too, took the opportunity to visit Le Tréport and other resorts. These were to be the final relaxed days of Ernest's life. He wrote to Annie of the 'many miles' he had travelled, with train journeys 'to a small village' from which the men had to walk 11½ miles in full pack, with ammunition in pouches in blazing sunshine. Military formation was not maintained, as twenty arrived first, with the rest arriving in 'driblets of 2, 3, 10 & so on'. Ernest expressed pride that his fitness had allowed him to be among the first twenty, through application of mind over matter, 'for I have never done as hard a day's work in all my life'. He acquired sore heels and a raw right hip bone from the effects of his water bottle rubbing the skin.

Ernest and his comrades were now within earshot of 'the boom of the guns', at a rest camp '30 mls or so behind the front'. Billeted in a barn with around forty other men, during the day Ernest was able to buy food and milk from local farmers, 'but change is very scarce'. Therefore, he requested that Annie send him French francs by registered letter. He had also tasted some French wine 'but didn't much care for it'.

The scenery reminded Ernest of the Belgian landscape the couple had enjoyed during their 1912 honeymoon. Scores of houses were partly ruined or occupied as billets by British troops but the vegetation remained unscathed. Ernest had 'had my bit of colour stitched to my back', as the battalion's commanding officer, Lieutenant Colonel Eric Benson, told his men they would soon be moving into a 'show' where it would be a case of 'up you go & the best of luck'. The green oblong cloth that would mark out the men of the 9th KRRC on the battlefield was attached 2 inches below the collar. Battlefield commanders would thus be able to distinguish the battalion from other units through the dust and smoke of action.

Lieutenant Colonel Benson had returned from hospital that day to reassume command from Major Porter. The CO had already been awarded a Military Cross for his actions at Hooge in July 1915. Two days later, orders arrived that the battalion was to move the following morning. Despite the growing tension of the anticipation of battle, Ernest expressed an inner calmness, bordering on fatalism: 'Somehow I feel very fit & full of life, & mean to go on enjoying myself as long as ever I can. There are gaping holes in the walls & any number of flies, but I don't seem to care a rap, & I can't tell why.'

Ernest had seen many different regiments, including some 'Bengal Lancers & fine swarthy fellows they seemed', reassuring himself and Annie, 'There are plenty of men here who have seen months of service & come through all right'. However, he yearned to receive a letter from Annie as 'I don't know when this will set off '.

Three days later, on 10 September, having still not heard from Annie, Ernest wrote again while on guard duty. He described conversations in broken French with civilians and taking part in a field day, attacking supposed German trenches then digging in: 'The work was very interesting.' News from home was sparse, with neither Ernest nor his comrades having received a communication for a fortnight. 'I think all our lads are alike, longing more for a letter than anything else.' He surmised that the absence of a missive may have been down to his transfer to a different battalion.

Men tried to maintain spirits with self-organised entertainment, a concert being held on the village green with men of the 9th Battalion performing in Pierrot costume. A piano had been requisitioned from a nearby village; 'so you couldn't expect an "Empire" performance, but it went off very well,' quipped Ernest, referring to the Empire Palace Theatre in Leeds, one of the finest variety theatres in England.

Regular baths were provided and four sprays had been fitted in the open air so several men could shower at once. They were supplied with a clean shirt and new socks; 'you may be sure we all enjoyed the change & comfort'. Additional gustatory pleasure was gained from the purchase of '6 or 7 fine big pears for a penny'. Ernest had also tasted locally brewed cider as well as red and white French wine.

Ernest's view of the war was formed from the positive spin of French newspapers: 'I have seen that all is going very well for the allies.' Thoughts of Annie's impending childbirth led him to advise her to invite friends for tea but let them prepare the meal. He implored her to spend any money necessary for her comfort 'as the war cannot go on for ever'. Ernest concluded, 'I have no idea as to when this will set off, but as I am on guard to-day, I thought I would take advantage of this opportunity & let you know how I am.'

These were Ernest's valedictory words.

Chapter 4

Dying and Missing

Over 7 million men were to serve in the British and Empire and Commonwealth Armies during the war. Nearly 900,000 would never return home. Circumstances of death were varied, most being inflicted via mechanised and anonymised warfare. Hundreds of thousands of bodies were obliterated when crossing no man's land, whilst others fell victim to a sniper's bullet. Just over 8,000 were asphyxiated by poison gas, whilst occasionally a man could be shot in cold blood by an enemy soldier. Establishing the exact fate of each man was an impossible task, especially of the missing. Following the maelstrom of battle, survivors' recall was sketchy and frequently contradictory. The greater the degree of uncertainty that hung over the man's fate, the longer the anguish suffered by families remained.

Lieutenant John Gillis Butt

'They came on in such numbers'

On 25 October 1914, a few miles east of Ypres, the shelling of 20th Brigade was so concentrated and heavy, with sixty shells per minute falling on the British lines, that many men suffocated under the weight of the soil from collapsed trenches. As the 1st Grenadiers' medical officer, Lieutenant John Butt strove manfully to do what he could for the wounded survivors. The Germans broke through and surrounded and captured the 2nd Battalion Scots Guards. 'Jack' Butt and his comrades were now in a desperately exposed position so were ordered to retire. By the evening of 26 October, a roll call taken in a bivouac in Sanctuary Wood revealed that nine officers and 301 men of the 1st Grenadiers had been lost. In such circumstances Jack would have been frantically working round the clock to organise his stretcher-bearers and medical orderlies, and provide what remedial treatment he could at his Regimental Aid Post before sending the wounded back to RAMC field units.

On 28 October, 20th Brigade was moved to a new position south of the Menin Road, where the trenches were in a poor state of repair. The remnants of 1st Grenadiers made their way up to the line via Gheluvelt. Some ten days before, they had been greeted enthusiastically by the inhabitants. Now it was a ghost town. Most of the houses and the church had been demolished and the roads were pitted with shell holes. Horse carcasses littered the streets. The German General Staff was determined that a significant breakthrough in the Allied lines was imminent, and one of the points of attack was to be the left of the line held by Jack's battalion.

That night was spent digging and repairing defences ready for a German attack. As morning dawned, a dense fog enveloped the level landscape. The 1st Grenadiers waited with tense expectation, but an immediate assault failed to materialise. British guns from the rear attempted to bombard the enemy, but many shells fell short, causing damage to the British-held line. After ninety minutes of shelling, it was decided a German attack was unlikely that day. As ration wagons could not be brought close to the front line, many supporting troops were sent back to collect their victuals, leaving those on the front line, including Lieutenant Colonel Earle and Lieutenant Butt, dangerously exposed. Suddenly the Germans attacked in close formation, using a mass of men concentrated on a narrow front. British troops were forced to retreat from the fire trenches to occupy the support trenches, and 'murderous fire' rained down on the remaining Grenadiers, who were outnumbered by about ten to one. Sir Frederick Ponsonby recalled: 'They came on in such numbers that an officer afterwards said the attacking force reminded him of a crowd coming on the ground after a football match. Shoulder to shoulder they advanced, much in the same way as their ancestors fought under Frederick the Great.'

The attacking Germans presented an easy target should the British keep cool heads. Leading by example in dashing counter-attacks, a few officers went out in front, with Major Stucley and Captain Wellesley being killed outright, and Major Weld-Forester and Captain Douglas-Pennant receiving mortal wounds. Having held on to a support trench for a further hour, almost encircled by the enemy, Captain Rasch ordered what was left of the Grenadiers to retire to a small wood. A further futile counter-attack was made until the handful of men remaining from the nearly 1,000-strong battalion were ordered to retire. Ponsonby's history recorded that the gallantry of the Grenadiers had deceived the Germans into believing that they were facing a far greater number of British troops than was the case. Thus they refrained from breaching the pitifully weak line, under the mistaken impression that there were large reserves to the rear.

Only four officers and 100 men of the 1st Grenadiers returned to billets at Hooge that evening. Men who had been left in the trenches, not hearing the order to retire, returned in dribs and drabs, bringing the strength up to 250. Lieutenant Jack Butt was not among them. Nor was Lieutenant Colonel Earle.

In the cover of a ditch a few yards from the main road, the battalion's commanding officer had been lying with a serious head wound sustained in the German onslaught. He had been carried there by his medical officer and a stretcher-bearer. In Jack's estimation it was too dangerous to move the stricken Earle, so the pair remained with him as their comrades were forced into further retreat. While Earle's wounds were being tended, a small group of German troops approached the British trio. Jack, along with the stretcher-bearer, was summarily executed by gunshot, his RAMC red cross arm brassard ignored. Earle, as a senior officer, had had his life spared, and it was to be from him, along with Coldstream Guardsman Private S. Venton, who came upon the tragic scene soon afterwards, that the truth of Jack's fate would be painstakingly extracted by his family.

Charles Attwood

'After a gas cloud had been passed over our trenches by the enemy, this solider was found dead at the bottom of the parapet.'

By the spring of 1915, the valiant efforts of men like Jack Butt had helped to hold the Ypres Salient. Nevertheless, the Germans remained determined to knock Allied forces out of Belgium and gain control of the Channel ports of Dunkirk, Calais and Boulogne. The Allies, as well as defending access to these strategically crucial ports, also realised the symbolic importance of retaining a toehold of the remaining Belgian city not in enemy hands. In front of Ypres lay a mass of sunken roads, sodden fields, woods and a trench system that had gradually developed since its inception in September 1914.

In preparation for the defence of the salient, the 8th Battalion (90th Winnipeg Rifles), the 'The Little Black Devils', was inspected at Steenvoorde on 8 April by Lieutenant General Alderson, commander of the Canadian 1st Division. Charles Attwood, who had emigrated from Europe in 1912 in search of a new life, now found himself living in the bombed-out hellscape outside of Ypres. Fires turned the sky red and the ground shook from the shells raining down on the desolate terrain.

In mid-April 1915, the 1st Canadian Division relieved the French Eleventh Division along a 4,000-yard section of the front line, an area that had seen minor conquests and subsequent reverses between the German and French armies. At this stage, there was no continuous line of trenches for the Canadians to defend, rather a series of unconnected ditches 2 or 3 feet deep protected by a flimsy breastwork of sandbags, which would frequently let through a sniper's bullet. Some trenches were littered with rotting bodies and human excreta, the debris of previous skirmishes. The openness of the positions and the shallowness of the trenches left the Canadians exposed to enfilading fire.

The objective for the Canadian Division was to maintain their position on Gravenstafel Ridge, near the village of St Julien. From 17 to 22 April, the Canadians spent time deepening and strengthening the flimsy trenches they had inherited from the French. Intelligence reports had been received that cylinders of poison gas were being stored in the German trenches. A German deserter had been found in possession of a primitive gas mask and a wad of cloth soaked in protective chemicals. He had disclosed the existence of twenty cylinders of chlorine gas for every 40 metres of front in the area. Although this information was passed on to the Canadians during the handover of trench duty, British and French commanders remained sceptical that the Germans would use such an indiscriminate and deadly weapon, which had been outlawed under Article 23 of the Hague Convention of 1899.

They were tragically mistaken. On 22 April, a fresh spring day quite unlike the weather Charles and his comrades had experienced on Salisbury Plain, the Germans released their canisters. At 5.00 pm, a drifting fog, variously described as grey, yellow or green by Canadian troops, spread across no man's land. More than 160 tonnes of chlorine gas had been released. The Canadian Division was holding territory that formed the intersection between the British and French armies, with the largely conscripted 45th French (Algerian) Division to their left. Once the first waves of gas began to choke and blind the Algerians, many of them broke ranks and retreated, as the heaviest concentration of gas had glided across the ground in their direction. The chlorine burnt throats, causing lungs to fill with foam and mucus, having a similar effect to that of drowning. One Algerian who stumbled through the Canadian lines was frothing at the mouth, before falling, writhing at the feet of an officer.

This frantic retreat left a 4-mile hole in the front line on the Canadians' left flank. Canadian and British battalions quickly moved to plug the gap and the salient remained intact, with Ypres being saved. The Germans in turn had rushed towards the gap the gas had prised open but were unable to proceed further as they had not planned for such an unexpected turn. Nevertheless, the Canadian troops were in danger of being encircled by the advancing Germans, yet in the early hours of 23 April they held firm. By nightfall, Charles had been issued with a cotton bandoleer and his battalion supplied with kettles of water behind the trench parapets. In the event of a further gas attack, the men were instructed to wet the cloth and breathe through it to filter out the worst effects of the gas.

In the early morning of 24 April, two German planes were seen flying over the Canadian-held trenches. At 4.00 am, enemy artillery opened up against the 15th and 8th Canadian battalions whilst German troops clad in miners' helmets could be spotted unfurling long hoses. A strong hissing sound was heard and the ominous green fog, 15 metres high, began its deadly drift towards the Canadian trenches. Men began to suffocate, their eyes and lungs burning. They collapsed into the mud, unable to breathe. Eyes bulged from sockets and skin began to turn blue, then a green-black. Terror was spread by what one officer described as 'this filthy loathsome pestilence'. German infantry troops followed in its wake and many Canadians who could still breathe abandoned their positions to dig in half a mile further back. Others sought refuge by laying face-down in the crevices of their trenches but succumbed to the drowning effects of the chlorine gas as it was heavier than air, filling the precious space between mouth and ground. A few men survived by holding urine-soaked cloths and handkerchiefs over their mouths on the instruction of medical officers. They were able to fight on despite being half-blinded and vomiting blood-tinged fluid through their constricted throats, managing to maintain their position on the ridge.

One 8th Battalion comrade of Charles's, Winnipeg native Lester Stevens, later recalled:

> [The gas] came up and went over the trenches and it stayed, not as high as a person, all the way across. Two fellows, one on my right and one on my left, dropped. And eventually they got them to hospital, but they both died. … I was a bit of an athlete in those days and a good swimmer, and I could hold my breath … as soon as I saw that gas coming, I tied a handkerchief over my nose and mouth. … That saved my life.

Stevens was taken to a military hospital with an increasingly tight chest and having difficulty in breathing. He was told the gas had also paralysed the nerves of his bowels: 'it tied me all up in knots, in my stomach. … I don't go to the bathroom only about every fourth day.'

Due to standing above the gas cloud, Stevens was less affected than many of his comrades, including Charles. One man collapsed and was placed in a dugout by Stevens, who was approached by another man to provide some water. Stevens gave the man the small amount of liquid he had remaining, but this, mixing with the gas in the man's lungs, killed him.

John Uprichard had completed a plumbing apprenticeship in civilian life, giving him a keen awareness of the need to instantly respond to the threat of a gas leak. In his platoon only two men used the technique of urinating on a cloth then placing it over their nose and mouth; 'we were run out of water … you weren't very fussy on what you done then'. Men in other platoons, on the advice of Captain Bell, did the same thing.

On the arrival of the cloud, Uprichard recalled:

In ten, fifteen, twenty minutes, fellows would be spluttering and coughing and choking. Some of them collapsed in the course of time and others as I say, tried to cover their mouths up and do various things. I think that the few that probably covered themselves by using their first aid bandages, they more or less escaped it somewhat but not completely.

For some reason, Charles was either not quick enough to cover his mouth or did not manage to follow the advice to soak a handkerchief in urine, and was one of those who fell repulsing the German attack. It was at this moment that the life of the Somerset-born printer who had sought a new life in Winnipeg came to a protracted and painful conclusion. His military record states: 'After a gas cloud had been passed over our trenches by the enemy, this solider was found dead at the bottom of the parapet. The trench occupied by his company was later evacuated and fell into the hands of the enemy.'

Although the 24 April attack had opened serious gaps in the Canadian lines and forced the retreat of several battalions, the battered First Division held the ground outside Ypres, buying time until French and British reinforcements could be brought in. After four days of intense fighting, most of the Canadians were relieved on 25 April.

Charles's 8th Battalion comrades were among those who had ensured the successful defence of Ypres. clinging on to the Gravenstafel Ridge. The cost was enormous. By the end of the battle on 25 May, more than 6,500 Canadians were reported killed, wounded or missing. They included Sergeant Frederick Hall, another Winnipeg man, who had lived a short distance away from Charles on Pine Street. Hall was to be awarded the Victoria Cross posthumously for his actions on the evening of the 24th, having repeatedly ventured into no man's land to rescue wounded men. Charles Attwood had made his contribution to a previously untested army, a hastily assembled division that had proved itself to be a determined fighting force against the might of the German Army, complete with its deadly new vaporous weapon.

Percy Pope

'Forward 41st. Get at 'em, Welsh'

By 25 September 1915, Second Lieutenant Percy Pope was, along with his comrades in the 1st Welsh Battalion, in the Nord-Pas-de-Calais region of France. The battalion formed part of 84th Brigade within the 28th Division, tasked with playing their part in the biggest British assault of 1915, the Battle of Loos. Having learned a grim lesson from the use of chlorine gas against the Canadians back in May, this engagement also marked the first use of the weapon by the British Army, 150 tons of chlorine gas being released from 5,243 cylinders. The battle was an attempt to break the stalemate that had developed during 1915 and reignite a war of movement.

Another technological innovation at Loos was the beginning of tactical bombing raids by the Royal Flying Corps, commanded by Colonel Hugh Trenchard. Despite the huge amounts of ammunition and innovations, Allied gains were to be minimal, with British casualties at Loos nearly twice as high as German losses. The Germans called the battle the 'Leichenfeld von Loos', the 'field of corpses of Loos'. One of those corpses was to be the Dorchester brewing magnate's son, Percy Paris Pope.

The battle had begun on 25 September with an attack by the London Irish Rifles, with Major Beresford blowing his whistle and crying 'Irish – up and over'. As they walked into no man's land, it was reported that the troops kicked a football towards the German trenches. This initial three-day attack had created more than 48,000 British casualties. The severity of the fighting caused Roland Leighton, Vera Brittain's fiancé, to write:

> Let him who thinks War is a glorious, golden thing, who loves to roll forth stirring words of exhortation, invoking Honour and Praise and Valour and love of Country … let him but look at a little pile of sodden grey rags that cover half a skull and a shin-bone and what might have been his ribs, or at this skeleton lying on its side, resting half crouching as it fell, perfect but that it is headless. …
>
> Who is there that has known and seen, who can say that victory is worth the death of even one of these?

By 28 September, the British had lost all previous gains taken during the battle. The formidable Hohenzollern Redoubt, located on a slight slope that afforded excellent observation and fields of fire for the Germans, took the form of a salient that protruded into no man's land. The redoubt was linked to the German front line by two trenches, Big Willie and Little Willie, both deep, well-fortified positions that contained several machine-gun positions. Big Willie trench was partially occupied by the British, a trench block being the only barrier between the two sides.

A counter-assault was to be made around the redoubt by 28th Division. From 28 September to 4 October, repeated bombing offensives took place, with the division sustaining losses of 146 officers and 3,231 other ranks. Initially, the 83rd Brigade and 85th Brigade had attempted to regain the lost ground but were repulsed by the Germans from 28 to 30 September. By 30 September, only three-quarters of the western face of the Hohenzollern Redoubt and Big Willie trench remained in British hands.

On 1 October, 84th Brigade relieved 85th Brigade. The 6th Welsh Battalion, led by Lieutenant Colonel Lord Ninian Crichton-Stuart, took over the old British front line opposite the Hohenzollern Redoubt, with 2nd Cheshires on their right. There had been much damage not only to the front-line trenches, but to the connecting communication trenches. Some of the dead had been built into the hastily patched-up parapets. Many of these too would eventually join the ranks of the everlasting missing.

At 3.00 pm on 1 October, Percy's 1st Welsh Battalion was ordered to take over the trenches occupied by 6th Welsh, and to mount a night attack over the open ground towards Little Willie trench, and on the western face of Hohenzollern Redoubt. Little Willie trench was to be taken – according to a report written by the battalion's commanding officer, Lieutenant Colonel G.P. Hoggan, and circulated amongst relatives of the missing – 'at the point of the bayonet regardless of all costs'.

The 6th Welsh were to sit in reserve to the rear of the old British front line trench, leaving Percy and his comrades to attack a front of about 400 yards, over a distance of 300 yards, the assault to commence at 8.00 pm. Hoggan, who had commanded his battalion since 15 June, assembled his officers, explained the situation and had them synchronise their watches so the advance could begin in silence at precisely the same moment across the line.

Due to damage to the communication trenches and the crowding during the crossing over with the 6th Welsh Battalion, Percy and his comrades did not arrive at the jumping-off trenches until after dark, therefore no proper reconnaissance of no man's land was possible. Barbed wire had been removed from the parapet of the British trench to enable a smoother passage, and at precisely 8.00 pm the move forward began in perfect silence. Hoggan recalled the battalion 'crept over the parapet like one man. Officers in line with the men. The second in command, Major Hobbs, in the centre of the line.'

The battalion attacked with A, B, C and D companies ranged from left to right, with Percy being towards the centre of the assault in B Company, close to Major Hobbs, the battalion's second-in-command, and Lieutenant Colonel Hoggan. The latter's report described the next few moments of tension followed by a burst of action:

So silently was the advance carried out that the Regiment was within 100 yards of the enemy before being discovered. Then from both flanks machine guns spurted flame, and the whole length of the opposing trench opened rapid fire. The C.O.'s voice rang out, 'Forward 41st. Get at 'em, Welsh.' In 20 seconds there were 250 men and many officers on the ground. The remainder were in the enemy trenches bayoneting those in the trench and firing at the retreating Prussian Guards.

Fifty enemy troops were killed, nine taken prisoner and a machine gun captured, 'a gallant little affair', but two serious mishaps had already occurred. Firstly, the four companies had not been spread widely enough. Due to the lack of reconnaissance, A Company had drawn too much towards the others, meaning six bays of trench on the left flank containing about fifty Germans had not been attacked. Thus, the advancing Welsh were cut off from the head of a sap, which had been run out towards the German trenches in order to carry supplies of food, water and bombs. The Germans then gained control of this sap.

The second misfortune occurred at the opposite extremity of the advance. D Company had lost touch with C Company, leaving a gap of about 40 yards between them. Despite D Company, led by Captain W. Owen, gaining their objective in Little Willie trench, about forty Germans were left in between them and the right of the rest of the Welsh line formed by A, B, and C Companies. Owen's men attempted to link up with C Company, fighting along 70 yards of German trench, but their bombs often failed to ignite in the wet weather.

Meanwhile, the Germans on both flanks started bombing, with the supply of bombs for the attacking Welsh being 'very limited' to about 600 missiles. The failure to take the left flank meant that the attacking force found itself cut off from supplies of food, water and, worst of all, bombs. Testimony provided by those who took part in the attack would suggest that Percy Pope was one of those who successfully made it to Little Willie trench in the first phase of the action. Volunteers were called for to go back to the British lines for more bombs, and a further 600 were secured.

As the attack had not fully realised its objectives, Captain Egerton was sent back to the supporting battalions with a message requesting reinforcements. Fifty men led by one officer were sent up to the right in order to try to plug the gap left between C and D companies. In the darkness they arrived too close to C Company, meeting no resistance, leaving D Company still isolated. Another group of reinforcements was requested to be despatched to the left flank to support A Company in pushing out the enemy from the remaining section of Little Willie trench. However, this request was not granted, instead an officer being sent back to brigade headquarters to explain the situation.

Meanwhile, an attempt was made to connect the captured section of Little Willie trench with the old British front line trench by digging a new communication trench. The 6th Welsh dug forwards whilst the 1st Welsh dug backwards to link towards the centre of no man's land. This proved a dangerous task, with men under persistent German sniping and shellfire. They lay prone in the shallow trough of the sap, gradually digging away in the darkness. One messenger attempting to run across the 30-yard gap was shot by two separate snipers, indicating that the enemy had their sights clearly fixed on this endeavour. In all, fourteen men were killed in completing this communication trench, each shot through the head by eagle-eyed German snipers. It was finally completed by 2.30 pm on 2 October.

The first two days of October were spent in bombing battles on either flank. According to Hoggan, 'The Welch had the best of these battles, wounding or taking prisoners,' but by 10.00 am they had exhausted their supply of bombs, with the enemy seeming to have an unlimited supply. Around forty men now lay wounded in the trench previously held by the enemy. The Germans gradually encroached into the parts of trench taken by the Welsh, using Minenwerfer shells, 'sausage up'; that is, once the shell had reached its regulated distance, it dropped perpendicularly down. Usually it could be seen during its descent and dodged, but the British troops were so congested in Little Willie trench that it was impossible to evade. Hoggan wrote: 'When one lands in the trench six men in the vicinity disappear. – Major HOBBS, second in command, was magnificent – cool & collected – he held the men together & kept their spirits up in a wonderful manner.'

Sergeant Major C. Mudford undertook nine perilous journeys between the two trenches to fetch more bombs, earning the Distinguished Conduct Medal for his bravery. Private C.C. Grant won the same award for acting as a runner, helping the wounded before sustaining serious wounds.

Shortly after the completion of the communication trench, a third German bombing party attacked the centre of Little Willie trench, coming down a communication trench from their main position. Hoggan and Hobbs collected men together, leading them with rifle and fixed bayonets, and counter-charged this, attacking Germans. A hail of bombs destroyed and scattered the men following them. It is possible that this was the moment that Percy Pope was wounded, as Hoggan was to relay in a letter to Alfred Pope. Both Welsh flanks were rapidly being pushed into the centre. This situation was becoming hopeless, so the order was given to move out of Little Willie and to reach the newly dug communication trench. As the retreat began, machine guns opened fire on the Welsh, followed by more shells.

The 6th Welsh had also made dispositions to stop this rush of bombers, forming men and machine guns across the traverses. The CO, Lieutenant Colonel Ninian Crichton-Stuart, was shot dead while observing and directing the fire of one of his machine guns. The 1st Welsh reoccupied the old British front line trench, remaining there for a further twenty-four hours. By now the surviving men were exhausted, having been on the move and then in the trenches for a full eight days and nights. In such a condition of enervation it is not surprising that subsequent accounts of who had been killed, wounded or captured became confused and contradictory. Most had been without food or water for forty-eight hours. A night-time search of the communication trench was made by stretcher-bearers, who found Second Lieutenant Ruthven Pomfret Hore, an officer attached from the Dorsetshire Regiment, who died from his wounds soon afterwards, and Captain Egerton, who was very seriously wounded in the head. Hore had been a colleague of Percy's in the Inns of Court OTC. Lieutenant Weber had been badly wounded in the right forearm but remained on duty through the night of 2 October, until ordered back by Hoggan. Captain Warren, it was believed, had been wounded and taken prisoner. A subsequent attempt to recapture Little Willie trench by 1st Suffolks and 2nd Cheshires proved unsuccessful.

Hoggan concluded his report on the action in the unit war diary by testifying that 'All officers behaved magnificently but the casualties were very severe'. Three hundred and seventy NCOs and fifteen officers had been killed, wounded or gone missing, including his second-in-command, Major Arthur Hobbs. Hobbs had been wounded in the hand during the retreat through the communication trench, emerging into clear sight and not having been heard of since that incident.

Hoggan listed the following casualties amongst his officers:

Major A.H. Hobbs missing
Capt J.L.E. Warren ditto
2 Lt Hore, R.P., wounded – since died
2 Lt Davies, G. missing
Davies, T.J.C., wounded
White, H.T. ditto
Pope, P.P. ditto
Heard, R.D., ditto
Lt Kinnaid, C ditto
Lt Newington, E ditto
2 Lt Weber, C.T., ditto
Capt Egerton, G.W. ditto
2 Lt Hazell, M, missing
2 Lt Lord, A, wounded
Lt Toller, R.A., wounded

On 3 October, 1st Welsh were relieved and marched back to Vermelles. Hoggan was taken to hospital suffering from rheumatism and evacuated back to Britain. Percy Pope was not amongst those who made the weary journey back from the trenches. In the chaos of battle, his fate was unknown. He had, in the eloquent phrase of his brother-in-law, the Reverend Richard Bartelot, 'disappeared within that cloud of mystery which veils the "missing" in this stupendous war'.

Arthur Greensmith

'Two years in the making. Ten minutes in the destroying.'

1 July 1916 was the blackest day in the history of the British Army. On that fine summer's day, more than 57,000 men became casualties, with over 19,000 deaths. Whole communities, whose husbands and sons had volunteered to serve in the Pals battalions that made up much of the attacking forces, would mourn the loss of a generation of young men.

The Somme had been chosen as the location for a massive summer offensive as both British and French forces could take part, the area being at the conjunction of the operational areas of each army. The undulating countryside was reminiscent of Salisbury Plain, where many of the troops had trained the previous summer. The land was interspersed with large, dense woods and small villages. The Germans had the advantage of occupying the high ground and had turned a series of villages into strong fortresses along a robust defensive line. They had also manufactured deep dugouts that could withstand heavy shelling.

The 12th Battalion York & Lancaster Regiment, the Sheffield City Battalion, had spent the days preceding the attack observing the intense bombardment of the German positions. Although Private Arthur Greensmith and his pals knew that some would not survive the big push, an air of nervous optimism pervaded as they had been led to believe there would be little resistance offered by the enemy after such an artillery onslaught. However, some felt a sense of an impending appointment with destiny. Corporal D.E. Cattell, who had been brought up as a Christian, singing 'boy and man' in the choir at Sheffield Cathedral, thought it prudent to attend a communion service held prior to the battle:

> Up to that point the forthcoming event hadn't bothered me, but at that church service held in the wood, seeing as we could the build-up of marching men, guns and horses moving towards the front, then I had this feeling of awe. It must have been the effects of the service and seeing all this movement that you got this feeling, just as if something was coming at you.

At 3.00 pm on 30 June, the fateful message was received confirming the attack for 7.30 am the following day. The objective for the men of 31st Division was to take the village of Serre, one of the fortified settlements in German hands.

The village, about 5 miles north of Albert, was situated at the most northern point of the main thrust. Men were to go into action in Field Service Order, minus their large packs, instead carrying a small haversack slung on their back. This would contain mess tins, one day's rations and iron rations for emergency use. They also carried a spare pair of socks, a cardigan and a 'housewife' sewing kit. Each rifleman carried 150 rounds of ammunition in pouches and an extra bandolier of fifty rounds in his pack, four empty sandbags and two grenades. These were not to be thrown but passed as required to trained bombers. They also carried two gas masks and a rolled groundsheet. By the time they were ready to go into battle each man would be carrying at least 60 pounds, with some detailed for extra equipment a load of 90 pounds. Each man also carried a pick or shovel fastened on his back.

At 7.20 pm on 30 June, the battalion set out for the front line. At the crossroads north-west of Courcelles they received tea laced with rum and ate half a day's rations. Arthur's D Company was in position by 3.50 am, reaching the assembly trenches in an exhausted state, with three and a half hours of nervous tension to endure before attacking. D Company had been detailed to be in the third wave, beginning their 500-yard journey forwards to the front line at 7.29 am, with an anticipated time of 7.35 am to go 'over the top'.

Right on cue, Arthur and his comrades moved in column and in clear view of the German artillery, suffering 50 per cent casualties before reaching the front line. It is possible that Arthur was killed or mortally wounded before leaving the trenches. Soon afterwards, D Company left the trenches and ventured into no man's land.

The battalion war diary recorded:

> They were immediately met with very heavy machine gun and rifle fire and artillery barrage. The left half of 'C' Coy was wiped out before getting near the German wire, and on the right the few men who reached the wire were unable to get through. As soon as our barrage lifted from their front line, the Germans, who had been sheltering in their Dug-outs immediately came out and opened rapid fire with their machine guns.

Richard Sparling vividly described the action during which Private Arthur Clarence Greensmith, mining engineering student, son and dearly loved brother, vanished from the earth:

> The 1st of July, 1916, will be remembered as one of the saddest and most tragic, yet withal one of the most glorious pages of Sheffield history, for on that day there fell in battle the largest number of Sheffield men ever known. Around it sacred memories will ever cling as citizens recall the

gallant men who in a few minutes put to the test their long months of training. ...

The man who was present at the battle for Serre will at their mention see again the day before the battle – the toilsome journey through the trenches, half-full of water; see again the tired slumberers of the dawn, the beautiful summer morn, the faultless parade on the parapets, and the unwavering quick march into the hail of bullets and shells; see again those brave comrades mowed down as grass before the scythe, and those odd parties crossing the German trenches, alas! never to return.

He will see again the lightening shell-bursts, hear their stunning crashes and feel the shaking of tortured earth. He will recall the mangled, blackened bodies and hear the groans of ghastly wounded and voices of grey-faced soldiers as they said to themselves 'Let us hush this cry of "Forward" till one thousand years have gone.'

As his thoughts travel he will clench his fists at the recollections of the enemy riflemen sniping the wounded who showed any signs of life, and making target practice of the dead. He will feel again the burning ray of the brilliant midday sun, and see on every hand in dreadful No Man's Land those glittering triangles, every triangle a symbol of dead, dying and wounded. He will think of the parched lip and throat, and hearts of anguish, pain, and suffering, and then of the welcome sunset and more welcome shades of night, which enabled the living and hysterical wounded to reach our lines, some by crawling, some by crouching runs, and some by painful dragging of bodies ...

In this tangled mess of human misery Arthur Greensmith vanished from history:

This is a jumbled, vague story which has been told. But no clear narrative seems possible. The record consists merely of fragments picked up and pieced together: from what the men tell me of their little bits of the battle, from what one saw through the waving July grass on a trench top, from what the observers and airmen saw in the brief glimpses through the murky cloud of dust and smoke. In the regimental records there is a long list of well-remembered men with nothing but the word 'missing' marked against them. They went, and they did not come back. That is all. It is so different from one's dreams.

Those who made it to the German wire found it to be almost intact, as the seven-day artillery bombardment had had minimal impact. The German machine guns effected the end of life to those who found themselves stalled at the wire. A few survivors who had not been not cut down by the gunfire sheltered in shell holes for the rest of the day and made their way back to the British line once darkness fell.

On 2 July, two patrols went out into no man's land to assess the situation and to bring in further wounded men. A roll call taken on 7 July recorded 201 men from the battalion as 'missing', forty-two of them from Arthur's D company. The war diary of 94th Brigade recorded that the third and fourth waves of the attack, which had included Arthur, had suffered so greatly that they had lost half their strength before reaching no man's land. Eighteen of the 201 would eventually be found to be alive. In total, 248 men of the Sheffield City Battalion were killed on 1 July 1916, with 165 of them never to be identified. We shall never know if Arthur's life was destroyed behind or forwards of the British front line. What we do know is that at some point after 7.29 am on 1 July 1916, he disappeared from history. To this day, Arthur Greensmith's remains either lie out on the battlefield in front of Serre, or in an anonymous grave marked 'A Soldier of the Great War – Known unto God'.

Ernest Blackburn

'The word "RETIRE" will not be used under any circumstances.'

Alongside early volunteers for the Pals battalions like Arthur Greensmith who were thrown into the Somme Offensive were those who had been coerced into enlisting under the Derby Scheme, or conscripted under the Military Service Act of 1916. One such Derby volunteer was Leeds schoolteacher Ernest Blackburn, who would perish at the Battle of Flers-Courcelette.

Having been recently transferred to 9th Battalion King's Royal Rifle Corps, at 5.00 am on 11 September, Ernest and his new comrades marched the 7 miles to Airaines and entrained at 12.30 pm. Dis-entraining at Méricourt, the battalion marched through Buire and Dernancourt and the men were finally allocated a field north of the railway on which to encamp. The following day the battalion moved nearer to the firing line, camping to the south of Bercordel. The weather was foreboding, with stormy showers the order of the day. Under literal and metaphorical darkening skies, the battalion practised attack formations in the afternoon.

General Douglas Haig had formed the belief that, due to the success of the Brusilov Offensive on the Eastern Front, the time was right to renew the pressure on the German armies in France, pressing home the advantages gained during the first two periods of the Somme Offensive. The first tanks were now deemed ready for action, albeit without time for their crews to have undergone full training, and despite the reservations of Lieutenant Colonel Ernest Swinton, whose brainchild they were.

On the 14th, orders were issued for the big attack that was to commence the following morning in co-operation with the French, and at 6.20 pm the men moved up to Pommiers Redoubt. Ernest's new battalion formed part of the 42nd Infantry Brigade with the 14th (Light) Division, which was to attack with the Guards Division to their right and the 41st Division to their left. As those surrounding divisions were composed of fresh troops who had not previously been engaged on the Somme, Major Porter esteemed it 'a very great honour' for the battle-hardened 14th Division to have been selected to take part in the attack. The 14th (Light) Division, under Major General V.A. Couper, was to attack the small German salient east of Delville Wood, assisted by three tanks. Tank D1 was to advance at 5.15 am from the Pilsen Line.

The orders, issued by battalion adjutant Captain C.D. Lacey, identified the task of the 14th Division to capture Gueudecourt and establish a line to the north and east of the town. Four objectives were to be captured in turn, with descriptions of each objective issued to every officer. The attack was to begin at a yet unspecified 'Zero hour on Z day'. Ernest's battalion was to form a second wave of advance, operating behind the 9th Rifle Brigade and 5th Somerset Light Infantry and alongside 5th Oxfordshire and Buckinghamshire Light Infantry. At zero hour the front two battalions were to advance, with the second two moving up to replace them in York Alley and Check Line. Then, one hour forty-five minutes after zero hour, 9th KRRC was to leave the trenches to clear Delville Wood. Further advances were planned after that.

The ground for the assault had been well prepared with a three-day bombardment, which gradually intensified as the time for the attack arrived. Major Porter provided a preliminary perspective on the new weapon:

A new form of armoured motor car was employed for the first time during this attack. They were known as 'Tanks' and were able to move over any kind of rough ground, being able to cross shell holes or trenches, climb banks and get over sunken roads.

In appearance they were most uncouth with caterpillar wheels passing right over them. They were armed with 6lb guns as well as with several machine guns and were a formidable adversary to meet.

Ernest had been assigned to the battalion's C Company, which was to be in the second line of advance behind A and B companies. It was emphasised: 'It is most important that Companies keep their direction and occupy the whole of the objective allotted.' Compass bearings were given to all officers and aeroplanes would continually monitor progress from the air. Red flares would be lit on reaching each objective. No orders, sketches, letters or papers likely to be of use to the enemy were to be taken into action. All ranks were to be warned against the danger of drinking water found in the enemy lines until it had been passed fit for consumption by a medical officer.

The army's commanders did not indicate complete faith in the mettle of many of the new additions to the ranks. A police post was to be established to collect stragglers, who would be sent to their units, their names having been recorded and an extra mark made against those without rifles or equipment. The battalion would form a guard led by Sergeant Jordan with six men at the junction of Angle trench and Longueval Alley to turn back all stragglers. This party would accompany the battalion until it arrived at Delville Wood. The orders emphasised: 'The word "RETIRE" will not be used under any circumstances.'

Men were warned that those returning from the firing line 'with so-called "Shell-Shock" or light scratches will be tried by Court Martial and severely dealt with'. Death or glory was to be Rifleman Blackburn's fate.

Zero hour was 4.30 am on 15 September, at which time Ernest and his comrades moved from Pommiers Redoubt to Montauban Alley, each platoon advancing in file, keeping an interval of 50 yards to the next one. Two Vickers machine guns and Stokes mortars were carried at the rear. At 6.20 am the battalion moved up from Montauban Alley to York Alley and Check Line, with 5th Ox and Bucks to their left and behind the 9th Rifle Brigade. Forty minutes later, the men moved further forward to achieve the final objective of gaining ground north-east of Gird Support and digging in a line of trenches.

The battalion advanced in a north-easterly direction, with Waterlot Farm to their right and Delville Wood to the left. Pivoting left, it swung round well clear of the north-east corner of Delville Wood, behind the 9th Rifle Brigade and in touch with the 5th Ox and Bucks to their left. Although it was anticipated, no German shellfire was encountered. Around 7.15 am, two hours and forty-five minutes into the action, Lieutenant Colonel Benson, who had been up with the leading companies directing the advance, returned to battalion headquarters, to be replaced by Major Porter, who joined A and B companies. Ten minutes later, these two leading companies came under 'heavy hostile machine-gun fire' from a German gun about 80 to 100 yards from the right flank of the battalion. The gun 'did a great deal of execution, particularly to the two leading companies of the battalion and also caused several casualties amongst Battn Hdqrs in the rear'.

This machine gun was eventually silenced by two Lewis guns assisted by a party of 9th Rifle Brigade bombers, but not before it had accounted for the lives of dozens of men including, in all probability, Rifleman Ernest Blackburn. The advance continued, with very few officers left, and with death, being no respecter of rank or education, having claimed Lieutenant Colonel Eric Benson. Benson had been a contemporary of Percy Pope's at Winchester College and had, like Percy, progressed to the University of Oxford. Benson's body, like Ernest's, would never be identified, and the name of the former scholar of an elite public school would be forever commemorated within a few inches of that of the Board School-educated Ernest on the Thiepval Memorial to the Missing. Another family that would experience the loss of a son that day was that of Prime Minister H.H. Asquith. He would soon learn that his son Raymond had been killed serving with the 3rd Grenadier Guards, a short distance to the right of where Ernest Blackburn fell. The great and the good mourned alongside those of modest backgrounds. The desolation of death was democratic.

It is possible that Ernest was one of the 350 men who remained under the command of Major Porter, who had managed to amalgamate the remnants of the by then leaderless 9th Rifle Brigade into his battalion during the latter part of the morning. A further artillery bombardment at 5.45 pm was encountered, prior to an abortive German attack, but Major Porter did not report significant losses of men at that time. Porter and his men were eventually relieved by the Somerset Light Infantry.

The remnants of the battalion arrived back at Montauban Alley at about 5.00 am on the 16th, where it remained all day in support of the 43rd Brigade. The day was spent trying to reorganise the battalion as the casualties had been heavy. Lieutenant Colonel Benson and Lieutenant Meek had been killed, whilst nine other officers had been wounded. Of the 231 other ranks reported as casualties, 22 were killed and 143 were wounded, whilst 66, including the Leeds schoolteacher Rifleman Ernest Blackburn, were missing.

Four days later, the exhausted 14th Division was withdrawn from the Fourth Army, drawing words of acclaim from General Rawlinson. Rawlinson desired to 'convey to every officer, NCO and man my gratitude and congratulations for the admirable work they have done'. Ernest and his comrades had 'displayed a fighting spirit and dash which is worthy of the best traditions of the British Army, whilst their discipline and self-sacrifice has been beyond praise'.

A Special Order of the Day, issued by Major General Victor Couper, commanding officer of 14th (Light) Division on 24 September, heaped further commendation on the fighting unit of which Ernest had been part for a mere fortnight:

> [T]he GOC congratulates all ranks of the 14th (Light) Division on the high character they had earned for dash, discipline and hard work. The Division had proved that the New Army is in no way behind the Old Army in fighting qualities and the names of the famous Regiments represented

in the Division have, by the hardships endured and sacrifices triumphantly made, acquired new and undying honours.

Such laudatory words, if they ever reached the heavily pregnant Annie Blackburn in her Leeds terraced house, would have been of little comfort for the chilling anxiety into which she was plunged at news of her husband's disappearance.

Frank Mead

'a note to help make Xmas a bit merry for you in the circs'

From the first faltering deployment of tanks at the Battle of Flers-Courcelette, the engagement that claimed the life of Ernest Blackburn, the succeeding year saw the development of the Mark IV tank, with shorter-barrelled six-pounder guns and its fuel stored in an external tank to improve crew safety. By November 1917, 432 Mark IV tanks were available for the British Third Army's push towards Cambrai. However, more than half were out of action by the end of the first day, despite British forces making advances of about 5 miles. The soldiers were forced to retreat over the coming days and by early December more than 80,000 men were either wounded, missing or killed. Amongst the missing was Private Frank Mead of 1/23rd (City of London) Battalion.

On 21 and 23 November, Frank had witnessed the presentation of fourteen gallantry awards to battalion members who had excelled themselves during a raid on German trenches two-and-a-half weeks previously. On 24 November, the battalion paraded and marched to Gommecourt, where the men were billeted under canvas. High winds meant many tents were thrown down. The following day the men marched via Bapaume to a Nissen hut camp at Barastra. On the 27th, now under the command of Major W.H. Murphy, the men of 1/23rd marched to a tented camp near Cambrai.

The 29 and 30 November were spent in trenches in a forward area, and some men were instructed to reconnoitre German defensive positions before being relieved by the 1st KRRC. At 6.00 pm on 2 December, the 1/23rd Battalion moved to Sunken Road trench to relieve 1/6th London Battalion and support a counter-attack to be made by 1/8th London Battalion. Frank and his comrades were in place by 8.00 pm. B Company was positioned on the Fontaine-Bourlon road whilst the other companies remained in Sunken Road trench. This position was held during the night of 2/3 December and through most of the following day. During the night, heavy artillery fire killed five men: Privates Frank Mead, Henry Wallington, John Steele and Benjamin Stanborough, and Lance Corporal Ernest George. An additional thirteen men were wounded by shelling.

Forty-eight hours later, after sustaining further casualties, Frank's comrades began their withdrawal from the front line, completing their evacuation on 5 December. At some point between 3 and 5 December, Frank Mead, Henry Wallington and one other man were hastily buried by their comrades, their personal possessions having been carefully removed in order to return them to family members back in London.

As Frank was going up to the Sunken Road trench to face his death, a letter posted on 1 December from Reg was making its way across the Channel. He had been relieved to hear his brother was 'all right, and hope you will continue so'. Reg was 'hoping you have been able to keep warm' in the cold weather. He passed on news of William Cambray, who had visited Elfindale Road for tea recently, 'has been having a ruf [sic] time of it in the way of near shaves, by what he says'. Cambray was now undertaking a six-week pilot training course. A native of Herne Hill, he had first served in the London Regiment, seeing action in France. In 1916 he had transferred to the Royal Flying Corps and qualified as an observer, being credited with bringing down six German planes between May and October 1917 and awarded the Military Cross.

Reg went on to describe an air raid over London: 'On Thursday morning we were awakened by guns about 5 'o' clock by a visit of the Gothas. They left their cards at Dulwich Pk, Vauxhall & Stockwell so not far from us. Two were brought down as you have read in the papers.'

Reg lamented the continuation of the war, 'and us all have our Xmas dinner at home worse luck'. Stoically, the teenager reflected, 'well we must cheer up & look for the best'. A war that would drag on into 1918 would mean 'next June I suppose I shall be in karkhie'. After relaying information about the health ailments of various acquaintances, including their boarder, Miss Ada Lewis, who was 'not up to much. She does not seem to keep away from the floo', Reg enclosed 'a note to help make Xmas a bit merry for you in the circs'. He hoped that Frank was 'keeping fit & good luck'. When his letter was returned via the War Office nine days later, it was starkly clear to Reg that Frank's well of good luck had run dry. His lovingly crafted letter had gone unread by his dear brother and the heart had been ripped out of the closely knit Mead family.

Gilbert Donnelly

'The men who knew no fears, the Munster Fusiliers'

As the war entered its fourth grim year, there was hope on the Allied side. The USA, after much persuasion from President Woodrow Wilson, had formally declared war on Germany on 6 April 1917, and the first units of the American Expeditionary Force had fought at the Battle of Cambrai in November. By the spring of 1918, General Pershing had four American divisions to support the French Army. Further reinforcements were flooding across the Atlantic Ocean to bolster the efforts of the flagging Allied forces.

Despite hopes of a pivotal shift of fortunes in favour of the Allies, on the Eastern Front, the withdrawal of Russia from the war following the new Bolshevik government signing the Treaty of Brest-Litovsk meant that fifty German divisions could be redeployed to the Western Front. In a race against time, before American power would render the war unwinnable for Germany and her allies, General Erich Ludendorff launched what he hoped would be a conclusive offensive in the spring of 1918. It would be during this great push of German forces that Lieutenant Gilbert Donnelly of the 1st Battalion Royal Munster Fusiliers would be killed.

A flavour of life in the battalion in the days before the Spring Offensive of 1918 was provided by the chaplain, Captain Thomas Duggan CF. Duggan had arrived in Flanders in 1917 and had initially been posted to a Casualty Clearing Station some distance from the front line. Upon his transfer to an Irish regiment, he quickly developed strong bonds with his predominantly Roman Catholic flock. On 4 March, the battalion moved out of the line for a rest. Duggan wrote, 'The poor men want it though I have been very comfortable here.' They had been forty-two days in the line but 'we are having a very easy time now'. On 9 March, he wrote home: 'The weather here is glorious. I have spent all yesterday and today hurling. Where we are at present you'd never dream there was a war on. We are having Benediction this evening. Needless to say I am in good voice.'

Ten days later, the men were still unsure as to what the next phase of the war would bring: 'Nothing doing here. There are all kinds of rumours of offensives, counter offensives but nothing ever happens. I am still in that little village from which I started for home the last time. However, the place is so quiet now that we no longer sleep in a cellar. In some ways I miss it. Especially the dirt.'

Duggan described the 1st RMF's high spirits on St Patrick's Day 1918:

We celebrated St Patrick's Day in great style. We meant to have an open-air Mass but when we arrived at the place selected there were four German sausages [observation balloons] gazing down at us so we decamped another half-mile to a hut. The boys sang 'Hail Glorious St Patrick' til they were black in the face. Of course, I had to tell them that St P. (as might be expected from a man of discernment) held the men of Munster in a special esteem. As a matter of fact I believe he boycotted them.

After dinner we had a hurling match (which I refereed). Most of the spectators were from Cork city. You'd think you were at the Athletic

Ground to head the shouting 'Go on Tarry', 'Go on Busty'. The warriors referred to are known in their official capacity as Sergeant O'Donoghue (from de Marsh, Fader) and Sergeant Busteed (from de sout side).

After the match they consumed 20 barrels of beer and weren't a bit the worse for it. It is only the light French ale and has no effect on them. I went down to their concert about 9 o'clock. I made for the biggest knot of men. That was where the beer-barrel was. About twenty yards away there was a much smaller crowd. That was the stage were someone was singing of

'The men who knew no fears
   the Munster Fusiliers'

I was talking to one of them the other day. He was temporarily in bad humour about something. 'If I was once back in Cork, Fader, with Bull's cap off me, the divil [sic] himself wouldn't drag me out again.' They always refer to the Empire as 'Bull'. It is great to hear them when both artilleries are bombarding. 'Go on Jerry', 'Go on Bull' 'One up for Bull' etc etc.

The 16th (Irish) Division had been charged with holding a 4-mile section of front forward of the village of St Emilie. The 48th and 49th brigades were on the front line, known as 'Blue Line', whilst Gilbert and his comrades waited in reserve some 400 yards in front of the town on 'Brown Line'. The Germans were to open Operation Michael – their great 1918 Spring Offensive – in this sector with a gas bombardment.

At 4.30 am on 21 March, 1st RMF took up their battle positions around the village of St Emilie, sustaining casualties from gas and shelling while moving up. Lieutenant Donnelly, as an officer, assumed the dangerous task of acting as a spotter for a Lewis machine-gun crew. One subsequent account stated that Gilbert had been killed by shelling between 10.00 am and 11.00 am. At 11.00 am, information was received that the enemy had occupied Lempire and Basse-Boulogne to the north-east, and the Munsters were ordered to counter-attack Red Line at once in co-operation with 6th Battalion Connaught Rangers. The order was quickly cancelled, although this directive did not reach Lieutenant Colonel Rowland Feilding, commanding officer of the Connaughts, whose battalion attacked without the expected support of the Munsters. Lieutenant Colonel Kane, commanding officer of the Munsters, received orders to occupy the Brown Line trench and hold it against the enemy's expected advance.

The enemy attack began at 5.00 pm but got no further than the wire in front of the trenches, with many German casualties. These attacks were repeated each half hour. It is possible that in the intervals between these attacks, Gilbert, looking out across no man's land to anticipate the next attack in order to direct the fire of his Lewis gun, was shot by a German sniper.

In the rapid German advance of the following days, Gilbert's body did not receive a formal burial. However, evidence later came to light which verified that thirteen men killed during the attack had been hastily buried under German direction. Chaplain Tom Duggan and Captain Bisset, the RMO, were later listed as having been taken prisoner, suggesting that they stayed with the dead, dying and wounded to provide spiritual and medical succour to their stricken comrades. Duggan may well have had the opportunity to say prayers for the deceased, as he was not captured until 22 March.

Following Gilbert's death, the 16th (Irish) Division suffered horrendous losses, the highest of any British division during that period. Within a day, 1st RMF had been reduced to seven officers and 450 men, and by the time of the final general withdrawal across the Somme in early April, just 290 men were available for duty. The roll call of dead, wounded and missing officers confirmed the deaths of Lieutenant Donnelly and Second Lieutenant John Fullin MC. Six officers were listed as wounded and five as missing. The 1st RMF was a shadow of its former strength and was eventually transferred to 57th (2 West Lancashire) Division for the remainder of the war. Captain Duggan survived captivity, and forged close links to the Irish nationalist movement of the 1920s. Aged 50, he volunteered for service in the Second World War, being awarded a Military Cross for his gallantry during the retreat to Dunkirk.

Alan Stirling

'I am like Johnny Walker – still going strong.'

Former Wolverhampton warehouseman Private Alan Stirling had completed two years' service in the Army Ordnance Corps before being transferred to the 10th Battalion King's Royal Rifle Corps. Upon the disbandment of this battalion in early February 1918, Alan was one of a draft of ten officers and ninety other ranks which awaited the arrival of the 12th KRRC in camp at Reninghelst, 9 miles south-west of Ypres, as they came out of the front line. Lieutenant Colonel L.G. Moore DSO returned from leave to resume command of the battalion. Alan was assigned to C Company and the men marched to a camp just east of Wippenhoek, behind the Ypres Salient. The battalion war diary recorded the camp as 'not bad … clean and neat. Every man had a bunk.'

The following day was spent on marching drill, gas drill and short route marches, but this training was recorded as 'unsatisfactory' due to the weather, lack of training stores and poor-quality parade grounds. Alan's new battalion was to be deployed to staunch the German Spring Offensive, the Kaiserschlacht (Kaiser's Battle). The attacks would commence on 21 March 1918, with the aim of breaking through the Allied lines at the weak hinge point between the British and French armies near Saint Quentin and outflanking the British forces.

Alan and his comrades were to face storm trooper units, trained in infiltration tactics to penetrate and bypass enemy front line units, leaving these strongpoints to be dealt with by follow-up troops. The storm troopers were to press on and disrupt enemy headquarters, artillery units and supply depots in the rear areas, making rapid gains in territory. Word had reached the British high command that a major offensive was due, and the 12th KRRC, operating as part of 60th Brigade within 20th Division, spent much of February 1918 on trench duty on the Ypres Salient before transferring to Arras to await the German offensive.

On 8 February, the battalion marched for two and a half hours to Malplaquet Camp, just south of Dickebusch, and the men were able to take baths in the afternoon. The following day, a cold and windy one, was spent on squad and platoon drills and inspections. Sunday, 10 February saw the customary church parade take place in the camp's recreation hut at 11.30 am. Spiritual solace was sorely needed at 10.15 that evening as a considerable volume of artillery fire began, the heaviest part concentrated on the Messines neighbourhood. This proved to be men from the Australian Imperial Force carrying out a successful raid near Warneton and a British bombardment of Polderhoek Chateau. The following day saw Alan and his C Company comrades being trained in wiring, range practice with rifles and Lewis guns, and rewarded afterwards with 'dining out'.

Alan experienced his first taste of trench duty on 13 February, when 12th KRRC went into the front line in the Polderhoek Sector. Entraining at Dickebusch station at 2.45 pm, arriving at Manor Halt an hour later, the men were provided with tea before marching on to the front line via Sanctuary Track, the appropriately named Stirling Track and Polderhoek Track, and were in position by 9.00 pm. Nearly three years after the first German gas attack of the war at Ypres, during which Charles Attwood had perished, Alan Stirling was subjected to a gas shell assault in the evening of the 15th. Members of C Company were 'obliged to wear their box respirators for an hour' to avoid the tragic fate of the Canadians.

After 12th KRRC batteries had bombarded Polderhoek Chateau during the afternoon of 16 February, Alan and his pals were replaced on the front line by the 6th Bedfordshires that evening, arriving at West Fire Camp by 9.30 pm to have their feet washed, socks changed and enjoy hot tea and porridge.

The battalion's railway journey to Nesle on 21-22 February was delayed by a derailed truck. On reaching the station the men were given tea and 'were received in very respectable billets'. The area, located in the Somme Department, had been in the hands of the Germans until March 1917, 'and the inhabitants had interesting accounts to tell'. The following week was spent on cleaning parades, church services in the recreation hut, musketry training and practising depth defending and counter-attack. Captain M.T. Sampson, the battalion's adjutant, noted, 'The country, being for the most part grass-covered and not enclosed, with undulating hills and sunken roads, was both useful and pleasant for training of all kinds.'

The afternoon of 27 February was a half-holiday and inter-platoon football matches were organised. The war diary from 5 to 20 March briefly recorded: 'Battalion prepared the defences of Offoy.' It was on 6 March that Alan Stirling wrote his last recorded words:

Dear Mother, Father, All,

Just a line to let you know I am like 'Johnny Walker' – still going strong after a return to this land of milk and honey.

Hope that all at home are keeping well and father better than when last I heard from home, by the way I haven't heard from you lately, the reason being I think – is because I have been posted from the 10th to the twelfth batt.

Here is the address.
Rfm A Stirling 204366
No 10 Platoon
C Company
12th K.R.R.
B.E. Force
France.

I must wish you many happy returns if it was your birthday last month and I hope that they will be many and happy. Am sorry I haven't a card to send but here is a big birthday kiss X.

Weather out here is fairly decent, one thing I don't think we shall experience another winter like last.

Well dear mother father and all @ home in conclusion let me ask you to keep smiling. I know things must be very hard for you, but we have got to stick it.

Best love and kisses to each one.
Your Loving Son
Alan
XXxxxxxxxxxxX

The final thirteen kisses were one for each of his eleven siblings and his parents.

On 20 March the battalion was 'stood to' until 9.30 pm when the men returned to billets. The launch of Operation Michael began at midnight along the whole front, with a very heavy bombardment which gradually increased in intensity until it reached its maximum at about 4.00 am. Finally, at 2.30 pm on 21 March, the order came through from brigade headquarters to 'man battle stations' and at 3.15 pm, Alan and his comrades marched off via Sancourt, Villers-St-Christophe and across the fields to a sunken road about 500 yards north-west of Douchy.

The area was being heavily shelled and brigade headquarters ordered 12th KRRC to remain in situ awaiting further instructions. At midnight on 21/22 March the order came through to move to battle stations. A peculiarly dense mist had fallen, making movement extremely difficult. The initial disposition placed Alan and the rest of C Company holding the strongpoints, behind A and D Company on the front line and B Company poised ready for a counter-attack. The 12th KRRC was at the extreme left of the brigade, with its right flank resting in the town of Fluquières and its left just south of Vaux. The 12th Rifle Brigade was to the immediate right of the 12th KRRC.

The night passed quietly but during the morning reports arrived that the Germans had broken through the division holding the forward line, and that the 12th KRRC should expect an attack in the afternoon from the direction of Vaux. At 3.50 pm, a long drawn-out bugle call from the enemy lines heralded an attack 'of very great force' against both of the battalion's flanks. German storm troopers penetrated the battalion lines, creating a gap in the wire. Still the companies hung on, as four attempts to rush through the wire were repulsed by fire from two Lewis guns that had been pushed out in front. The diary noted, 'their every effort was frustrated'.

However, the battalion was sustaining heavy casualties, mainly in A Company. It will never be known at what point during the actions from 22 March onwards that Alan fell as it was not until 2 April that the adjutant was able to assess losses. In the maelstrom of German attacks, British retreats, entrenchments, counter-attacks then further retreat, it became impossible to keep track of the fates of individual men.

By the end of the first day, the British had lost 7,512 dead and 10,000 wounded, and the Germans had broken through at several points on the front of the British Fifth Army. By the evening of 22 March, 12th KRRC's position was fast becoming untenable. Many officers had been wounded or killed and the men were forced to retire. Marching back towards Villers-St-Christophe through a dense mist, the officer in charge had to rely on a compass bearing to make their revised position. Meanwhile, German aeroplanes flew overhead, firing down lights but not inflicting damage. On arrival at Villers, C Company was deployed to the south-east of the village with the remnants of A Company. There was to be no respite from the Germans, as storm troopers made a frontal attack at 11.00 pm: 'they were on top of us almost before we realised their presence, having crept up under the cover of the mist.' A wedge was driven between the right and left halves of the battalion, making a further retirement unavoidable. At this point, several members of 12th KRRC were taken prisoner. Thus, when the tally of the missing was eventually compiled, many families, including the Stirlings, were left with the possibility that their loved one had been captured.

The new defensive position, by a belt of wire in Villers, was taken up with a view to the battalion being able to delay and harass the enemy. However, this line had been occupied for barely an hour when, in the early hours of 23 March, orders were received from Brigade to take up a new position on the southern bank of the Canal de la Somme and to hold a bridgehead at Offoy. Difficulty was experienced in crossing the river Germaine as the bridge had previously been blown up, 'and our task was in no manner simplified by the close and organised pursuit of the enemy'. The battalion reached Offoy at dawn, finding it lightly held by elements of the 61st Division. On reaching the bridgehead, men were ordered to fall out so they could fill their water bottles while the officers snatched a few minutes to discuss the situation 'and to obtain a coherent account of what had been happening' before crossing the bridge, which was subsequently destroyed in an attempt to prevent further German incursions.

Alan's C Company was left guarding the remains of the bridge, holding on with 'great gallantry and courage'. The day of 23 March passed uneventfully, but no sooner had darkness set in than 'a great noise of traffic and shouting' arose in Offoy. British Vickers and Lewis guns fired in response, but at various places on the opposite bank of the canal the sound could be heard of Germans driving stakes into the ground and moving planks. It was obvious to the men of C Company, probably at this stage still including Rifleman Stirling, that the Germans were planning to throw out bridges in order to continue their assault. They were successful in planking the Offoy Bridge, and repeated attempts were made to rush it. The battalion war diary recorded that 'C Coy held on successfully and earned a great and well-merited praise'.

After two days of Operation Michael, the Fifth Army was in full retreat. As they fell back, many of the isolated redoubts were left to be surrounded and overwhelmed by the following German infantry. The right wing of Third Army became separated from the retreating Fifth Army, and drew back to avoid being outflanked. On 24 March, about 1,200 yards east of Offoy, the Germans managed to bridge the canal. Fifty men of the Royal Warwickshire Regiment and two Lewis guns were sent to harass them. Despite this effort, 'the enemy completed his task and poured over the canal'. Confronting the Germans were men from the Irish Young Citizen Volunteers and Royal Irish Rifles from the Ulster Division, who broke at once in disorder. Attempts to rally them proved futile, leaving the right flank of 12th KRRC exposed. B and D companies mounted a counter-attack: 'It was a great charge. The bayonet was used to wonderful effect,' driving the Germans back to Canizy but not back across the canal. The foe 'came on in greater numbers than before'. Meanwhile, Alan's C Company was being severely trench mortared, but was saved from having to evacuate their position by the decisive actions of the men of the Royal Flying Corps, nose-diving to a height of about 200 feet, dropping bomb after bomb on the German gunners, putting them completely out of action.

At 3.00 pm the Germans crossed the river at Voyennes, 2 miles north-west of Offoy, forcing the battalion to withdraw once more under heavy shell and machine-gun fire from both flanks. Several casualties were sustained at this point before the remnants of the battalion were distributed across a 1,000-yard frontage. Further casualties were sustained by British guns firing short, then, at 10.15 pm, the Germans opened a terrific machine-gun fire from Bazancourt without reply from British artillery. As the morning of 25 March dawned, 12th KRRC's rearward positions were subjected to an intense bombardment at point-blank range by enemy field guns. Before noon more casualties were inflicted 'by our own artillery who seemed incapable of finding the correct range'.

Although no precise numbers were recorded due to frequent retreats and retrenchments, it appears that most fatal casualties for 12th KRRC were sustained from 22-25 March, making this the most likely period that Rifleman Alan Stirling was killed, the severe trench mortar attack on his C Company on 24 March near Offoy being the strongest possibility.

If he did survive a further few days, he would have either witnessed or heard about the bayoneting of a German officer who was dressed in a British uniform. The men under his command succeeded in surrounding the battalion headquarters, capturing the whole of its personnel. The remainder of the battalion was caught in shell and machine-gun fire, ending in a rush and rout. On 26 March the vestiges of 12th KRRC were formed up under Captain N.W. Paddy MC and marched westwards in column, arriving at Roye at 3.00 am, acting as a rearguard for the whole division. Still, the enemy closed in on them, as the division was forced to retreat via Arvillers and Le Quesnel. Two more German officers wearing British uniform were encountered, one being killed by gunfire, the other being captured while cycling into Arvillers. By now the retreat had ceded nearly 30 miles of ground to the Germans.

A counter-attack was staged at 4.00 pm on 29 March, which recaptured Mézières, taking many prisoners and machine guns in the process. This gain was short-lived as forces to the left gave ground and were attacked from the left rear, sustaining numerous casualties. By this time units had become very mixed in the confusion of rapid retreat. Cookers were brought up from the rear and men were given hot meals during the night of 29 March. On the afternoon of 30 March, the Germans recaptured Little Wood, but a counter-attack made by an admixture of men from 12th KRRC and 12th Rifle Brigade regained the lost ground, seizing forty-nine prisoners and nine machine guns as they went.

Once again, British lines broke on 31 March. The 12th Battalion's D Company was attacked from the rear, 'almost annihilating it', as those who could escape were forced back to Hourges, 'and made one last stand on the slopes from Rifle Wood'. This position proved unfavourable and the battalion was finally withdrawn to the rear at Domart that night.

On 2 April 1918, the bedraggled remnants of 12th KRRC arrived at the village of Quevauvillers, to the west of Amiens, where the men were provided with a 'good hot meal in a field'. No billets being available, they moved 3 miles north-east to the village of Revelles, where a full account could be taken of the losses sustained over the past fortnight. The figures made grim reading.

Six officers were known to have been killed in action, with a further eleven listed as wounded but whose presence was known. Five were wounded, believed to be prisoners of war, including the battalion's commanding officer, Lieutenant Colonel L.G. Moore. One missing officer was believed to have been taken prisoner. Of the men in the ranks, 216 were confirmed as killed or wounded, with a further 207, including Rifleman Alan Stirling, recorded as missing. Six men were known to have been wounded before going missing, with only one member of the battalion reported missing, believed to have been killed.

It proved impossible to establish individual death dates for many of those who had gone missing, with those members of 12th KRRC whose precise fate remained unknown being officially recorded as having died on 2 April 1918. Rifleman Alan Stirling, former grocery warehouseman, was never to be heard of again. After two and a half years in the army, destiny had called him home to his God.

Chapter 5

Searching for the Missing

Minds and hearts agonisingly turning over the possible fates of a missing relative became all too common an experience during the war. Distraught families would expend considerable effort attempting to elicit answers to their own personal mystery. The most protracted search of the eight families in this book was conducted by the family of Lieutenant John Gillis Butt.

John Gillis Butt

> 'It is awful for relations being kept in suspense.'

It was while tending the wounds of Lieutenant Colonel Maxwell Earle, as they sheltered in a ditch near to the Kruiseik crossroads, that Lieutenant Jack Butt and a corporal medical orderly had been shot through the head by a German soldier. Both men were subsequently buried by German troops, unbeknown to any of their comrades in the 1st Grenadiers.

Jack's name appeared on a list of missing. Instantly, his father, Edward Ormiston Butt, a retired lieutenant colonel who served with distinction in the RAMC, made contact with his old commanding officer, Sir Alfred Keogh, Director General of Army Medical Services. Keogh replied to Edward on 14 November, unable to provide definitive information but keen to indicate the prospect of a positive outcome:

> My Dear Butt
> Just a line to say to you & Mrs Butt how distressed I am. At the same time these cases of 'missing' are nearly always cases of capture by the enemy. So don't worry.

Meanwhile, the strain of uncertainty was being felt across the family. Jack's mother, Helen Butt, referred to 'Poor Gladys', Jack's twin sister, who 'will be fretting dreadfully'. However, the understanding amongst his relatives was that 'many people are reported wrong, it's very likely he is a prisoner'. Despite that ray of hope, 'It is awful for relations being kept in suspense'.

Edward had inserted a notice in *The Times* newspaper, requesting information about his son. This had been seen by Elizabeth Stewart, a nursing sister serving at No. 1 London General Hospital in Camberwell, who wrote to him on 29 November. One of the patients in her ward was a Private Regan of 1st Grenadiers. Regan had been sent to the hospital that week from the front line. Elizabeth had enquired if he knew anything of Jack, and received the following reply: 'Four days after we retired [to] Armerik, a village in Belgium, Pte Lambourne, stretcher-bearer, 1st Grenadier Guards, told me he had seen Lt Butt shot – he thought fatally – by a sniper – while he (Lt Butt) was attending to the C.O. – Colonel Earle.'

Although this second-hand account was, Elizabeth felt, 'not very definitive or satisfactory information to send you', she nevertheless hoped that the Butt family could use it as a basis of further enquiries as 'every bit of news that can be given is precious and must not be held back'. Furthermore, Elizabeth provided Private Regan's regimental and home addresses should the family wish to contact him.

Edward Butt had also made enquiries of the Red Cross Society in Geneva. The organisation made a record card of Lieutenant Butt's particulars. They were to endeavour to trace the whereabouts of John Gillis Butt, an English military doctor and a lieutenant in the Royal Army Medical Corps, attached to the 1st Battalion Grenadier Guards, who had been reported 'disparu' on 28 or 29 October at Gheluvelt near Ypres. His next of kin was recorded as his father, Colonel E.M. Butt, residing at Douglas, Bothwell, Scone. One Red Cross record suggested that Jack had been captured at Le Cateau and might possibly have been 'fait prisonnier' at Döberitz prisoner of war camp in Brandenburg. This card, created in December 1914, gave an additional family contact as Mrs Helen Butt of Crumlin Lodge, Datchet.

Edward Butt received word from the society in December informing him of the good news that 'J. Butt' was being held in Döberitz. These joyful tidings were quickly overshadowed by the realisation that the man in question was in fact Private J. Butt of the Grenadier Guards, not Lieutenant J.G. Butt of the Royal Army Medical Corps. Edward Butt replied to the society's secretary on 14 December to request that a further search of prisoners be made for his son, who 'was last seen unwounded in German hands with a lot of other prisoners'. Edward enclosed a cheque for £1 to support the work of the society, and to expedite their staff 'find[ing] out where he is interred'. Thus, the Butt family was insisting on the 'where', not the 'if', of Jack's incarceration.

During the Yuletide of 1914, as families across Britain were forced to accept the reality of the war not being 'over by Christmas', Edward received a letter from Gertrude Bell, the secretary of the British Red Cross Wounded and Missing Bureau, based in the Rue Victor Hugo in Boulogne. Her letter stated that evidence had been received on 23 December from a Lieutenant J. Teece:

'He says that Lt Butt was last seen with the Commanding Officer, who was afterwards wounded and taken prisoner.' Gertrude's suggestion was that it was 'probable that he may have been taken a prisoner also, as he was with the Colonel'. Optimistically, she concluded, 'Lt Butt had been doing excellent work. I cannot help hoping that Lt Teece's conjecture may be correct and that Lt Butt may be heard of in Germany.'

However, as the new year dawned, no word came from Jack. By early March 1915, Helen Butt was under severe emotional strain. She wrote to Gladys, then living in Calcutta with her husband Robert 'Bob' Hodgson, 'I have just got over an awful headache attack, so I feel very flat & depressed.' The prospect of her husband making the long journey from Scotland to Datchet for a weekend visit did provide a glimmer of positivity, and there was pride in his continued contribution to the war effort: 'I saw his name mentioned in *The Times* for his splendid work he had done in Scotland in hunting up men for the army. I am glad they recognize his good work for he certainly does work hard.' Edward was evidently still not a man to be trifled with, Helen averring, 'if he could only do it without getting everyone's back up all would go well for him'.

In his absence, Jack's name appeared in the *London Gazette* in March 1915, announcing his automatic promotion to captain. Medical officers who were 'missing' remained on the Army List until their deaths were officially confirmed. By the high summer of 1915, Helen Butt's life continued in anxious uncertainty. With her husband in Scotland, her daughter in India, the fate of her son still shrouded in mystery and international post frequently being delayed or lost, she had to cling to what hopeful conjecture she could muster. Writing to Gladys on 18 July, Helen referred to a family friend who had written to her giving:

> a wonderful account of a missing officer that was discovered by his sister in Germany. And you will see that this was told to Elsie by a friend of the Officer's family – so you see the Germans can hide men and prevent them writing home when they want to. So I will never give up hope about Jack till the war is over. I feel sure he is hidden away some where and that he will turn up all right.

Helen believed she had extra grounds for hope of Jack's safekeeping, being the mother of twins:

> I still think that if anything had happened you would have felt it as you are his twin. There is wonderful sympathy between twins so the following story proves.
>
> I was talking to my solicitor here, Harrison, about proving dear papa's will and when I had settled up our affairs, he asked me if I had anything

of Jack. No, but I will never give up hope till the war is over, and his twin sister agrees with me & feels that he is alive. So he said 'it is curious that you should have told me that about his twin sister, for it reminds me of an occurrence that took place in my office some months ago. I was talking to a client – a young officer of 19 – when in the middle of our conversation he suddenly jumped up off his chair exclaiming "My brother is killed I Know it! I am sure of it!"' Mr. Harrison thought the boy had gone mad, but it was afterward found that his twin brother had been killed at that same hour and same day in France. This clearly proves that there is a bond between twins.

Helen implored her daughter to:

Pray for dear Jack every night that he may be taken care of wherever he is – think of him and send him cheerful loving thoughts every day. And they will reach him. This is what I try to do every day – and as well as helping him you will be helping yourself. ... Read that book I sent you and it will explain to you the importance of thought and how it travels to those we are thinking of.

Positive thoughts were not enough to bring news of Jack, so in August Helen began another enquiry, writing to Alfonso XIII, King of Spain, whose country had remained neutral in the war, imploring him to make enquiries via channels unavailable to the British authorities. She received a reply from Don Emilio de Forres, the King's private secretary at the Palacio Real de Madrid:

Madam

I am ordered by His Majesty my August Sovereign to answer your letter petitioning His Majesty to cause inquiries to be made with regard to your son, Mr John Gillis Butt.

Although His Majesty's embassy in Berlin is charged only with the interests of France & Russia His Majesty being desirous nevertheless, of demonstrating his interest in British subjects, has graciously acceded to your request, and has commanded the Spanish Ambassador in Berlin to communicate with Great Britain's representative there, the United States Ambassador, in order that in conjunction with the latter, the necessary investigations may be made. His Majesty earnestly hopes that these inquiries may be the means of procuring satisfactory information for you.

Inevitably, this offer of regal assistance yielded no further news of Jack.

More than a year since any definitive news had been received, and with the swelling hopes and disappointments of possible sightings yielding naught, Helen resolved to contact Edith Earle, the wife of Jack's commanding officer.

On 16 November 1915, Helen received a letter written from Edith's Eastbourne home promising that she would help in any way possible 'to have news of that dear boy of yours'. Edith agreed that:

> it does seem a curious veiled story – as far as I can make out Max was hit through the head early on the 29th and your son with a stretcher-bearer carried him to a ditch where your son bound or was binding up Max's head wound when a German came and at a range of 3 feet shot the stretcher-bearer through the back. … from what Max remembers his instinct was that your son was shot at the same time and Max lay on top of him. As he said he felt he became very still.

Although this account pointed towards the worst possible news, the words 'from what Max remembers' and 'instinct' left a sufficient space in which forlorn hope could still germinate. Edith also mentioned a Coldstream Guardsman, Private S. Venton, who had been detailed by his platoon commander, Lieutenant Granville Smith, to remain with her husband, and with whom she had corresponded. Smith had reportedly told Venton, 'there's a good fellow stop and look after him'. Venton, whose fate as a prisoner of war was sealed by this order, had recalled that Earle was so 'covered with slime' that he could hardly get a grip on his body. The ditch in which Venton tended the Colonel and watched over his two dead comrades was evidently the stinking drain from the farm.

Edith noted that no trace had been found of the other officers wounded at the same time as her husband – Lieutenant Charles Douglas-Pennant, Captain Guy Rennie and Lieutenant Philip van Neck – but promised to send Helen a map of where she understood the shooting incident had taken place. Although her husband was in the relative safety of captivity, Edith had other burdens to endure. She confided to Helen that 'the child is improving wonderfully but the news of my poor husband is not at all good, he suffers terribly from his head and his leg is quite crippled'. Sadly, Evelyn Earle, her invalid daughter, would die less than two years later.

A flurry of correspondence that had taken place between Lieutenant Colonel Earle and his wife relating to Jack was shared with Helen. On 5 December, Max Earle wrote, 'I wonder if you could see if anything is reported to have happened to Butt who was my doctor, I do not know his initials. … If nothing definite is known of him I am sure he is killed …' On 7 December, Earle wrote, 'my impression is those around me were killed' but 'I only had intervals of consciousness'. On 5 January 1916, he recalled, 'it was my impression he [Butt] was dressing my head and was shot. … I have a recollection of him being very still.' On 6 February, his view was less conclusive: 'it is very difficult to know what happened when I was shot … I remember feeling wet when Butt was doing up my head and looking at my second wound and seeing a lot of mud on my boot.' A week later he veered towards the view that Jack had almost certainly been killed: 'I was still resting against Butt who lay perfectly still and his assistant lay over my legs with his head beside my stomach. I was as sure as anything that both were dead …' Whilst Earle's recollections gave a strong indication that Jack had been killed, there remained sufficient doubt in Helen Butt's mind, arising from the fact that he had admitted to drifting in and out of consciousness during the course of the morning due to his wounds.

Concurrent to Helen Butt's enquiries about her son, the wheels of officialdom sought to grind towards a conclusive resolution of the issue. On 10 December 1915, the War Office contacted Edward Butt, requesting confirmation that no further news had been received by the family. In the absence of any additional information, the official view was that the Army Council 'will be regretfully constrained to conclude that he died on or since [29 October 1914]'. Helen Butt was not yet ready to accept that conclusion. She replied on her husband's behalf on 15 December, pointing out that it was she who had been making all recent enquiries regarding the fate of her son, as her husband was currently 'doing duty' at the Hotel Metropole in Brighton. Helen compiled a summary of the facts that challenged aspects of the official narrative.

• She queried the fact that the battalion was said to have been fighting at Gheluvelt on 29 October 1914. Helen had ascertained that Earle and her son had been at a brickfield some yards from the Kruiseik crossroads and provided a hand-drawn map she had received from Mrs Earle to explain her doubts.
• Furthermore, had Lieutenant Granville Smith, who had ordered Private Venton to remain with the injured Colonel Earle, seen Jack's body, he would have reported this.
• As Mrs Earle had been told by official sources that 'her husband's life had been saved by the stretcher-bearer and by a man in the Coldstream Guards', the possibility remained that the German who had shot the stretcher-bearer had taken Jack prisoner before the Coldstream Guardsmen had arrived. By shooting the stretcher-bearer at close range, it appeared to Helen 'as if he [the German] tried to spare the Doctor in order to capture him'.
• An account received 'about a year ago' from Colonel Corkran of the Grenadier Guards had suggested that Jack had been seen alive on 31 October near Gheluvelt, in German hands.

Mrs Earle had also been passed a letter written by the German surgeon who first dressed her husband's wounds, an epistle that had been written to a family

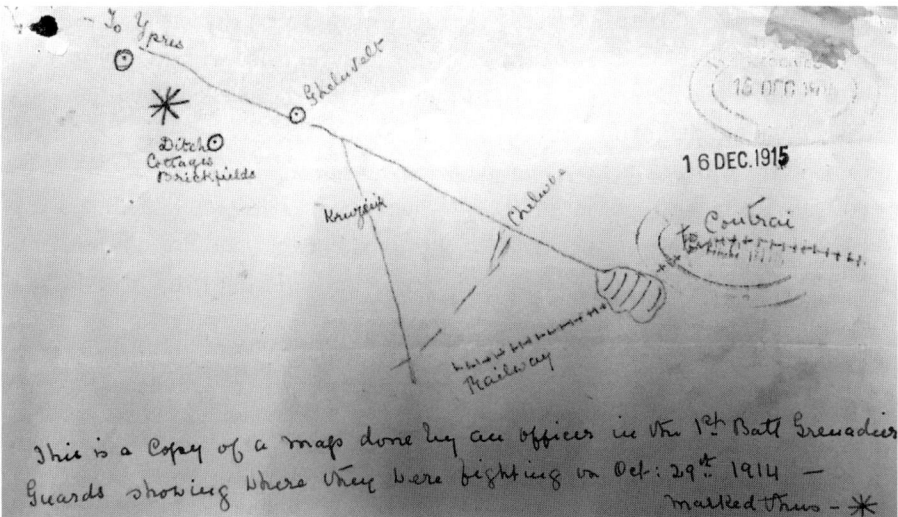

Hand-drawn map showing the location of Jack Butt's death. (*Courtesy Nick Previté*)

friend of the Earles' in Germany. The surgeon recalled: 'An English wounded officer, Lt Col Earle, whom I dressed on the battlefield on 29th Oct 1914 at Gheluvelt about 7 Kilometres east of Ypres asked me to send you news of him.' The delay of over a year in expediting Earle's request had been caused by the surgeon mislaying his pocketbook, recently recovered. The doctor had been attached to Regiment 247 of Reserve (Württemberg) in the 2nd Battalion as assistant surgeon. The battalion had been ordered to advance along the Menin-Ypres high road in the direction of Gheluvelt. Their attack began at the break of day, gaining possession of a road crossing:

> In a house at the 4 cross roads about a kilometre east of Gheluvelt I established a collecting station. In consequence of the artillery and machine gun fire it was not possible to send to rear the wounded. About 9am 2 stretcher-bearers brought me a wounded Englishman [Earle] as well as a soldier who was not wounded [Venton]. They had found them both not far away in a ditch. The officer was shot in the head and right leg, the latter wound being fairly big and very painful. I put on a temporary dressing and lay the officer with our wounded in the house which was somewhat ruined and made him as comfortable as possible.
>
> As the road crossing was an important military point it was under a heavy artillery fire all the day and during a portion of the day it was within the gun fire of the English. The wounded had to remain the whole day in house and could only be moved to the dressing station at night fall. It was here that I handed my wounded to my surgeon. The dressing station was in a farm at Vieux Chien and Lt Col Earle was put in a barn on

some straw with German Officers. The following day we dressed him again. He without doubt suffered much but his general state was good and he was grateful for the treatment. ... I had the feeling that he feared he was mortally wounded, with a kindness that was touching the English soldier showed for the officer, he remained crouching in the most uncomfortable position for hours together in order to help and ease his officer. From what I learnt the man was moved with his master to the rear and not with other prisoners.

Earle had given the surgeon the address of a female family friend in Hamburg to whom he could relay this account. Earle had noted discrepancies between his own recollections and the surgeon's. He had not recalled seeing a German surgeon during the day and had thought it was one of 'his own people' who put him in a house. Earle was taken to Courtrai, where he was placed on the railway station waiting room floor, 'where I suffered from hunger and thirst'. His leg and head wounds were again dressed in the corn market at Courtrai, from where he was removed to Brussels on 11 November, leaving the Belgian capital eight days later. 'I am particularly pleased the surgeon mention Venton's devotion ... a care and attention worthy to be classed with that which a mother shows her child.'

Meanwhile, on 15 December, Helen Butt wrote to Sir Alfred Keogh, recalling their meeting some years previously in Dublin:

[S]o I venture to write to you about my son who has been 'missing' since the 29th of Oct 1914. As he is in the Corps, I would like to make known to you the information that I have had of him from time to time, so I am sending you the enclosed – I did not make these facts known before, as they were so indefinite. ... For some reason I can't explain, I always feel my boy is a prisoner in Belgium, and if the Germans are working him they don't care to let any information of him come through – so I am quite prepared not to get any definite news till the war is over.

It is sad but still I am proud that I had a son to help in this great struggle, and from what Colonel Earle has written of him he did his bit well. I enclose you his photograph – I should like you to see it, these perhaps you would kindly pass it on to the Casualty Department. If it were kept there it might bring forth some more definite information.

The following day, Helen wrote a further letter to Keogh, apologising for troubling him again and enclosing further information that she would be forwarding to the War Office. She persisted in challenging what was becoming the officially accepted version of events, that her son had been shot and killed while tending the wounds of Lieutenant Colonel Earle. On 31 December

1915, she replied to the casualty section of the War Office, having received a letter informing her that 'full lists of missing Soldiers are sent to Germany for distribution in the Camps and Hospitals for ascertaining whether a man is a prisoner of War. Individual enquiries for missing men are accordingly no longer sent to Germany.' Her impression remained that her son had been taken prisoner, alongside Private Venton and Colonel Earle, with the unknown Grenadier medical orderly alone being killed. Therefore, Helen requested that a special enquiry form be sent to Private Venton asking him targeted questions to draw out his precise recollections of that fateful morning. Venton would need to be asked about 'a medical officer' in the ditch, rather than a specific name on the list, 'Lieut J.G. Butt'. Helen had not yet written directly to Private Venton, 'as I think if he were approached officially we would be more likely to get the real facts'.

On 1 January 1916, Private Venton, in a letter to Edith Earle, confirmed he had seen 'the young doctor' and he felt 'confident he was dead'. Venton also recalled Earle being taken to a cottage and given a cigarette by two German officers, but that the wounded officer had lapsed into unconsciousness 'for some hours' after that. Venton had been 'afraid he could not live but he had a good heart'. In response to Helen Butt's plea that Venton be contacted directly by the War Office, he was asked to provide his recollections of 29 October 1914, in particular if he remembered seeing an RAMC officer and a wounded stretcher-bearer near him, and if the medical officer had been taken prisoner at the same time as Venton himself and Colonel Earle. Venton sent his response on 1 February 1916 from Stendal PoW camp:

> Sir
>   In answer to your letter C.2 Casualties 21091/1 I beg to state that on 29th Oct 1914, when I was with Col. M. Earle, Grenadier Guards, I did see a medical officer close to him and who I am convinced was dead, also a medical orderly near him.

Thus, there appeared an inconsistency between two versions of events provided by Venton, written just a month apart. In the first, Jack was 'lying under' Colonel Earle. In the second, he was 'close' to him. This discrepancy was enough for Helen to maintain hope. The War Office was not of the same opinion. On 28 February 1916, Helen was informed that their official conclusion, based on Private Venton's recent testimony, was: 'It is regretted that it would appear to confirm the report of death of Lieutenant Butt.' She was asked if she now wished to acknowledge official acceptance of her son's death. The discrepancies in Venton's reports meant that Helen was not yet willing to accede to this request.

She responded on 2 March, expressing her thanks and gratitude to the Army Council for their 'kind expressions of sympathy on the subject of my missing son'. However, she stated that she thought the statements of Private Venton to be 'not very reliable'. Therefore, she was 'not inclined to place much credence in what he has written in reply to your enquiry'. Helen was 'quite prepared to wait patiently for events to develop which will throw some definite light on the present sad uncertainty'. Helen received a further letter from the War Office on 6 March, stating that 'in accordance with your wishes, no further action will be taken at present'.

A third letter, written by Private Venton to Mrs Earle on 15 April, thanked her for a parcel she had sent him, and for one sent by Colonel Earle's mother, which had contained a book, 'which I think is splendid'. Venton also stated that he had received a letter from Mrs Butt:

> She thinks now that may not have been her son that was near Colonel Earle. I am sorry to say I don't know, under the circumstances it was impossible for me to take any particulars of him, but I have my reason why I felt sure the officer was dead, which I will tell her if I get home some day.

Venton had evidently attempted to spare Helen the grisly specifics of what he had seen, treading an agonising line between the instinct to give conclusive confirmation of death, whilst sparing the lurid details necessary to remove any doubt from the minds of the relatives. This slight equivocation left sufficient space in the mind of Helen Butt to reject the notion that her son was dead.

She contacted the War Office again on 29 May 1916, enclosing a copy of Venton's correspondence. Helen claimed it as proof that Venton's statements 'are not of much value' and therefore she was refusing official recording of her son's death. Helen summarised Colonel Earle's recollections of the incident

– that his head had been resting across Jack's thighs while dressing his head wound, when a German had approached and shot the stretcher-bearer at a range of 3 of 4 feet through the back. As this bullet passed through the orderly it entered Earle's ankle, rendering him unconscious.

Private Venton's narrative had traced the next part of the action, claiming that the Coldstream Guards had passed the ditch on their way up to the front at about 5.30 am. Venton had been told by an officer to fall out and stay with them. Venton and Earle were taken prisoner, and a German doctor who attended to Earle stated that they had been brought to his dressing station by two German stretcher-bearers at about 9.00 am. Helen found it 'strange' that Private Venton had not discussed his version of the incident with Colonel Earle when they were being held prisoner in Brussels, and queried the fact he could so positively assert that he had seen that Jack was dead without providing any further particulars. She had therefore written to Venton asking for specific details about what he had seen; whether the doctor who had been attending Earle had been dark or fair, and to say where he had been hit. This information had not yet been forthcoming.

Helen concluded:

> Venton's letters read untrue and as if he were keeping something back, but it is possible as he is a prisoner that the Germans will not allow him to write the true facts. I still think that my son is alive and that he was likely taken prisoner by the German who shot the stretcher-bearer before Venton came on the scene.

A War Office official drew up a summary of the information gathered thus far: firstly, that the possibility remained that the German who shot the stretcher-bearer had taken Jack prisoner while Colonel Earle had been unconscious; and secondly, that Colonel Corkran, who assumed command of 1st Grenadiers after Earle's capture, had made enquiries about the fate of Lieutenant Butt, and had been told by one of his men that Jack had been seen unwounded with another wounded prisoner in German hands on 31 October near Gheluvelt, but the man who had seen him had subsequently been killed. Rumour swirled around rumour, with each well-meaning attempt to shed light on the course of events serving to further muddy the waters of compiling an accurate account. Two quartermasters in the 1st Grenadiers were stated to have written a year ago to the British Red Cross Society at Boulogne, informing them that Lieutenant Butt was last seen by several men in the battalion walking out towards the firing line with the CO. Nothing had been heard of Jack since he had been reported missing.

It was Earle who was able to provide the denouement in the long search for news of Jack. Due to lingering health problems caused by his wounds, he had been transferred to an open prison, the Pension Morier in the Chateau d'Oex region of Switzerland. Earle had written to the Secretary of the War Office on 30 June 1916, citing the 'gallantry and devotion to duty displayed by Lieutenant J.G. Butt'. He also provided a detailed and definitive account of Jack's death, which he also proposed to send to the Butt family:

> On 29th Oct 1914 1st Bn Gren Gds was holding a line of trenches, about 1 mile east of Gheluvelt near Ypres, running SW from the Ypres-Menin road. Between 5 & 5.45 am I saw from the Bn HQ trench the enemy were successfully attacking the trenches of the unit on my left. I sent my 2nd in Comd to my supporting company to prepare that unit for action & telling the rest of HQrs to remain in the HQ trench, got out myself to see the

ground which was new to me & to observe the enemy with the view of delivering a local counter-attack.

I had, however, not gone far before I was wounded by a stray shot in the head & shortly after fell. When I regained consciousness I found myself in a shallow ditch, my head being dressed by someone, and I saw my Bn sick orderly kneeling at my feet facing me. I enquired who was bandaging me & I recognized the voice of Lt Butt who replied that it was he. I said 'Look out Butt we are well in front & we shall be taken.' He answered that we were all right & begged me to remain still. I cannot say how long I had been unconscious. I presume however from the increased daylight about 15 minutes.

I had some further conversation with Lt Butt when 2 or 3 Germans came up to us. I heard a loud shot 2 or 3 feet away & felt Lt Butt, who was kneeling on his left knee & supporting my head on his right thigh, collapse.

A German then fired down on the back of the sick orderly. The ball passed through the man fell forward onto me. I lay there sometime. I know not how long but never moved or spoke, I subsequently lost consciousness.

My object in writing this is twofold:-

(1) To say that I am convinced that Lt Butt was killed.
(2) To ask, should the Army Council from other evidence be satisfied of Lt Butt's death, if a letter can be sent in the name of the Army Council to Lt Butt's relatives expressing approval of his self-sacrifice in helping his Comd Off.

I was able when in hospital in Germany to get home through a private channel the names of certain officers under me who had distinguished themselves in action during the previous days of fighting & these names I now find appeared in dispatches. I purposely did not name Lt Butt because his action was a personal one to me.

I believe that when I spoke to Lt Butt the enemy had already passed over us.

I further believe that as a British counter attack was seen approaching and the Germans deliberately tried to kill all the officers & men of the Bn over whom they had passed & that I am the only survivor of the episode. The counter attack did reach me & I have some slight recollection of being taken to a hut … by my own people.

I feel that Lt Butt's action was most brave in that he went out to tend me & stopped by me when he might have escaped. I consider he gave his life for mine. I hold the view however that in so exposing himself he was not acting in the best interest of the service.

I know not if the Army Council accept this view but I feel certain that they will admit that Lt Butt's conduct was of great personal bravery & self-sacrifice and consequently thoroughly in keeping with the best tradition of the RAMC. I therefore hope that a suitable letter may be sent to Lt Butt's relations.

The delay in making this report is due to my having only been sent to this country from Germany a month ago & to my having been somewhat suffering since my arrival.

I have not communicated with Lt Butt's relations. I am about to write to them now but I shall not mention that I have written to you.

I beg to be excused for writing to you direct. The incident is somewhat a personal one, it took place a long time ago, I am in a somewhat unusual position here & the ordinary channels of communication have, owing to the fortunes of war, been a good deal changed … since I was shot.

The following day, Earle wrote to Helen Butt, giving further contextual detail of the events leading to her son's death. On the evening of 28 October 1914, Earle had selected a venue for his headquarters near a spot that intelligence information had told him was due to be attacked the following morning. A small trench had been dug. Between 5.00 and 5.20 am he noticed that the regiment on his left was being heavily attacked and was in fact giving way. Earle left his trench to get a better view of the battlefield, and 'walked some little way', leaving Butt in the trench.

I was then struck in the head by a stray shot and soon fell. I believe your son saw me fall and at once came with his orderly to my assistance. I believe shortly after he reached me the Germans were rushing over where I lay with your son and his orderly and we were not touched.

Earle went on to explain that some time later he had heard a gunshot close to his head:

and I felt your son collapse … I am sure he was killed instantaneously for he never spoke to me or moved. … I sincerely wish that I could hold out to you any hope of it being otherwise. I consider that he was murdered in cold blood contrary to all laws and customs of civilized warfare. … It was just like him not to think of himself but to expose himself and sacrifice himself for another. Though I had known him but about 5 weeks I in common with all my officers had learnt to like and admire him very much. We had been in close action from 19th to 26th during the greater part of which he had been incessantly at work day and night. We all recognised his devotion and skill.

Earle was keenly aware of the fretfulness the word 'missing' could produce, and therefore was earnest in his desire to deliver the fatal news directly to Helen:

I always feel in war the worst thing for friends and relations at home is to have a loved one 'missing'. The hoping against hope must be terrible. This uncertainty I fear must have been your lot through many, many months. Of course I cannot say that I saw your boy dead but I cannot disguise from you the fact that I can hold out no hope that he survived that morning. Would that I could say to you that perhaps he was only insensible and that he was taken prisoner. He had his 2 red cross brassards, that I know and of course he had his officers' uniform. I or Venton must have heard of him if he had been taken to a field hospital. It is I fear quite impossible that he could have been hidden away in Germany without the knowledge of the American Ambassador who has I think done good service for the British.

He had hoped to have been able to deliver this tragic news to Helen in person, but despite the relatively lenient terms of his captivity, which would allow him to have his family over to Switzerland to visit, and to take a house in that country until the end of the war, he was not permitted to return to England. 'I wish that I was allowed to go home in order that I might tell you this sad story which is painful to me to write, and must be still more painful to you to read, but this cannot be.'

Earle's keen awareness of the agonies of uncertainty pertaining to men lost in battle had its roots in his own personal bereavement:

I lost a brother in the Cape War and although I was fighting on the same field I was never able to obtain really definitive news of his end and I know the feeling that always kept coming over me that it must be a mistake, someone thought he fell, he might be mistaken for someone else etc etc. I fear you know only too well all the hopes, doubts and fears. I, of all men, who owe your son so much, would willingly be spared telling you that I can hold out no hope to you.

Let me say that you have my very deepest sympathy, I know only too well how empty these words are and how nothing that I can say or write can alleviate your loss and sorrow.

In a later account, given to the War Office after his release from captivity, Earle emphasised that his RMO had been the victim of a war crime:

The lieutenant was wearing Red Cross armlets when I saw him last, a few minutes before I was first hit; it was then sufficiently light to see 150 yards though the morning was misty. ... Lieut. Butt, owing to his armlets and to the position he was in, kneeling and supporting my head, could not have been mistaken for anybody but a doctor tending a wounded man. I can offer no reason for his murder, unless it was that a counter-attack was either feared or seen approaching.

Earle recorded that his own greatcoat, jacket, shirt and vest were taken by the Germans, but that thanks to the presence of Private Venton, his watch and money were not stolen.

More than a year and a half had passed since Jack Butt had been reported missing. During that time his parents had contacted the Red Cross Wounded and Missing Bureau, the Director General of Army Medical Services, the King of Spain, relatives of other troops, eyewitnesses to his final known moments and the War Office. No stone had been left unturned in their extended quest to ascertain news of their dear son. That period of unbearable uncertainty had come to an end.

On 20 July 1916, the Military Secretary of the War Office wrote to Helen, informing her that 'information has now been received from Colonel M. Earle which makes it clear that Lieutenant J.G. Butt of the Royal Army Medical Corps was killed on the 29th October 1914'. Helen replied the following day, accepting the inevitable: 'I fear there can no longer be any doubt of my son's death, so you may consider him killed on Oct 29th 1914.' She implored that Jack's name be kept out of the casualty lists in the newspapers, in order to avoid the triggering of a second wave of sympathy letters 'which I would rather avoid'. Jack's loss would be keenly felt amongst a wider circle of friends and family, but the stress that his mother had endured had taken a heavy toll on her health. She would not live to see the end of the war in which her only son had become an early and inexcusable casualty.

Charles Attwood

'Your son was one of those whose life was blotted out by this dastardly method'

The actions of the Canadian Division at the Second Battle of Ypres had been met with acclaim, their courage and tenacity in holding the Gravenstafel Ridge in the face of a fearsome envelopment of chlorine gas establishing the reputation of the dominion's troops as worthy warriors. The cost had been high: 6,500 casualties, 2,000 of them fatal. Far away from war's horrors, at Somerton's police station, consternation was mounting about the cessation in the steady flow of letters that Superintendent Henry Attwood and his wife Emma had been receiving from their eldest son, Charles. Rather than impotently await news, Henry wrote to the Canadian Record Office in London for information. His worst fears were confirmed on 8 May when a telegram was received informing him of Charles's death, the news having been reported by the 8th Canadian Infantry Battalion's adjutant on 1 May. Henry and Emma readily accepted the veracity of the communication, and the sad news of Charles's death was reported in the local press.

The *Western Chronicle* of 21 May reported:

KILLED IN ACTION
We regret to report the death of Private Charles Attwood, who was killed in action in the recent fighting in France. The fallen hero was the eldest son of Superintendent Attwood of the Somerton Police Force. He enlisted at the beginning of the war, coming across the Atlantic with the Canadian contingent. Deep sympathy is extended to the bereaved family in their great sorrow.

The *Central Somerset Gazette* of 28 May 1915, in a fuller report, described Charles's passing as a 'gallant death', and the 'heavy blow which has fallen' on the Attwood family. Charles had been 'doing well as a printer' in his new life in Canada. He had been a 'regular correspondent' whose letters were 'always cheery and full of patriotic spirit that inspires men of the British armies'. The 'official intimation of regret that Charles Attwood had been killed in action near Ypres on the 23rd April [was] received with much sorrow in Somerton, where Pte Attwood was well known and popular. He was an excellent athlete and member of the Somerton Rifle Club. He made many friends in Canada, as well as his native land.'

Emma Attwood needed little convincing that Charles had died during the gas attack at Ypres, maintaining throughout her life that she had heard his voice call 'Mother' at the moment of his passing. However, the lack of definitive information of the circumstances of his death and the yearning to know his final resting place continued to gnaw away at them. Four months after Charles had been killed, Emma wrote a letter requesting such details be provided, and whether she could receive any personal effects of Charles's that had survived the fighting on Gravenstafel Ridge. This message was passed on to the battalion's adjutant, Captain O'Grady, who responded on 2 October 1915:

Dear Madam
I have made inquiries and have been able to obtain the following information regarding your gallant boy whose death we all immensely regret.

He died as a result of gas & poisoning following the attack made upon our line on April 24th, where as a prelude, volumes of poisonous gas drifted across our lines, choking and suffocating those who were unprepared to withstand it. Your son was one of those whose life was blotted out by this dastardly method.

We were unable to procure any of his sentimental effects, as in the rush and confusion of attack, counter-attack and retirement it was impossible to attend to the numerous dead. Every effort was made to pay our last respects to our fellow comrades but in no instance were we able to obtain any of personal effects.

The brave fellows who survived were so weary that they cast aside all but the barest necessities. ...

Extending to you my heartfelt sympathy in your bereavement I am,

Yours truly

O'Grady had given emphasis to the fact that Charles's comrades would have 'made every effort to pay our last respects' to assuage Emma's torment, whilst making abundantly clear the impossibility of arranging a formal burial in the circumstances that had pertained during the attack.

Henry and Emma's craving to learn more of the circumstances of their son's death, and the faint hope that his body may have an identified grave, continued into 1916. On 14 January, Henry received a letter sent on behalf of the Lieutenant Colonel i/c records of the CEF, based in Westminster House, Millbank, London. The missive could only reiterate previously provided information:

Dear Sir

I beg to repeat the following official report, which has been received from the Officer Commanding 8th Battalion in connection with the regretted death of the soldier named in the margin (No. 26 Pte. C. Attwood 8th Battalion).

'I have caused enquiries to be made in connection with the death of the marginally noted man, and I am informed that Pte. Attwood died on the morning of April 24th from the effects of the gas the Germans were using. A few moments after the gas cloud passed over, Pte. Attwood was seen by his comrades lying at the bottom of the parapet dead. The trench this company were in was evacuated later and fell into the hands of the Germans, so that the body was not buried by us.'

I am sorry to say that no report of burial has been received from any other sources.

Charles's military record curtly noted, 'Body not recovered for burial'. There was little else his family could do except mourn his passing in the knowledge his body lay somewhere in Flanders soil. Henry Attwood would articulate the emotional attachment he felt to the land of his son's death by donating money to support the welfare of Belgian refugees, but this altruistic act would not protect him from further heartache. The IWGC would not identify Charles's body when they undertook the removal of battlefield corpses following the cessation of war. The faint hope held by Henry and Emma Attwood that there might be a grave to visit in the foreign field where their son had perished was extinguished. All that remained were memories and the hope of a heavenly reunion for the God-fearing Attwoods.

Jim Attwood, who disappeared in mysterious circumstances. (*Courtesy Robin Williams*)

Just as Alfred and Elizabeth Pope would have to bear the heartache of two of their sons having no known grave, so Henry and Emma Attwood would experience further anguish over the disappearance of Charles's younger brother James. 'Jim' Attwood had joined the Merchant Navy in 1916, aged 17. His war record was distinguished, serving in seventeen missions transporting explosives from the USA to Britain, dodging German U-boats in the Atlantic. He had served on board the *Escalona* and the *New York City*, earning the British War Medal on account of having served for six months or more at sea between 1914 and 1918, with the addition of the Mercantile Marine Medal due to having made voyages through a designated danger zone.

The *Western Chronicle* of 22 August 1919 recorded Jim's rapid rise through the ranks:

SOMERTON. Early Promotion. —Mr. Jim Attwood, son of Superintendent Attwood, has been appointed to the rank of fourth officer in the Merchant Service. This is somewhat a record. Mr. Jim Attwood is only 20 years of age, and has only just completed three years out of his four-year apprenticeship. He is one of the youngest officers in the Mercantile Marine.

Jim continued to serve on the *Escalona* following the conclusion of the war, before working on board various vessels owned by the Bermuda and West Indies Steamship Co. and the Pan American Petroleum and Transport Co., carrying cargo and passengers between the Caribbean, Mexico and New York. In April 1920, Jim applied to become a naturalised American citizen, and in May 1923, his final recorded voyage took place as a cook on board the *George W. Barnes*, sailing from Tampico Mexico into New York.

In June 1925, Jim wrote to his younger brother Henry from South Street, New York City. He held out the prospect of a job that could be arranged by a friend, 'Bill'. Employment would be available 'as soon as you hit N.Y.' However, this job would not be directly with Bill 'as things are rather slack with the "R.R.s" until the weather gets a little bad outside'. Nevertheless, it would pay around $7.50 per hour (an hourly rate of over $110 dollars at 2019 value). Henry was to bring a little money with him as Jim 'might not be in town when you arrive, as very often we pull out on a minute's notice'. The potentially generous remuneration on offer for a young man setting foot in New York, the fact that Jim and his associates had to remove themselves from the city at short notice and the reference to 'R.R' (Rum Running) suggests that Jim had become involved in the illegal smuggling of alcohol into Prohibition America.

News of Jim dried up in September 1927, his last communication being a postcard sent from Saint Pierre and Miquelon. The French-owned territory, an archipelago situated in the Gulf of St Lawrence near to the south-western coast of Newfoundland, had become a hotbed of alcohol smuggling during the 1920s, with over 1.5 million gallons of Canadian whisky being shipped into the USA annually. US coastguards were keenly aware of the practice, and deadly games of cat and mouse would occur between them and the Rum Runners, often with fatal results.

Twelve years after the disappearance of one son in tragically heroic circumstances, Henry and Emma Attwood were to experience further years of torment over the uncertain fate of their second son. One promising lead was a letter sent by a Virginian lady, Pearl Trimmer, who, like the Attwoods, was searching for news of her beloved 'Jimmy'. Henry and Emma were as keen to learn what she knew of Jim's life as she was to seek information from Somerset. She wrote them a long letter on 30 January 1929, which provided them with an insight into his final years.

Pearl was 'more than sorry that you have not heard from Jimmy as yet'. She went on to explain that she had first met him in September 1926 when he was 'working on a boat that went from New York to some place south of Florida'. On one trip his boat had experienced engine trouble and docked at Norfolk

City, Virginia, for repairs. Jim Attwood and his associates were forced to stay in the city 'for quite some time'. Pearl disclosed that 'he and I got be more than just friends'. In fact, Jim had asked her to marry him, with the couple planning to become engaged in the spring of 1927. He had left Norfolk in February, eventually reaching New York in April, and had made the time to visit Pearl.

At this time, he had wired his parents to send him money, which Pearl had found puzzling, 'as he to my knowledge was getting along fine and was not wanting for anything'. Then Jim had set off for what Pearl believed would be his final voyage before returning to Virginia to collect her before they both began a new life together in Britain. She continued to hear from him until September 1927, when the boat he was on 'went to an island some place above Canada'. After a lacuna in communication from Jim, Pearl feared that 'maybe he had transferred his affections to someone else and so I tried to forget him, which was impossible'. As he had not written to her for the forwarding of his personal effects, she endeavoured to trace Jim's whereabouts, which had led her to write to his parents. The anxiety over Jim's disappearance was now shared on both sides of the Atlantic. 'I can't express just how I feel, knowing that you too have not heard from him … my heart is full and I am more than anxious to hear from you.' Pearl treasured her memories of him, and of the photographs of his family he had entrusted to her.

The fact that Jim had urgently needed money despite benefitting from seemingly lucrative employment would suggest that he had encountered business troubles, possibly incurring a debt that needed swift repayment, as he was known to be poor at handling money. On 12 September 1929, Emma Attwood wrote to Daniel Miller, the American vice-consul to the UK, who replied eleven days later. Miller's suggestion was that the family contact the United States Shipping Commissioner with detailed information of the vessels Jim was known to have sailed on. Henry Attwood acted on this advice but received a reply from the commissioner stating that a consultation of his records had 'fail[ed] to disclose any information regarding the whereabouts of Mr Attwood'.

The Attwoods continued their search for news of Jim for many years. On 7 July 1933, T.L. Petty, the Inspector of Detectives at the Division of Police Detective Bureau in the City of Norfolk, Virginia, wrote to Emma Attwood to report that one of his officers had managed to trace Pearl Trimmer, who was now married to a James Brady. The information relayed was thus: 'She states that James Attwood was in Norfolk, Virginia, from July 13th to Nov 26th 1926, and during that time he called to see her several times. She further states that she has not seen him since nor does she know where he is.'

In June 1936, Emma Attwood contacted the headquarters of the Salvation Army, which placed an appeal in the American edition of *War Cry* seeking news of Jim, but none was forthcoming. The trail was running cold. Henry was forced to accept the conclusion that his second missing son had either been shot on sight by US coastguards while engaged in smuggling illicit alcohol into America, or that he had been assassinated for failing to honour a debt. No record of his death has ever been found. Henry Attwood lived until 1956, dying at the grand age of 89. His policeman's lot was not a happy one, with his later years being spent caring for his granddaughter Jean after his daughter Edith's premature demise aged 49. Despite this, family members who remember him recall a kind, warm-hearted man.

The loss of Charles and Jim is still felt keenly within the family to this day. Charles had died nobly, his memory appropriately honoured and his sacrifice memorialised. Jim had vanished in suspicious and probably ignoble circumstances. Nonetheless, ties of kinship meant his loss was felt no less intensely. In 1986, the brothers' niece, Robin Williams, took her daughter Nicola to visit Langemark, in the vicinity of where Charles had perished in 1915, an experience she found 'deeply, deeply moving'. Yet there was still an unfulfilled yearning to know precisely where Charles fell. Additionally, Robin has made extensive enquiries to fill the hole in the family's knowledge of the fate of her Uncle Jim. Scraps of evidence have come to light, but nothing that definitively lays to rest the memory of Jim Attwood. After decades of ambiguity, this family, like so many others, are yet to attain a sense of closure over the loss of their loved ones.

Percy Pope

'I am so sorry to be unable to give you any news about your laddie.'

The telegram that would devastate Dorchester's Pope family, and instigate months of arduous effort trying to trace Second Lieutenant Percy Paris Pope of 1st Battalion Welsh Regiment, was sent from the War Office at 9.20 am on 9 October 1915, arriving at the Dorchester Telegraph Office at 10.16 am:

Regret to inform you that 2nd Lieut P.P. Pope Welsh Regt is reported missing Between Oct 1st and 4th.
This does not necessarily mean he is wounded or killed.
Secy
War Office.

This was both inconclusive and disturbing. If Percy was not killed or wounded, where was he? If he had been wounded, had he been taken to a British or

German military hospital? If he had been killed, why the doubt as to his fate? Alfred set to work to find answers to these questions. Four days after the receipt of the telegram, the War Office wrote assuring him that should any further news of Percy emerge, it would at once be communicated to him.

Meanwhile, Alfred engaged in a flurry of anxious correspondence between surviving members of the 1st Welsh Battalion and the relatives of those reported missing. One of his first correspondents was Lieutenant A. Holt, who, still serving with the battalion, confidently asserted: 'Your son was reported missing, but I am very pleased to say that he has since been reported as having passed through a Clearing Hospital.'

Whilst hoping that Alfred would, in the meantime, have received a letter from Percy, Lieutenant Holt had no further corroborating information regarding the clearing hospital.

'We do not know, once wounded, what Hospital or where they are sent so that I regret I cannot give you any further information.

'I trust your son is doing well & that his wound was not serious. ... I was very fond of your boy.'

Meanwhile, Percy's mother, Elizabeth, had written to Lieutenant Colonel Hoggan, the battalion's commanding officer. Hoggan had been evacuated to Scotland following the actions of 1–3 October at the Hohenzollern Redoubt. Writing precisely three weeks after he had seen over a third of his battalion wiped out, Hoggan regretted that 'I am so sorry to be unable to give you any news about your laddie.'

Hoggan's recollection was that Percy was amongst those overwhelmed in the final rush of German bombers on 2 October, proffering the view that he 'must' have been taken prisoner. Whilst this information would have given Alfred and Elizabeth Pope a firm hope that their son would one day return, it stood in confusing contradiction to Lieutenant Holt's assertion that Percy was safe in a British military hospital.

Hoggan advised it could take up to three weeks before news would reach England, but in the meantime a letter to the battalion's adjutant might elicit word from those who had fought alongside Percy. Hoggan enclosed a detailed account of the assault on Little Willie trench during which Percy had gone missing, providing further leads that Alfred and Elizabeth would investigate during the autumn and winter of 1915/16. Acting upon Hoggan's advice, a letter was sent from South Court on 31 October to Captain Edward W. Bryan, 1st Welsh's adjutant. By the middle of November, the battalion had been transferred to Salonika and Bryan sent a hastily written letter on army filing paper. Having consulted his records, Bryan's stated: '[Y]our son P.P. Pope was wounded on 1st Oct during the attack on "Little Willie" trench which adjoins the Hohenzollern Redoubt on the North Side. From records I find that he was evacuated from the 85th Field Ambulance on 2nd October and after that date I cannot trace his movements.'

Bryan had interviewed Percy's batman, who claimed to have visited the Casualty Clearing Station in Bethune, where he was informed that Percy had left about ten minutes before his arrival. The man handed Percy's pack to an orderly then returned to the battalion to relay the news. From the clearing station, once remedial treatment had been given, a man would be passed down the line to a field ambulance. Bryan had received notification from No. 85 Field Ambulance that Percy had been assigned to them on or around 5 October, two days after the 1st Welsh's retirement from the old British front-line trench.

The adjutant had also gleaned 'from various sources' that Percy had been wounded in the lower jaw and leg, 'both gunshot wounds'. Bryan's summation was: 'In all probability PPP is now in some hospital in England, or if not sufficiently recovered to move, is still in hospital in France.' He apologised that he was unable 'to further relieve your very natural anxiety' but hoped that by the time his letter reached Dorchester more definite news would have emerged.

The shock of learning that Percy had been doubly wounded was tinged with the relief at the firm testimony, albeit at third-hand, that he was under the professional care of a named RAMC unit.

Captain Bryan explained to Alfred the difficulty in providing definitive information from confused recollections:

> The trouble is that, during an action, the wounded have to take care of themselves (for obvious reasons) until they can be collected. What happened was that your son probably walked or crawled back to the trenches of another unit and was passed back by them. He did not pass through our own Medical Officer's hands.

Bryan signed off: 'your son was greatly esteemed by us all, and we that are left, hope for his speedy recovery and safe return to us.'

Spurred on by the suggestion that Percy had been admitted to No. 85 Field Ambulance, Alfred duly made enquiries of that unit. However, a letter sent from France on 20 December proved a hammer blow: 85 FA's commanding officer, Lieutenant Colonel J.R. Whait, maintained that he could 'find no trace of his having passed through to this Field Ambulance & therefore can give you no information about him'. The unit had not been in the Vermelles area at the time of Percy's disappearance, having handed over to No. 6 Field Ambulance on 1 October. It was possible that he had been received by that unit. Another possibility was that Percy had been evacuated to a prisoner hospital, therefore that a communication to the Director General of Medical Services would be in order, as names of all wounded officers were passed to him. Finally, Whait hoped that Percy would not suffer permanent damage from his wounds, his battalion having done 'splendid work' despite being 'badly hit'.

A further enquiry to the commanding officer of No. 33 CCS, which had been operating behind the 1st Welsh lines in early October, evinced the reply that 'I regret there is no trace of your son 2nd Lieut P.P. Pope having been through this Clearing Station.' Alfred's letter was passed on to other clearing stations in the vicinity, but this had proved fruitless, as a subsequent brief note sent from the O/C No. 33 CCS informed him. Alfred sent a further letter on 10 December, instigating additional enquiries amongst military hospitals and field ambulances, but no one had been able to trace Percy or his kit.

Whilst unit records stated that Percy had passed into the hands of the RAMC, others of his comrades thought he had been taken prisoner. Pursuing a line of enquiry via Cox & Company, a firm that managed the financial affairs of many army officers, Alfred had been given the address of the hospital in which Lieutenant Arthur Toller, one of the officers listed as 'wounded' on Hoggan's report on 1–3 October, was convalescing. Elizabeth Pope wrote for information, receiving a reply from Toller on 22 October. Frustratingly, Toller was only able to provide second-hand information that had come his way: that Percy had been wounded on the night of 1–2 October when the 1st Welsh had made their charge and taken the trenches of Hohenzollern Redoubt and Little Willie. The suggestion that Percy had been wounded in the initial assault stood in contradiction of Hoggan's belief that he had been injured when the Germans had rushed the communication trench on the afternoon of 2 October.

Toller explained that the wounded had to be left behind when the battalion was forced to retire, at about 4.00 pm on 2 October as, 'if we had taken our wounded back it would have had to be across the open, which as you can see means not only certain death to the stretcher-bearers but also to their patient.' He saw 'no reason why you shouldn't have every hope of hearing from him in, say, a fortnight's time – as he is I think undoubtedly "wounded & a prisoner"'.

Given that eventuality, Percy's prospects looked relatively positive as:

What may be more reassuring than anything to you is the fact that of late the Germans have been known to treat our prisoners very so much more kindly – especially those who are wounded – and the Bavarians (who were opposite us) have never been anything like so unkind as the Prussians – around whom nearly all the stories of atrocities centre.

Arthur Toller had been a Charterhouse School contemporary of Percy's brother Jack, and had therefore become a 'great friend' of Percy's when serving in the same battalion. Despite his wounds, Toller was 'getting on well & hope to get the operation over in a few days from now on my leg'.

Another convalescing member of 1st Welsh to receive a letter from Elizabeth Pope was Lieutenant Weber. Weber wrote from his bed at the Royal Free Hospital that he could provide little information but expected that Percy had been taken prisoner on the night of 1 October 'with a good many other fellows'. Weber continued in optimistic vein: 'I think you will find he is alright as I hear the Germans on this day were treating our wounded and prisoners very well indeed. I sincerely hope you will hear from him soon and that he will be alright as he was one of the best of good fellows.'

Reassuringly, Weber advised, 'If taken prisoner you will always have the consolation of knowing that he will not be back in the firing line.' Weber requested that Alfred inform him when, not if, news was heard of Percy. He suggested that many prisoners would write on the back of a cheque when communicating with their friends at home, so to be watchful of any financial transactions in Percy's name.

The letter concluded with a hint at the seriousness of Weber's injuries:

I have written the above at Lieut Weber's dictation as he cannot manage to write yet. I am his fiancée.

M.E. Morgan

Fired with the suggestion from two sources that Percy may have been taken prisoner, Alfred and Elizabeth Pope noted the contents of a bulletin issued from General Headquarters in France on 23 November 1915, circulated in the British press, stating that Lieutenant Alfred M. Hazell of 1st Welsh Battalion was 'Previously reported missing, now reported wounded and prisoner of war'. Hazell had previously served as a lance corporal in the 1st Canadian Divisional Cyclists, being awarded the 1914–15 Star before being gazetted as a temporary second lieutenant in August 1915 and transferred from the Canadian Expeditionary Force to the 1st Welsh.

Alfred found Hazell's Monmouthshire address and wrote to his wife, Daisy. She replied on 12 December, assuring Alfred and Elizabeth they 'have my deepest sympathy in this trouble [sic] time of anxiety and suspense'. She was unable to provide news of Percy, whom she confirmed had been alongside her husband on 2 October, the day he had been wounded and taken prisoner. Daisy had written to her husband three weeks previously, asking for any information about not only Percy, but Captain Warren, Lieutenant Davies and Major Hobbs, but she was not expecting a swift reply, as it had already taken a month for previous letters to reach her husband.

Five weeks later, another letter from Daisy was received at South Court, apologising for having held off writing due to a lack of communication from her husband. She still held out hope that 'I shall have some good news for you and the relatives of the other missing officers in my next letter'. A stream of letters was passing between the relatives of those men wounded, missing or taken, with Daisy having just received a letter from the mother of Lieutenant Davies.

Daisy's next letter was sent on 7 February 1916, with Alfred and Elizabeth 'still in suspense with respect to your missing son'. Sadly, she confirmed that her imprisoned husband 'was unable to give me any news of any of the other "missing officers", as he was rather badly wounded in the head and did not remember anything after being "hit"'. Daisy thought it would be odd if he were the only captured battalion officer who had managed to make contact with his family whilst others were not able to. Despite this hint that there were no other 1st Welsh officers being held by the Germans, Daisy thought it 'more than likely that your son is a prisoner only no doubt badly wounded and unable to send to you'. Whether this was her true belief, or she did not want to be the person who gave the stark reality four months since Percy and the others went missing, it is hard to tell. If Percy were in such a badly wounded state, many more months of anxiety and suspense would await the Popes. Still, the War Office had not received official news from Germany as to her husband's location, even though she had been receiving letters from him. Daisy passed on the address of the camp – Fürstenberg-in-Mecklenburg.

A fortnight later, Daisy wrote thanking Alfred for the *Daily Mail* photographs of his serving sons. Her husband had been able to confirm that he and Percy had been in the same company and were together 'on the fateful afternoon'. However, he had not seen Percy once the attack had begun. Daisy agreed to visit addresses that Alfred had requested, presumably in the South Wales area, of relatives of members of 1st Welsh also lost that day. She would also undertake to visit members of the battalion convalescing locally, including a Private R. Lewis. Alas, these enquiries yielded no further news of Percy's fate.

While the correspondence with Daisy Hazell was ongoing, Alfred once again wrote to Lieutenant Colonel Hoggan, who replied from his home in Colinton, Midlothian, on 12 January 1916 that he was 'so grieved to hear you have heard nothing more of your brave laddie Percy'. Hoggan had received no further news of any of the missing men previously under his command, and bemoaned the reluctance of the German authorities to pass on news of prisoners: 'It is a most ghastly & heartrending war, void of chivalry. The Germans pride themselves in frightfulness and withhold news of prisoners for this purpose.'

Pursuing the prisoner of war line of enquiry, Alfred corresponded with Robert Davies, father of Second Lieutenant Griffith Davies, another missing officer. A resident of Blaenau Ffestiniog, North Wales, Mr Davies had, like Alfred, searched for information from the prison camps of Germany, but:

> Up to now I have received no news that he is a 'Prisoner of War' but on the contrary I received a card from Amsterdam yesterday informing me that although searching enquiries had been made in Germany, they have proved futile. It appears from the card that I am to expect a fuller reply from the 'International Agency Geneva'.

Davies was in communication with several agencies, including the Queen Victoria Jubilee Fund Association, Geneva, who had circulated his son's photograph through all the hospitals and camps in Germany and Belgium. Sympathising with the Popes in the trying circumstances, Mr Davies was gradually succumbing to despair: 'I very often feel that we shall never see him again, but at other times we try our best to keep up, and to continue hoping for some good news. Should we receive any further clue as to the fate of any of our sons I shall communicate with you directly.'

In a further letter in early January, Davies lamented: '[T]he reports are conflicting. One was to the effect that Capt Warren & two other wounded officers, one believed to be 2nd Lieut T.J.C. Davies were captured. Another was Lieut Davies is a prisoner of War with Capt Warren & Hobbs who were taken in a trench retaken by the Germans after bombing.'

Mr Davies had been in communication with the parents of Captain Warren and Lieutenant T.J.C. Davies, and passed on their addresses to Alfred, whilst commending him that 'your family has contributed nobly to the cause of our Country'.

Robert Davies proved as unrelenting, ingenious and assiduous as Alfred and Elizabeth Pope in attempting to find a trace of his son. He wrote to a friend, a lieutenant in the Royal Engineers serving in France, who made enquiries on his behalf. This had turned up an account from Sergeant E.J. Morgan, Company Sergeant Major of A Company of 1st Welsh. Writing from Salonika on 13 December 1915, Morgan recounted that:

> 2nd Lieut Griffith Davies was shot in the stomach during the Charge at Vermelles about 8pm the 1st Oct.
> A couple of men of his Coy offered to take him back ... but he refused and told them to go on. Our Battalion took the German trench but they could not spare any men to look after the wounded that night, about four pm the following afternoon the Hun drove our fellows out and they

had to fall back on the old line. So Mr Davies was left out, what has become of him I don't know.

Remaining yours sincerely E.J. Morgan

Sadly, Mr Davies had taken that piece of news as final confirmation that his son must have subsequently died from those wounds, adrift from his comrades and without succour. The tragedy was magnified by the fact that owing to the lack of men that night to collect the wounded, they were left unattended on the battlefield. For Griffith Davies's family, 'Our hope that we shall see him again is rather remote, as I am afraid that the Germans will not take any trouble with the seriously wounded of our men.' After wishing the Popes good luck, Robert Davies signed off with the statement, 'I remain in sad bereavement'.

On 18 November 1915, Mrs Kathleen Warren wrote to Alfred on paper bordered with the black of mourning. Her son, Captain James Warren, had, like Percy, been attached to the 1st Welsh from 3rd Welsh and had been reported missing following the action of 1–2 October. From her five-storey terraced Hampstead town house, Kathleen, the wife of church missionary the Reverend John Warren, wrote thanking Alfred for the loan of a copy of Lieutenant Colonel Hoggan's report of the action. Mrs Warren had given up hope of her son being found alive, as she beseeched Alfred to pass on his name to Major Alec Pope of 3rd Welsh, who was undertaking searches in the area for Percy. Mrs Warren hoped that Alec 'might possibly come across [her son's] grave in looking for his brother' in the area of La Bassée. Any searches Alec may have undertaken proved as fruitless as those in search of Percy, as James Warren's body was never recovered.

On 18 January 1916, Mrs Agnes Davies, whose 'dear boy', Second Lieutenant T.J.C. Davies of 1st Welsh, was also missing, wrote to Alfred Pope. She had seen the *Daily Mail* report of his several serving sons, noting that Cyril Pope had been taken prisoner in November 1914. Agnes bemoaned the lack of news she had received since the initial missing telegram. Piteously, Agnes implored Alfred to 'Forgive me for troubling you but I am his mother & he is my only son'. Alfred responded promptly to Agnes's plea, as three days later another letter was sent to South Court, this time from her husband, John Davies, thanking him for having forwarded letters from other 1st Welsh family members. Alfred had also proudly included the photo sheet of his sons in military service, prompting the laudatory comment of 'an outstanding instance of loyalty & devotion'. Mr Davies had shown the photographs to a 1st Welsh sergeant, who had been immediately able to identify Percy, but supplied no further information beyond that previously given 'that they were all left in a trench & must be prisoners'. The sergeant had relayed that Percy was in B Company whilst he had been in A, and could not recall many members of Percy's company, being a former South Wales Borderer who had not been long attached to 1st Welsh.

Davies forwarded correspondence received from Mrs Hazell and Mrs R. Davies. Still the flicker of hope remained amongst families in limbo, with Davies mentioning an acquaintance who had not heard from a family member missing since May 1915 but who was 'not at all despondent as it is well known that no letters are allowed to come through from the War Zone & there are over 500 British Officers in and around Brussels'.

Davies drew comfort from the fact that Daisy Hazell heard from her husband 'only by a lucky chance, with speculation that the letter had somehow been smuggled out or escaped the vigilance of the Germans'. Although still hopeful, for Davies, 'time is dragging on & it is weary waiting'. Despite holding out the hope that 20-year-old Thomas John Carlyle Davies might have been taken prisoner, eventually John and Agnes were forced to accept that he too had died in the same action as Percy, his body never to find an acknowledged resting place.

The final piece of correspondence kept by Alfred Pope from a relative of a 1st Welsh officer was sent on 30 March 1916 by Lieutenant Colonel (retired) Arthur Hobbs. Hobbs wrote to Alfred, thanking him for his 'kind letter' and expressing sympathy 'in regard to the fate of our sons'. Arthur had received a telegram stating his son, Major Arthur Hobbs, who was second in command of the 1st Welsh, was '"wounded and missing" but not a word from them since'. Like Alfred and Elizabeth, Arthur Hobbs had spared no effort in attempting to trace news of his son, making 'every enquiry possible such as British Red X, Queen Victoria Jubilee Fund' but had uncovered no further information. Still, five months on, he held out the hope that both Percy and Arthur were prisoners of war 'and will return to us when this terrible struggle is over'. Arthur too had received letters from Hoggan and Bryan, proffering the view that 'all' the missing officers were prisoners. The information suggested that his son had been seen leaving the trenches capless, bleeding from one hand while firing his revolver. Alas, Arthur and Agnes Hobbs would never see their son again.

Alongside the sharing of information between families, enquiries were made of organisations that had access to information about wounded and captured officers. Cox & Company handled the financial affairs of about 250,000 army officers during the war, clearing up to 50,000 cheques per day. By the end of the war, a staff of 4,500 spread around the world was needed to cover the huge workload occasioned by the exigencies of the conflict. Alfred Pope had been advised that a missing officer's cheque was often the first intimation of his being a prisoner of war, and that all cheques cashed by officers held in Germany passed through the hands of Messrs Cox & Co. The company had established an enquiry office in September 1914 for the purpose of giving general advice and information regarding the wounded to the relatives of officers of the original BEF.

As the casualty lists grew throughout 1915, and in consequence of the unparalleled strain placed on the Casualty Department at the War Office, Cox & Co.'s organisation was found to be of considerable benefit in obtaining fuller details of individual cases and also in conveying messages to and from wounded officers still in hospital in France. The company developed a system of obtaining available information regarding 'missing' officers and was frequently in the pleasurable position of being able to give the first glad tidings that a missing officer was safe.

Alfred Pope turned to their expertise to seek information about his son. On 15 October 1915, he heard from Cox & Co. that the last communication from Percy had been on 11 September, when a cheque had passed through their hands. His name had not appeared on any of their hospital lists from France or England, but the office did provide the names and addresses of four fellow battalion officers who could possibly be in a position to provide further information to Alfred and his family: Hoggan, Weber, Browne and Toller. A letter written by Alfred on 7 December 1915 to Percy's Barclays Bank branch in Oxford received the immediate reply from the branch director that they had received no news of him.

Cox & Co. wrote on 7 December to say they had 'received from the Expeditionary Force one package of kit B.R. 2353 in the name of 2nd. Lieut P.P. Pope, 3rd, att: 1st Welsh Regiment'. After completing the relevant paperwork, Alfred was told that the War Office had instructed the company to return Percy's effects. By April 1916, Alfred was in the process of winding up Percy's financial affairs, withdrawing £273 1s 4d sitting in the Barclays account and £88 18s 5d held by Cox & Co. In June 1916, a dividend of £103 2s 6d was paid into Percy's domestic bank account, in respect of his shares in the Eldridge Pope brewery.

In addition to contacts with Percy's former comrades, fellow-suffering families and firms with financial links to their son, Alfred and Elizabeth Pope did not eschew the more widely available sources of information about missing soldiers. On 9 November 1915, Alfred received a handwritten letter from the International Committee of the Red Cross regretfully informing him that 'your son's name has not yet appeared on our German lists', but that it was still early to expect news, holding out hope of future information. Alfred had offered to personally fund the society's work in trying to trace Percy, but he was assured that 'Our work is entirely gratuitous; we are only too glad if we can in any way help to mitigate the mental agony that accompanies war'. Equality of anxiety was to be shared by families of all classes, regardless of the means at their disposal to expedite further enquiries.

On 11 January 1916, the War Office informed Alfred that 'there is little hope that he is still alive' but that in view of the information that he had collected about possible sightings in a field ambulance, or suggestions he had been taken prisoner, further enquiries would be made. On 18 March, a further letter was issued regretting that no further information had been obtained. Many units had left France for the Middle East. If the information Alfred had received from No. 85 Field Ambulance was correct, the letter continued, it was to be feared that Percy died in one of the field ambulances or in transit from one to the other, and his death was not properly recorded, owing to the very heavy casualties that had occurred about that time. Further effort would be made to verify Captain Bryan's statement that Percy had been evacuated through the medical lines. Inevitably, this yielded no results.

Like Helen Butt in her search for her missing son Jack, Elizabeth Pope wrote to the King of Spain. On 21 January 1916, Elizabeth received a letter from the representative of Alfonso XIII in response to her 'petitioning H.M. to cause inquiries to be made in Berlin with regard to Mr P.P. Pope (your son)':

> Although the Spanish Embassy in Berlin was charged only with the interests of France and Russia, H.M. being desirous, nevertheless, of demonstrating his interest in British subjects has graciously acceded to your request and has commanded the Spanish Ambassador in Berlin to communicate with Great Britain's representative there – the United States Ambassador – in order that, in conjunction with the latter, the necessary investigations may be made.

Despite this kindness on the part of a foreign sovereign, inevitably it drew no trace of Percy.

Ten months after news was first received of his absence, the War Office issued official notice of his death. The hammer blow letter, sent on 23 August 1916, read:

> On the subject of Second Lieutenant Percy Paris Pope, 3rd Battalion attached 1st Battalion Welsh Regiment I am commanded by the Army Council to inform you that as the latest official report regarding this officer is to the effect that he was missing on the night of the 1st to 2nd October 1915, this Department is not in a position to issue a formal certificate of death. Looking, however:
>
> 1. To the length of time that has elapsed since he was officially reported missing.

2. To the fact that his name has not appeared in any last of prisoners of
war received from the German Government –

The Army Council are regretfully constrained to conclude that Second
Lieutenant Pope is dead, and that his death occurred on or since the 1st
day of October 1915.

I am to add that the Army Council have unfortunately no doubt as
to the death of this officer. … I am to express the sympathy of the Army
Council with you in your bereavement,

A further official letter was received at South Court from the Keeper of the
Privy Purse, expressing 'deep regret' on behalf of the King and Queen and 'to
assure you that during the long months of uncertainty Their Majesties' thoughts
have been constantly with you and those who have been called upon to endure
this exceptional burden of anxiety'.

The extraordinary endeavour expended by Alfred and Elizabeth Pope had
yielded little except the reassurance that they were far from alone in their
anguish. Although Percy's death had become an accepted fact, the family could
not retreat into the gloomy solitude of mourning one lost son. Anxiety as to the
welfare of the rest of their large brood remained high, with Cyril still a prisoner
of war in Germany, long lacunae in news of Decimus, who was fighting in Iraq,
and another son, John Allen, suffering shell shock.

Less than a year after the final confirmation of Percy's death, Alfred and
Elizabeth had to absorb another hammer blow when they were informed that
their fourth son, Captain Charles Alfred Whiting Pope, RAMC, had been
reported missing on 4 May 1917 when the British troopship *Transylvania* was
torpedoed in the Mediterranean by a German submarine. It sank within fifty
minutes, with many nurses, soldiers and crew escaping on the ship's lifeboats.
However, twenty-nine officers and 373 other ranks were lost. Initially it was
hoped that Charles had been amongst the survivors.

Marion Pope, Charles's wife, had received the dreaded telegram, informing
her that her husband was 'reported missing believed drown May fourth' on 16
May. Although the well-meaning but false rumours that surrounded Percy's
disappearance were mercifully not to be repeated in the case of Charles, Alfred,
Elizabeth and Marion still instigated enquiries so they could receive eyewitness
confirmation of the full circumstances of his death.

Captain Lestock Livingstone-Learmonth of the 14th Black Watch (Royal
Highlanders), who had not been with Charles at the time the first or second
torpedo hit the ship, wrote to Alfred, 'I am very sorry to have to think that
anyone who has not been traced by this time must have been lost.' One sergeant
wrote to Marion that he had been with Charles in the ship's hospital. Having

made sure that the patients were safe, they both went on to the parade deck. Shortly afterwards, on hearing that there were several men below who had been wounded in the blast, 'Captain Pope went down with a party of men to try and rescue them and dress their wounds – that thus he died the death of a British Officer and Gentleman – at his post.'

Another colleague wrote, 'He was in charge of us on the *Transylvania* and was missing when we landed. He died as every Britisher likes to die – doing his Duty and went down with the ship whilst dressing the wounds of the poor fellows who were hit by the explosions.'

Definite confirmation of Charles's death came in this letter, with the words 'I happen to know this as I was working with him up to about three minutes before she sank, when he ordered me over the side'. Official notice of death was received from the War Office on 21 September 1917, and he left behind not only his grieving parents and widow, but two sons and a daughter. One of these sons, John Gorton Pope, was also lost at sea while serving as an officer in the RAF in 1942. The Popes gave more than their share of sacrifice in the wars of the twentieth century.

Arthur Greensmith

'I hardly know how to begin to write to you, my heart is well nigh bursting, first with hope & then despair.'

On 18 July 1916, having received no news of Private Arthur Greensmith of the Sheffield City Battalion for over a fortnight, his sister Cecilia wrote him a distraught letter on behalf of the family. The Sheffield press had carried extensive reports of the battalion's part in the big push on the Somme at the beginning of July but the Greensmiths, like dozens of other local families,

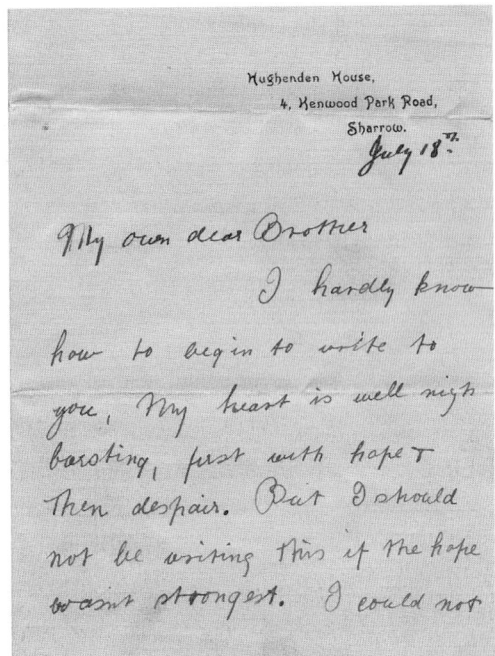

Hughenden House,
4, Kenwood Park Road,
Sharrow.
July 18

My own dear Brother
I hardly know how to begin to write to you, My heart is well nigh bursting, first with hope & Then despair. But I should not be writing this if the hope wasn't strongest. I could not

Letter written by Cecilia Spittle to her brother Arthur Greensmith on 18 July 1916. Arthur had perished seventeen days previously. (*Courtesy Rosemary Gregory*)

were left in a state of severe anxiety. Beginning with an entreaty to 'My own dear Brother', Cecilia revealed:

> I hardly know how to begin to write to you, my heart is well nigh bursting, first with hope & then despair. But I should not be writing this if the hope wasn't strongest. I could not possibly tell you what your silence has meant to us. I am convinced of this if you could have written nothing on earth would have prevented you. That we hear no news is no reason why we should not drop you a line to cheer you up. We know what you have been going through & can just imagine to ourselves your bravery through it all, God grant that you will [be] spared to come back to us.
>
> Every moment of every day I am praying for you & trying not to lose faith. Keep baby's photo on you it may prove lucky. The day she was born a stray black cat persisted in being in my bedroom, therefore she is a lucky baby.
>
> Write as soon as possible
>
> God bless you always
Cecilia

In desperation and helplessness, Cecilia was clinging to the hope that Christian prayer would sustain her and her brother. Running alongside this traditional invocation of celestial support was the folk superstition of the luck a black cat and a photograph of a baby could bring.

Nine days later, Cecilia's letter arrived back in Sheffield, addressed to:

'Cecilia'
4 Kenwood Park Road
Sharrow
Sheffield

On the reverse, an adjutant had noted:

Missing France
Relatives informed
Return to sender.

Sheffield families whose loved ones had been reported 'missing' would press soldiers home on leave for information. Those who had endured the agony of the Somme had to bear the further strain of the emotional pressure and disbelieving reactions of their comrades' families. Corporal D.E. Cattell recalled, 'It was a harrowing time for me with the mothers of my friends asking for information about their sons. When I told them that they had been killed or were missing, they wouldn't believe me. In fact in some cases it cost friendships.'

The local press carried photographs of the missing, appealing for information. Private J.W. Norton, reading one such plea while convalescing in a Bristol hospital, was able to confirm the death of his comrade Private Frank Nichols, a machine-gun team leader. Acting on behalf of the city, the Lord Mayor of Sheffield, Councillor Frederick Warlow, wrote to the War Office requesting that further searches be made that might bring some relief to his suffering citizens. He received a reply in August, explaining that lists of the missing had been sent to Germany via the Red Cross for circulation around hospitals and prison camps. Warlow collated the details from relatives of the missing through his own office, acting as a conduit of information between them and the War Office, and the Greensmiths duly submitted Arthur's particulars to the Lord Mayor.

In the days between the despatch and return of Cecilia's letter, the *Sheffield Daily Telegraph* published a copy of a letter sent by Private J.C. Thompson of the Sheffield City Battalion, who was then convalescing in a Kent VAD hospital. Thompson had written to the Reverend George H. McNeal, Superintendent of the Sheffield Wesleyan Mission in Norfolk Street, thanking him for his 'kind letter [it is] so nice to feel that one is not forgotten'. Thompson went on to recount his recollections of 1 July:

> I was very lucky indeed to get off so easily. My heart bleeds when I think of our poor lads who fell that awful day. Still, I am tremendously proud of them. There is one thing I should like to tell you Sheffield people, and that is that a finer and more gallant battalion never went into action.
>
> When the full story of that day becomes known Sheffield will be very proud of her City Battalion. The boys climbed on to the parapet under a murderous hail of machine-gun fire and straight on through a perfect hell of bursting shells, both high explosive and shrapnel, and for not one moment did they hesitate, but drove straight on to their goal. Falling at every step still they went on, talking to each other and smoking, of course, as they went.
>
> Alas! Only a mere handful got to their objective, but get there they did. Oh, they were fine!
>
> Men that have been through Loos, Hill 60, Neuve Chapelle and Ypres said that the battle on July 1st was infinitely the worst and hardest they had ever seen, so you can imagine what the boys went through.

Cecilia cut out Thompson's letter and kept it in her scrapbook. Meanwhile, as the Greensmith family waited anxiously for news of Arthur, her younger sister Gwyneth performed at an 'excellent programme' at the Third Northern General Hospital in Wadsley, singing vocals backed by the orchestra of the Trinity

Wesleyan Methodist Church. The 'well-chosen selections' were 'admirably rendered'. The same page of the *Sheffield Daily Telegraph* that reported this musical event also carried news of the hundreds of wounded Sheffield men who were being returned from France to the very same hospital. How Gwyneth must have wished that Arthur were among them.

On 22 July, Second Lieutenant Frank Westley, the officer commanding D Company of the 12th Sheffield City Battalion, wrote to Arthur's father in response to a letter he had received from the family. Westley had not been with the rest of the battalion on the fateful 1 July, but had made enquiries upon his return, and 'it is with regret I have to inform you that he was killed in action on July 1 16 during the great advance made by this Battalion'. Westley had been given this information 'by men of [Arthur's] own platoon, who were with him all the time'. Westley went on to express his 'deepest sympathy at the time of stress and trouble', hoping that the family would 'be able to bear this great shock'. The letter struck the delicate balance between being definitive in its assertion that Arthur had been killed, citing 'men' who knew him well had been eyewitnesses to his death, whilst sparing the Greensmith family the details of the exact circumstances of his demise; whether it had been instant or prolonged, and the nature of Arthur's fatal injuries. Therefore, the letter, despite containing seemingly conclusive proof of Arthur's death, was not sufficient for the family to desist in their search for further news.

On 17 August, despite the grim news contained in the letter from Second Lieutenant Westley, the Greensmiths inserted a request for information in the *Sheffield Daily Telegraph*:

TOLL OF WAR
SHEFFIELD MINING STUDENT MISSING
News is to hand from the War Office that Private A.C. Greensmith, of 4, Kenwood Park Road, Sheffield, is missing, and his parents would be grateful for any information concerning him. He joined a local battalion of the Yorks and Lancs Regiment shortly after the outbreak of the war, and was in the assault on the 1st July, since which date he has not been heard of. On leaving Ashley House School, Worksop, Private Greensmith took up a position with a local firm of colliery owners, Messers J and G Wells Ltd, and was studying for the profession of mining engineer.

The *Trinity Wesleyan* magazine of August 1916, published by the church where the Greensmith family were active members, noted that July had 'commenced in great anxiety', with the City Battalion going into action on 1 July. Whilst thanking God that so many had come through the ordeal safely, and that a 'notable victory was won', sympathy was expressed to the parents of Tom

Gambles at the loss of their son. Gambles had died of wounds received in action on 28 June, while bringing in a wounded comrade from a raid. More heartening, Corporal A. Moore was recovering from wounds received on 1 July. Arthur Greensmith, it was stated, was amongst the missing and sympathy was extended to Mr and Mrs Greensmith. The author noted, 'As Wesleyan Chaplain to the Battalion whilst at Redmires, I feel deeply the loss of so many men to whom in other days I had the privilege of ministering.'

For many Sheffield families, the confirmation of their loved one's death came in the spring of 1917, when the Germans made a tactical repositioning to reinforce the Hindenburg Line, ceding the area that had been no man's land on 1 July 1916 to the British. It proved possible to identify and bury many of the bodies, but others were too badly mutilated to be able to put a name to.

The Greensmith family, however, did not have to wait until 1917 for definitive confirmation from the War Office that their son was assumed to have been killed. The *Sheffield Daily Telegraph* of 16 September 1916 carried the sad tidings:

NOW REPORTED KILLED
Another Sheffield man who was in the official list of 'missing' on the 1st July is now reported killed. Private Arthur Clarence Greensmith, of the York and Lancaster Regiment, son of Mr A.J. Greensmith of 4 Kenwood Park Road, was in the big advance on the 1st July, and then, with many others, made the great sacrifice. He was 22 years of age …

It had been a mere two months since Cecilia had sent her heartbreaking plea to Arthur, a letter he would never receive. Given the grim reports carried in the local and national press of the actions that had removed Arthur from the world, there was little chance that he had been taken prisoner, or was an anonymous casualty being treated by a field ambulance. The letter from Second Lieutenant Westley had confirmed this. Arthur senior received a letter from the office of Lord Mayor Frederick Warlow, who had been co-ordinating an official search for the news of Sheffield men, confirming receipt of a communication from the 'British Red Cross Society of St. John' dated 16 September, stating that Arthur Greensmith's name had appeared in the official lists of the dead published in *The Times* that day. Warlow expressed deep sympathy at the 'sad loss which you have sustained in the death of your son fighting so gallantly for his King and Country'.

Arthur's mother, Cecilia, prepared an insertion for the local press. It read:

Re: Pte A.C. Greensmith, 12/934 12th Batt York & Lancs Regt. Killed in France July 1st 1916.

Any information as to his resting place & a photograph if possible would be thankfully received by his mother at the above address.

The deep desire for a place that Mrs Greensmith could visit following the war, a plot of land where she could feel connected to her dead son, ached inside her. Sadly, no such information was forthcoming. There would be no known resting place for Arthur. No opportunity for his mother or sisters to place flowers on his grave. He would become one of the ranks of the disappeared.

Further official notifications followed. On 31 August, the Infantry Records Office at York stated that any surviving personal effects would be forwarded on. What may have been further consolation for Arthur's actively Christian family was a document sent to the family home on 1 July 1918, precisely two years after his death. Arthur was one of 300,000 men who had signed the YMCA's 'War Roll', a scheme initiated in May 1915 whereby men using the organisation's recreational huts could affirm their commitment to Christ. Enclosed with the letter was a membership card 'which we hope you will carry in your Pocket Testament as a constant reminder'. The letter framed the Christian's journey in militaristic terms:

If this is the first time you have faced the great call of the King of kings and given your answer by enlisting in His Army, we pray that you may be loyal to Him, and that you will manfully fight His battles. Be strong in the Lord and fear not. You will have to receive many a blow, but even if you should be bowled over, don't take it lying down. Get up again. Don't be beaten.

For the man who was already a Christian when he signed, 'we take it you re-consecrated yourself for service'. The YMCA 'would welcome a post card saying that you are trying to stand true. If you have any special difficulty in living the Christian life and need advice write to us.' The tragically obsolete final words of the letter read, 'Praying that God will keep you faithful to your covenant and that He will lead you all the way you have to go'.

Hope remained that Arthur's body might one day be found. Charles Appleby's son, Frank, who had served alongside Arthur in D Company, had been lost on the Serre battlefield, and once the war was over he travelled to France, searching the area for a trace of his son. Frank's body was eventually recovered and identified, Charles and his wife Mary choosing the biblical inscription 'He Fought the Good Fight With All His Might' for their son's gravestone in the Euston Road Cemetery. As a further memorial to Frank and other fallen soldiers who had been taught by his father at All Saints Church School, Pitsmoor, a scholarship fund was established in 1928.

Subsequent years would see the occasional Sheffield City Battalion corpse unearthed by French farmers. In 1928, the body of Private Albert Bull was found on the site of the old British front line at Serre. A memorial cross, which still stands to this day, was erected at the spot, whilst Albert's remains were buried at the Serre Road No. 2 Military Cemetery upon its completion in 1934. Sadly, the body of Arthur Greensmith has never been identified. His remains either lie on the battlefield, or in a grave marked 'A British Soldier of the Great War – Known unto God'.

Ernest Blackburn

'Our hearts are full of pity'

On 2 October 1916, a standard letter was sent from the KRRC Record Office in Winchester to the heavily pregnant Annie Blackburn in Leeds providing the somewhat vague information that her husband Ernest had been reported 'missing after the engagement at "not stated" on the 15/9/16'.

Following Ernest's previous advice, Annie placed his particulars in the *Leeds Mercury* of 7 October 1916 amongst those of others reporting missing or dead on active service:

Rifleman Ernest Blackburn (King's Royal Rifles), formerly a teacher at the Upper Wortley Council School, is reported missing since September 16th. His wife would be grateful for any news sent to her at 7 Moorfield Avenue, Armley.

On 9 October 1916, the KRRC's Regimental Paymaster wrote to Annie stating that, as Rifleman Blackburn had been reported missing in action, her separation allowance and pay allotment would continue to be issued for a further thirty weeks.

Ernest's family was quick to rally round with support for Annie. As brothers Harold and Herbert Blackburn set about writing letters to instigate the search for Ernest, the eldest brother, Albert, a railway porter in Campsall, near Doncaster, began organising practical support for their sister-in-law. Writing to her on 8 October, addressing her as 'Dear Sister', he expressed the 'heavy heart' with which he and his wife Jennie had received the news about Ernest's disappearance. Albert would 'not be able to rest' until he could see Annie in person to express his sorrow and sympathy, and he turned to the family's faith to state: 'Our hearts are full of pity, and in this your hour of trial, we will ask God to answer our prayer that he is still alive and a prisoner.'

Albert reflected on the sheer tragedy of the probable loss of the 'prospect of many years of happiness' that 'should be torn asunder through no fault of yours'. The 'sure hope' of a reunion had to be clung on to, but in the meantime, Albert vowed to honour the promise he had made to Ernest before he had left for war to 'be a brother not only in name but in deeds'. The strength of extended family ties was to be marshalled, with the Blackburns having agreed that Annie would not be left on her own in the forthcoming months. Ernest's siblings and their spouses would come to stay in Armley until Annie was 'in a position to get about again'. In addition to the emotional support, more prosaically, Albert promised that 'Jennie will also bring a chicken and some eggs and I will see that you get more chickens when required', before signing off with the 'hope that there will soon be glad tiding of Ernest and that God will answer our prayers'.

Further support was given by Ernest's father, James. Writing on 17 October, the day of the birth of Annie's second son, whom she named 'Ernest', he advised her to apply to the Secretary of the Leeds Teachers' Provident Society for a form that could be filled in to access any further monies due. James's letter was addressed to 'Dear Annie and the rest', showing that Albert's promise that she would not be left on her own was being adhered to. His practical nature also led him to echo his late son's previous advice regarding further administrative steps that needed to be undertaken, including the sending of a birth certificate to the paymaster of the King's Royal Rifle Corps in Winchester, in a registered letter, in order to claim a further three shillings and sixpence per week. Finally, the letter signed by 'Your affect[ionate] father' affirmed the 'hope that as one job is now comfortably over that you will still keep hoping for some good news'.

Harold Blackburn wrote to the British Section of the Bureau de Secours aux Prisonniers de Guerre in Berne, on 23 October 1916, providing precise and concise information to support his politely couched request:

> I shall be very much obliged if you will use your endeavours to trace the whereabouts of Rifleman Ernest Blackburn, 25080, D Company [sic], 12th Platoon, 9th Battalion, King's Royal Rifles.
>
> He is reported as missing as from the 15th September 1916, and as far as is known he would be in the great engagement at Flers when the Earl of Feversham was killed.
>
> He was 31 years of age and married and previous to joining the Army on May 29 1916, was an Assistant Master at the Upper Wortley Council School, Leeds. He resided at 7 Moorfield Avenue, Armley, Leeds.
>
> Previous to his marriage in August 1912, he lived with his parents at 68a Westgate, Dewsbury, and was very well known in regard to his connection with the Ebenezer Congregational Chapel, Dewsbury, where he was Captain of the Boys' Brigade, a choirman and assistant superintendent of the Sunday School.

Any news of him will be welcome.

Thanking you in anticipation of you being able to obtain any news of him

I beg to remain

Yours respectfully

Harold Blackburn

Lance-Corporal

King's Own Yorkshire Light Infantry

(Brother)

I enclose photo of him in uniform which is very characteristic.

This line of enquiry proved fruitless for Harold as in December he received a reply, signed on behalf of honorary secretary Nesta Sawyer, informing him that, as the War Office now had a 'new and comprehensive system of enquiry in the case of missing officers and men', enquiries via 'other sources' were to be discontinued. The photograph of Ernest was returned, along with the wish that the search for him should prove successful.

Another brother, Herbert, sent the same letter to the Queen Victoria Jubilee Fund Association (Inquiry Branch) Geneva, on 23 October, receiving a reply assuring him that the organisation had 'taken note of the particulars you have furnished' and assuring Herbert that Ernest's details would appear on their No. 20 bulletin and that his photograph would be reproduced on sheet No. 26. Both these documents would be sent to all camps and hospitals in Germany and Belgium to the Chief Medical Officers in the war zone of German occupation.

Harold Blackburn had also written to the Wounded and Missing Enquiry Department of the British Red Cross and Order of St John, receiving a bleak reply from the organisation's Carlton House Terrace headquarters dated 20 March 1917:

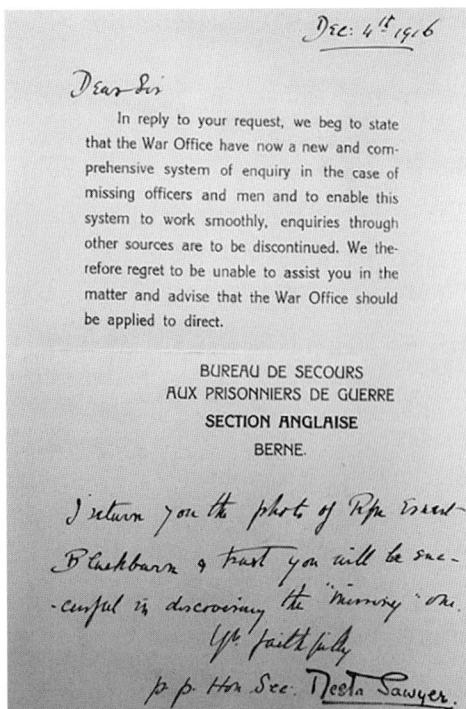

Letter from Nesta Sawyer to Harold Blackburn.
(*Courtesy the Blackburn family*)

Queen Victoria Jubilee Fund Association Missing Bulletin No. 20. Ernest Blackburn on second row, second from the right. (*Courtesy the Blackburn family*)

Dear Sir

I do not know if you are aware that the official list published in the "Times" of today contains the name of your brother as killed.

With much sympathy

The letter was signed on behalf of the Earl of Lucan.

The circulation of Ernest's name in the local and regional press had brought his case to the attention of Mrs Lily Daws of Scarborough. On 18 March 1917, she wrote to Annie after seeing an announcement 'in the Leeds paper' of the 'sad news' of Ernest.

Lily wished to know how long it had taken the War Office to inform Annie that her husband was presumed dead. Her own husband, Edmund 'Ted' Daws, a member of A Company, 15th Section of the 21st Battalion KRRC, had been reported missing on the same day as Ernest but she had heard nothing since the first notification of his loss. For Lily, 'the suspense is becoming more than I can bear', and she thought that Annie, being 'fixed the same', would understand her plight. She would not offer sympathy 'as it's such a cold thing', but assured Annie she could 'enter into your feelings as only those who have gone through trouble & anxiety can feel the same for others who are in the same trouble'. Bemoaning the state of perpetual anxiety in which probable war widows were being suspended, she proclaimed: 'It seems too cruel for words that us women should give our men & never get the satisfaction of knowing what becomes of them.'

Lily's husband, Ted, had been born in Scarborough in 1887, the sixth of seven children of parents who were boarding house keepers. Ted had attended St Martin's Grammar School before taking up an apprenticeship as a ladies' hairdresser. He and Lily had married on 18 November 1915. The 21st Battalion (Yeoman Rifles) KRRC had fought to a standstill at Flers on 15 September 1916. During a roll call taken the following morning, it was found that the battalion's commanding officer, the Earl of Feversham, a close friend of David Lloyd George, had been killed. Fifty-four other ranks had definitely been slain, 256 were wounded and a further seventy were 'missing', including Ted. His name had appeared in the 'Scarboro Casualties' listing of the *Scarborough Mercury* of 29 September, listed as missing.

Filled with dread, Lily had written to the War Office on 3 January 1917 asking for information. She had had a letter returned to her from France with 'Hospital' written across it, occasioning hope that Ted was still alive, but with no clue as to which hospital was being referred to. For Lily, 'The anxiety is getting terrible. Thanking you in anticipation.' Against all hope, she was 'still in good hopes even if we have to wait till the war is over. I feel a great number will return who have been reported lost.' This reluctance to engage with the awful truth had led her to resist seeking further information 'for fear they send me bad news'. The forlorn hope was even extended to Annie, whom Lily hoped would 'heal up as well as you can', but 'may even yet have brighter news'.

Annie replied to Lily, prompting a further response written on 25 March. Lily rated herself 'a real coward as your case is so very much harder than mine'. The poignancy of 'that dear little baby being born when you already know your husband was missing' was terrible. Christian faith was invoked, leading Lily to 'hope & pray that God will give you strength to keep up & that those two dear little ones may grow up & be a help & comfort to you'.

The troubles of women left without firm knowledge of their husbands' fate led Lily to question the purpose of the war: 'We are told to believe that everything is done for the best but it's hard to think so at the time – when we women have to face blows like these.' Lily had learned of the case of 'another poor little woman in Scarboro' whose husband had been confirmed as killed having been reported missing on 15 September. This widow had an 8-year-old son. This man, like Ernest and Ted, was in the KRRC, a triumvirate of tragedy, which caused Lily to state, 'I hate the name of that regiment now.'

Her suspense remained 'terrible. … I'm still waiting & hoping & yet dreading the fateful news.' Having given Annie her best wishes, she signed off, the last known contact between the two women. Whether or not Lily Daws did contact the War Office or any searching agency is not known. Ted was indeed confirmed as having been killed in action at Flers. Although there was no body for her to grieve over, a stone was erected in Scarborough's Dean Road Cemetery to act as a focus for family grieving and remembrance, inscribed with the words from Psalm 32:24: 'Be Strong and He Shall Comfort Thine Heart'.

On 19 May 1917, Annie received official confirmation of the news she had been dreading to hear for nine months. A certificate of death was issued by the War Office in London, stating that Ernest was assumed to have been killed in action in France on 15 September 1916. She wrote back the following day to ask if any of Ernest's effects had survived that could be sent to her but was informed that, to date, no effects had been received in respect of her late husband. No trace of Ernest was to be found.

Frank Mead

'The resurrection of the body, and the life everlasting'

As Frank and his four comrades had been killed by shelling in Sunken Road trench on the night of 2/3 December, amongst their 1/23rd London comrades there was no doubt as to their fate. Thus the Mead family were spared the months of high anxiety visited upon hundreds of thousands of other families. Thomas Mead received his son's unclaimed pay of £12 5s 2d on 1 May 1918 and five days later took delivery of an intimate grouping of personal effects that Frank's comrades had retrieved from his body before burial. This included two identity discs, some family photographs, a purse, some cards, a canvas wallet and a George II half-crown with the words of the Apostles' Creed written on the reverse, with the apposite words about ascending to heaven after burial:

> I believe in God, the Father almighty,
> creator of heaven and earth.

> I believe in Jesus Christ, his only Son, our Lord,
> who was conceived by the Holy Spirit,
> born of the Virgin Mary,
> suffered under Pontius Pilate,
> was crucified, died, and was buried;
> he descended to the dead.
> On the third day he rose again;
> he ascended into heaven,
> he is seated at the right hand of the Father,
> and he will come to judge the living and the dead.

I believe in the Holy Spirit,
the holy catholic Church,
the communion of saints,
the forgiveness of sins,
the resurrection of the body,
and the life everlasting.
Amen.

Gilbert Donnelly

'Lieut. Donnelly … was shot through the head and killed'

The sacrifice of war had already touched the Donnelly family via the death of Private James Nichol of 4th Battalion The King's (Liverpool) Regiment. James, a nephew by marriage of Gilbert's elder brother John, had been taken under the wing of John Donnelly junior and his wife, Mary. He had been killed in action on 3 February 1917, and was to be another of the perpetually missing. On 13 March 1918, John Donnelly senior learned that his 80-year-old mother, Jane, who for the previous two years had suffered from senile debility, had died. This grief his mother's passing was added to his anxiety over the safekeeping of his young son, Gilbert. John, who had sent and received

Lieutenant Gilbert Donnelly. (*Courtesy the Donnelly family*)

of hundreds of thousands of telegrams at Belfast's General Post Office, received the terrible news on 8 April 1918. The telegram tersely stated, 'Deeply regret Lieut G. Donnelly Munster Fusiliers killed in action March twenty first. The Army Council express their sympathy.' The telegram left no margin for doubt in John's mind. Gilbert was not missing, not severely wounded. There would be no false hope that he might be a prisoner of war or lying insensible in a clearing station or hospital. The news was swiftly relayed to the press. The *Northern Whig* of Saturday, 13 April reported:

Lieut. Gilbert Donnelly, killed in action March, son Mr. John Donnelly, Glastonbury Avenue, Belfast. He received his commission after a period of training with the Officer's Training Corps of Queen's University, and had been on active service since August, 1916.

A week later, the *Larne Times* printed a photograph of a resolute-looking Gilbert, a young man who would see more than his fair share of death and human misery during his twenty years:

> GILBERT DONNELLY. Lieut. Gilbert Donnelly, Royal Munster Fusiliers, killed in action 21st March … had been on active service since August 1916 and was engaged in the heavy fighting during the British advance from the Somme up to the capture of the Hindenburg line. A brother of the late Lieut. Donnelly was in the forces and served over two years in France with the Inniskillings.

Lieutenant Gilbert Donnelly. Note the change of expression after three years of war. (*Courtesy the Donnelly family*)

A private portrait of a slightly older Gilbert in his smart RMF uniform with eyes that held the horrors of war was in great contrast to that photograph that was taken of him in 1915 when he was a fresh-faced and confident, possibly even cocky, young recruit. In the months following Gilbert's death, Red Cross Wounded and Missing Bureau volunteers were able to piece together scraps of evidence from statements made by four members of his battalion. Private C. Kelleher, interviewed on 18 June at a Normandy convalescent depot, claimed to have seen Gilbert 'killed by a bullet in front of Ronsoy. We were holding the line at the time, and he was killed in the trench. The Germans took the ground and his body would have fallen into their hands.' In order to verify whether Kelleher was referring to the correct man, he was asked to provide a description of Gilbert, and he responded with: 'He came from the North of Ireland. He came, I think, from England December 1916. Dark hair, clean shaven, about 5 feet 5, medium build, about 26.' Kelleher had added several years to his age, due to a combination of the aging effects of months of front-line service had rendered on the 20-year-old Gilbert, and the air of authority and maturity of a junior officer.

Private F.N. Lightfoot gave a testimony on 2 August 1918 while convalescing aboard HMAT *Warilda* in Le Havre. Lightfoot recalled Gilbert was 'killed by a shell on the 21st March 1918 at Ronsoy', 2 miles in front of St Emilie, 'whilst going into a new trench between 10 & 11am. We were then retiring and I don't know what happened to his body.' To emphasise that he was referring to the correct man, Lightfoot added: 'He was the only Lieut Donnelly I know of in the 1st Battn.'

Private T. Foley, a member of Gilbert's Y Company, had been wounded during Operation Michael. Fortunately for Foley, he had remained in the hands of his comrades and by 9 September was convalescing at St Luke's War Hospital in Halifax. Interviewed by volunteer 'A. Farrar', Foley stated:

> It was at St. Emly [sic] where I saw Lt. Donnelly shot through the head by a sniper. It was daylight, morning of March 22nd and the enemy were advancing. I cannot say whether the body was picked up or left behind, as we were pushed back. Donnelly was observing for the Lewis Gun at the time of his death.

Foley also divulged, as part of his proof that he was referring to Gilbert, that Lieutenant Donnelly was known affectionately to his comrades as 'Charlie Chaplin', although the reasons for this remain unclear.

It is probable that John Donnelly received an amalgam of the recollections of Kelleher, Foley and Lightfoot. Although giving varying remembrances, it was clear that Gilbert had been killed by enemy fire. Despite the realisation that nothing would bring Gilbert back to his family, he was not ready to give up his search for the location of his son's remains. His correspondence with the War Office included a request that he be sent his son's new leather kitbag and contents, a Christmas gift. John was not even to receive this memento of Gilbert's life, selected with great pride and affection, as the War Office replied and said that none of his personal effects had been retrieved. The Germans had overrun the trenches and therefore all items were lost. John Donnelly returned to the War Office a return train ticket from Belfast that had been sent to Glastonbury Avenue to facilitate Gilbert's return to the front after a forthcoming period of leave. Travel administration had not kept pace with the casualty lists, delivering John the additional pain of what might have been.

Some small measure of comfort was possibly derived from a letter John received in mid-March 1919. His persistence had resulted in further enquiries being made by the Red Cross of Repatriated Prisoners of War. These had elicited information from Sergeant Michael Dooley, another member of Y Company. Dooley had been interviewed in January, recalling:

> I actually saw Lieut. G. Donnelly, Royal Munster Fusiliers, dead about 400 yards in front of St.Emily [sic] on the 21st March 1918. On the Ephy [Épehy] and Dronsoi [Ronssoy] Front on 21st March 1918, as we were holding the 3rd Line (Brown Line) and Lieut. Donnelly who was at the

time commanding my company was shot through the head and killed. I knew Lieut. Donnelly well. As a prisoner of war I was one of the party detailed to bury the dead and saw him buried close to St. Emily [St Emilie].

John now knew that Gilbert had been buried with some modicum of respect by men who knew and admired him. More than that, Gilbert's immediate family would never find out. As the decades passed, people who had known him personally passed away. John Donnelly died in 1935 without ever being able to visit his son's grave. The last of Gilbert's generation, his brother Hugh, died in 1976. It would take the dedication and persistence of family members three generations along from John and two from Gilbert to be able to conclude the search their great-grandfather had instigated but had lacked the information to close.

Stories of Gilbert's untimely death were retold through generations of his extensive family. Mark Gallagher, a grandson of Gilbert's elder brother John, was a frequent visitor to the battlefields of France and Belgium from the 1980s onwards. Upon mentioning the area to his mother, Eithne, she told him what little she knew of her Uncle Gilbert. Struck by the fact that his family lived a few hundred yards from the old Donnelly household on Glastonbury Avenue, Mark undertook further research, finding Gilbert's name on the Pozières Memorial. Realising that, sadly, interest in Gilbert's sacrifice 'had become low to non-existent' due to Ireland's problematic post-war history, he resolved to research as much of Gilbert's lost life as possible. Mark visited the National Archives on three occasions from 2005 to 2009 to gather information from Gilbert's war service file, sharing the information with his mother. He was astonished to discover that his great-uncle's name was on the Queen's University Belfast memorial, which he had passed hundreds of times during his own university career in the early 1980s.

Meanwhile, with the advent of the Great War centenary commemorations which began in 2014, another great-nephew, Dan Donnelly, the grandson of Gilbert's brother Billy, felt a duty to his relative to find as much information as he could about Gilbert's short life, and the circumstances of his death. This journey of exploration 'ended in a place I could only have dreamed of when I set out'. Dan, a Senior Lecturer in Molecular Pharmacology at the University of Leeds, used enquiry methods that had been unavailable to his great-great-grandfather, posting a question in an online war forum. His query was noted by James Uzzell, a military history researcher, who had been investigating the life of his own ancestor, Private Henry (Harry) Uzzell of 2nd Royal Munster Fusiliers, killed three days after Gilbert. Fortuitously, James was in France at the time he read's Dan's post, having just visited St Emilie Valley Cemetery, close to the spot where Gilbert Donnelly had been laid to rest by Sergeant Dooley and his prisoner of war burial party. James had been struck by one particular grave of an unknown lieutenant of the Royal Munster Fusiliers. His curiosity pricked, James quickly established that only two RMF lieutenants who had been killed in that area during the early stages of the Spring Offensive had not been identified.

This information set Gilbert's relatives on a quest that would last as long as the war itself. When he first came across the recollections of Sergeant Dooley and Private Foley that had been passed to John Donnelly, Dan found it 'a chilling experience. I cannot imagine the pain felt by his father when he read these accounts and no doubt realised that his son's final resting place would never be known – a needle lost in a very large haystack.' Using further online searching tools, accessing digitised records and contacting enthusiastic military history experts in order to locate 'this particular needle', Dan was able to piece together the post-death fate of his great-uncle.

While studying the war diary of 1st Munsters, Dan came across a handwritten appendix to the events of late March 1918, containing a list of dead, missing and wounded officers. The sight of Gilbert Donnelly's name affected Dan. 'I felt quite strange when I first found that note, written in the aftermath of such a terrible day.'

The grave that James Uzzell had identified, which might possibly contain Gilbert's remains, was in Plot 1, Row H, No. 15. James established that three multiple graves of British soldiers, buried in 1918 by the Germans, had been found just 500 yards away from the current cemetery location following the Armistice, and had been exhumed and buried, firstly in the St Emilie graveyard, then secondly in November 1920 by members of 83rd Labour Company under the direction of Captain W.E. Southgate RE to form Plot 1 of the Imperial War Graves Commission cemetery. The company was one of 183 formed towards the end of the war and assigned the task of exhuming the war dead. It was composed of men from the Liverpool Regiment, some of whom had volunteered to extend their army service post-war. Most of the men reinterred by the Labour Company were soldiers of the 16th (Irish) Division who had died during Operation Michael. All the men who were identifiable from personal items had been killed on 21–22 March 1918, thus it was a reasonable supposition that those who could not be identified had died at the same time.

The record of the first exhumation showed an 'Unknown (Lieut British) "MF"', with a comment, '2 stars on Tunic Sleeve', confirming that he was a first lieutenant. When the current cemetery at St Emilie was established in 1920, the burial was recorded as 'R.M. FUS UNKNOWN BRITISH LIEUTENANT'.

Further research amongst Commonwealth War Graves Commission records confirmed that there were just two first lieutenants of the Royal Munster Fusiliers killed in 1918 in France who had no known grave. Apart from Gilbert Donnelly, the other was Lieutenant W.S. Kidd of the 2nd Battalion, who led the defence of Malassise Farm, 2 miles north of Épehy. Known graves of soldiers who were killed contemporaneously to Lieutenant Kidd were buried at Malassise Farm, making it a reasonable supposition that he was too. This left Gilbert as the only missing Royal Munster Fusilier first lieutenant without a known grave. The 1st RMF's war diary confirmed that they had been '400 yards in front of St Emilie' at the time of his death, and Sergeant Dooley's testimony established he had been buried 'close to St Emilie'. The grave registration record stated that the body reburied in Plot 1, Row H, Grave 15 had originally been buried at St Emilie. These three pieces of information convinced James Uzzell and Dan Donnelly that the inhabitant of that grave must be the long-lost Gilbert Donnelly. Dan contacted the CWGC in July 2014 with his findings, which were passed on to the organisation's commemorations team. A year later, Dan was told to submit a comprehensive file of evidence, which ran to eighteen pages. A further fourteen months passed by before Dan was informed that his file would be forwarded to the National Army Museum's War Graves Adjudication Committee for a final judgment. By November 2017, as the ninety-ninth anniversary of the Armistice approached, Dan was still waiting for a response, so contacted the Royal Munster Fusiliers Association. Their chairman, Liam Nolan, contacted the National Army Museum, with the result that the case was prioritised, and on 5 January 2018, Dan was informed that the case for Plot 1, Row H, Grave 15 St Emilie Valley Cemetery being that of Lieutenant Gilbert Donnelly, 1st Lieutenant Royal Munster Fusiliers was accepted. The painful but necessary journey that John Donnelly had set out on a hundred years previously had achieved closure.

Alan Stirling

> 'At that time we were partly surrounded and it was a case of every man for himself'

Once news reached William and Emma Stirling of their son's disappearance, they were plunged into despair. The enormous volume of men who went missing or were taken prisoner during the Spring Offensive of March and April 1918 meant searching services became overwhelmed. Upon the signing of the Armistice on 11 November 1918, tens of thousands of British prisoners of war were released, meaning access to vast new sources of information as to the fate of missing men. This proved to be a double-edged sword for many families holding out the tiny hope that their loved one might still be alive but unable to communicate from a prison camp. Their non-return would be the final confirmation that their son, husband or brother was no more. It would take time for the recently released captives to be traced and quizzed, even as they tried to rebuild a semblance of normality into their dislocated lives.

It would be a further six months before final confirmation of Alan's death was received. Finally, more than fourteen long months after Alan was last known to have walked the earth, official ratification of his death was notified to the Staffordshire public. A newspaper cutting of 31 May 1919, still treasured by the family, read:

Rifleman's Fate
Former Ryecroft Soldier Presumed to Have Fallen
Official notification has been received by Mr and Mrs Stirling of 78 Ash Street, Wolverhampton that their son, Rifleman Alan Stirling, who has been missing since going into action with the King's Royal Rifles, is now presumed to have fallen. … Born at Cannon Street, Ryecroft, the deceased solder, who was 23 years of age, served for some time as a grocer's assistant in the employ of the late Mr T. Potts of Aldridge, prior to removing to Wolverhampton. He completed three years in the army, and was in the Army Ordnance Corps when transferred to the K.R.R.'s.

A final signing off of official attempts to locate Alan's whereabouts was received in December 1919 from the British Red Cross and Order of St John's Wounded and Missing Department:

Dear Sir

We much regret to say that not withstanding constant and careful enquiries, we never succeeded in hearing anything of:

[handwritten] Rifleman A. Stirling 204366. 12 KRRC

His name was on our lists for months, and we asked all the men of his unit whom we were able to see, both in English hospitals and at the bases abroad, but none of them threw any light on his casualty. We have also questioned released prisoners but have learnt nothing. We can therefore only send you a General Account of the action in which he was last seen, with sincere regret at our inability to help you any further, as this Office is now closed.

We wish at the same time to offer our sympathy to the family and friends.

Yours faithfully
CGB

Alan left £19 16 6 to his father in his will and was officially resumed to have died on 2 April 1918. Although no specific information could be gleaned from former comrades of Alan's regarding his fate, the Stirlings were sent an amalgam of statements from men who had been in his battalion during the actions of 21 March 1918 onwards:

> 12 King's Royal Rifle Corps March 21-April 2 1918.
> Our reports show that on March 21 1918 the 12 K.R.R.C. were holding the line in front of St. Quentin. This was the first day of the great German offensive, when, helped by the thick mist, the enemy attacked in overwhelming numbers and our troops were forced to retire for many miles. The line of their retirement can be traced by the following places, whose names are mentioned in reports which we have received – Houpy, Fluquieres, Foronte, Aubigny, Offoy, Hombleux, Breuil, Mezieres and Dumart, which is only 12 kilometres from Amiens.

The following accounts are from men who were present and give some idea of the confusion caused by the retreat. They show, too, how often it must be impossible for men to say exactly what has been the fate of their comrades.

> On March 21 we were in various posts on the St. Quentin front and at daybreak the Germans started their bombardment. At about 9.30 or 10.30 they made their big attack and we had to retire. We had to go back about 200 yards with the enemy close on our heels. Some time after this we were told to go back and retake the post and we did so. But later on it changed hands again and remained in possession of the Germans.
>
> It was on a canal bank on the St. Quentin front on March 21. At that time we were partly surrounded and it was a case of every man for himself. The Germans would be about a mile behind us.
>
> Near Fluquieres, S.W. of St. Quentin, the whole Lewis Gun Team was captured on March 21. It was a misty morning and they were located out on our front and were separated from us by a large area of old barbed wire, so we could not assist them when the Germans surprised them.
>
> On the 4th or 5th day of the retirement we were just this side of Roye, holdin an old trench. The Dressing Station was in a village about 500 yds to our left. That village was taken by the enemy in the afternoon. We retired about 5pm.
>
> On March 29 we made a counter-attack through a wood on the other side of Mezieres (E. of Moreuil). We got through the wood, but had to retire through it again, and the Germans were pouring some heavy shells into it.

We got shelled heavily and many men in trying to get back were shot down by machine gun fire. We were retiring and the Germans were only 500–600 yds behind us, so we couldn't bring away our wounded.

Two men were working a Lewis Gun at the time. One man was hit and dropped the gun, whereupon the other picked it up and continued working it by himself in the face of the advancing enemy. The Germans were all over them a few minutes later.

To this day, Rifleman Alan Stirling has never been found. An aching hole remains in the family due to the absence of a definitive resting place. Nothing, however, can remove the love and esteem in which his memory is treasured amongst subsequent generations of his family.

Chapter 6

Commemoration of the Dead

Once the work of the searching parties had been wound down, the question remained of how to provide some form of democratisation of memorialisation. Around half of bereaved British families would have a battlefield grave that they could visit, provided they possessed the financial resources to do so. But what of the relatives of the hundreds of thousands of men of whom no identifiable trace had been found? The scale of sacrifice demanded significant memorialisation.

Most of the men who would never return from the war were not soldiers at heart. Unlike nineteenth-century wars waged by the British Army, where commemoration of the dead had largely been the responsibility of individual families, or in the case of the Boer War, voluntary and community-based organisations, a war mobilisation that had been countrywide would require a national commemoration.

It had become customary to record the names of the 24,000 men who had died in South Africa in towns and cities as diverse as Crewe, Dewsbury, Dorchester and Hull. The Royal Engineers had recorded in situ the known individual burial places of those who had fallen, and the Guild of Loyal Women compiled the RE's lists into a register and oversaw the erection of simple cast iron grave markers in cases where the family could not afford to pay for a memorial. Thus, the principle had been established that the body of a man who had died in the service of his country should have a recognised resting place. The Great War accelerated the practice begun during the Boer War of ensuring the placement of named grave markers for the fallen. Post-1918, each man's grave would be identical, and the erection and maintenance of the cemeteries in which graves would be erected and names recorded would be paid for in perpetuity from the public purse.

War memorials were places where it was envisaged that people would grieve, both individually and collectively. It was Fabian Ware who established the template by which the dead of twentieth-century conflicts would be commemorated. After the furore surrounding the repatriation of Lieutenant William Gladstone's body, the army had moved to prohibit the removal of soldiers' remains for the rest of the war. This ban was later extended in perpetuity following the Armistice and agreements reached with the French and Belgian authorities for the granting of land in which to bury the dead.

In May 1917 the Imperial War Graves Commission was established by Royal Charter, charged with continuing the work of the DGR&E in peacetime, establishing conventions for the layout of British war cemeteries. Their work would be severely affected by the scale of the devastation that the great battles of 1916 onwards wrought on the ability of burial parties to collect individual particulars and achieve a degree of recognisable symmetry in the temporary cemeteries they constructed. Medical units were frequently overwhelmed with the volume of the mortally wounded, having to deploy precious and overstretched resources to the treatment of salvageable lives rather than the efficient recording and registration of the dying and dead.

Further behind the lines, greater care could be taken to correctly identify the dead and, as the fighting moved on, hundreds of cemeteries were established on former battlefields. Of paramount importance was parity of remembrance. Each gravestone would be identical, excepting a short personal inscription to be chosen by the family. For those whose relatives would be remembered on mass monuments, even this solace would be denied.

The thought that a son or husband would rest in a marked grave was often 'of great solace in our sorrow', as expressed by the family of Lieutenant Francis Mond, an RAF pilot shot down and killed in May 1918.

> [T]he misery that haunted so many others, that of a missing son, last seen going into action and not seen since. Saved too from the fear, common to so many others, that a son had suffered a lonely, agonising death in a shell hole, with no known resting place, no personal possessions to be retrieved and sent home.

Sadly, some of those who had been buried in named graves were posthumously assigned as missing as their resting places were destroyed by later fighting. In addition, due to mistakes made during the identification process, sometimes a soldier was recorded as having been buried in two separate places. On occasions, an exhumation would be carried out to confirm accurate identification; in other cases it was assumed the first burial was the correct one. A further impediment to the correct identification of the dead was the fact that many crosses that had been initially erected over the body of a dead soldier were blown down by the effects of war and then re-erected in broadly the same area but not exactly on the same spot.

Some private memorials to the missing, paid for by families, were placed close to the last known location of the dead soldier. Sometimes these personal expressions of grief were taken to military cemeteries with the nearest body found to the cross, the exhumers assuming the two matched up. The process of identification was confusing. One IWGC report noted: 'The establishment beyond all doubt of the correct identity is a lengthy process, requiring the close attention of highly trained personnel.'

In 1918, Sir Herbert Baker, Sir Reginald Blomfield and Sir Edwin Lutyens were appointed the IWGC's Principal Architects. After consultation with garden designer Gertrude Jekyll, they created the layout of a walled cemetery in a garden setting, with the headstones lined up in uniform rows, like regiments of soldiers. A Cross of Sacrifice for cemeteries containing forty or more burials, and a Stone of Remembrance for those housing more than a thousand graves were added. In 1918, the IWGC decided that 'whatever their military rank or position in civil life, everyone should have equal treatment in their graves'.

The IWGC's Honorary Literary Advisor, Rudyard Kipling, still grieving his own son Jack, proposed the Biblical inscription 'Their name liveth for evermore' for the Stones of Remembrance within each of the larger cemeteries. Edwin Lutyens designed the Stone in an abstract style that resembled an altar of sacrifice. His aim was to create a symbol that would endure in the landscape for many centuries to come.

Each individual soldier's grave was supplied with a headstone and families had the option of including a religious symbol such as a cross or the Jewish Star of David, and the addition of a personal epitaph of up to sixty-six letters, at a cost of 3½d. The intensely personal epitaphs would sit within the uniformly elegant layout of the cemeteries to inspire an admixture of sorrow and sublime awe. The work of the IWGC continued at a rapid pace, and by 1927 the memorials to the found were nearly complete, with 400,000 individual headstones, 1,000 Crosses of Sacrifice and 400 Stones of Remembrance in place.

Once the design for the perpetual resting places of identified and unidentified remains had been settled upon, there remained an acute need to commemorate the hundreds of thousands of the missing for whom there would be little prospect of a known place in one of the curated war cemeteries. The IWGC settled upon the idea of twelve monuments across the Western Front. However, the French authorities were reluctant to cede so much territory while their citizens tried to rebuild lives and businesses in their ravaged land. Therefore, some memorials to the missing, such as the Loos Memorial, which included the name of Percy Paris Pope, were incorporated into existing cemeteries.

At the eastern exit to the town of Ypres stands the Menin Gate Memorial to the Missing, containing nearly 55,000 names, including John Gillis Butt and Charles Attwood. Designed by Sir Reginald Blomfield, the memorial, straddling the old Menenpoort, was unveiled on 24 July 1927. It quickly become a focus of pilgrimage for families of the missing visiting the Flanders battlefields. Since

1928, the Last Post has been sounded at eight o'clock every evening under the memorial, save for a hiatus during the Second World War. The Tyne Cot Memorial to the Missing, designed by Sir Herbert Baker, was commissioned to commemorate nearly 35,000 men killed from 1917 onwards on the Ypres Salient, when there was no further existing space on the Menin Gate memorial.

The Thiepval Memorial, upon which are inscribed the names of Ernest Blackburn and Arthur Greensmith, was designed by Sir Edwin Lutyens and unveiled by the Prince of Wales in the presence of the President of France on 1 August 1932. In 1973, it was refaced with bricks from Accrington, Lancashire, to acknowledge the devastation wrought in the ranks of the 11th (Service) Battalion (Accrington) East Lancashire Regiment, the Accrington Pals, on 1 July 1916. The names of more than 72,000 men are inscribed on the memorial, alongside a large dedication which reads:

> Here are recorded
> names of officers
> and men of the
> British Armies who fell
> on the Somme battlefields
> July 1915 February 1918
> but to whom
> the fortune of war
> denied the known
> and honoured burial
> given to their
> comrades in death.

Annually, on both 1 July and 11 November, the collective sacrifice of the Somme is commemorated beneath the names of Private Arthur Greensmith, Rifleman Ernest Blackburn and their comrades.

The Pozières Memorial, unveiled on 4 August 1930 by Sir Horace Smith-Dorrien, was designed by William Harrison Cowlishaw and sculpted by Laurence A. Turner. The memorial was erected in 'memory of the officers and men of the Fifth and Fourth Armies who fought on the Somme battlefields 21 March–7 August 1918 and to those of their dead who have no known grave'. A total of 14,657 names of British and South African soldiers, including that of Rifleman Alan Stirling, adorn the memorial, which forms three sides of the perimeter walls of the Commonwealth War Graves Commission cemetery.

In addition to the grand national cemeteries and memorials established to commemorate the war dead, each community and family developed their own methodologies of mourning. The eight families whose stories have been followed in depth in this book have ensured their private and public memories continue to be cherished.

Percy Pope

'You know that I was fond of your boy whom I always thought an excellent
fellow and I deeply lament his loss.'

At the most personal level of commemoration, families received letters eulogising the lives of their lost loved ones. Even before the final confirmation that Second Lieutenant Percy Pope had been killed, letters of sympathy and condolence had been sent to Alfred and Elizabeth Pope at South Court, Dorchester. Sir Archibald Garrod, Regius Professor of Medicine at the University of Oxford and consulting physician to the army, had already lost two sons in the war, the most recent on 25 January 1916. Sir Archibald wrote to Alfred on black bordered paper on 19 February 1916, thanking him for his 'kind sympathy'. Garrod's third and only remaining son was 'in a line regiment, but not likely to be sent out this year, I am thankful to say'. Garrod recognised Alfred's 'intense anxiety, and sympathise with you in turn'. Sadly, Professor Garrod's remaining son, Basil, was, like Alfred's second eldest son Alec, to die in 1919, 'having passed through the perils of war'.

Letters of sympathy and admiration were not just received from the great and the good. On 3 January 1916, 12-year-old Amy Miller of Country Antrim wrote a charming letter:

When looking over the 'Daily Mail' I observed your photograph of your ten sons and son-in-law. I have never heard of truer patriotism. I have the photograph cut out, mounted and hanging in the sitting room. I could not refrain from writing to you to let you know what we think of you and your relations and how many hearts have been stirred by your noble sacrifice.

I am very sorry to read that one of your sons is missing and one a prisoner, but I trust they will be restored to you when this awful war is over. I am sure you will be awarded some day for all your friends are doing in these troublous [sic] times of war and sorrow. I am a little girl of 12 yrs of age but I am not the only one who is thinking of you at the present hour.

Your little friend
Amy J.C. Miller

Percy's former university and bar friends and colleagues were anxious to proffer their sympathy to his family. Emlyn Shaw, honorary secretary of the New University Club, wrote on 4 January 1916, expressing 'my sympathy in the anxious time you must be passing though since your son was reported to be missing'. One of the first of the Pope family's wide circle of contacts to express concern for Percy's whereabouts was Harry Pouncy, who worked alongside Percy at Quarter Assizes: 'I trust that your anxiety and that of Mrs Pope may soon be relieved by good news.'

Mr J.B. Clarke of Little Aston Hall near Sutton Coldfield, Birmingham, wrote on 4 January to congratulate the Popes on their son's war service: 'What a wonderful record you make & you have reason to be very proud. I am sorry to see one boy is missing & Cyril, whom I well remember, a prisoner. We trust he is being well treated & that you may have good news.'

The Clarkes' son, Noel, had himself been wounded but made a good recovery and returned to Flanders, whilst an extra layer of anxiety for them was caused by the lack of news coming from their German daughter. Despite having a close relative living in Germany, and sharing her desire for eventual peace, Mr Clarke was clear that 'Before absolution we must have repentance eh? & amendment & restitution as far as possible'.

A further letter congratulating Alfred on his sons' commitment contrasted their patriotism with 'the miserable "views" and acts of men who regard themselves as "great" and inspired by the highest sentiments, and who would withhold from the army men who are actually needed for our defence and protection. It is truly sickening.' The correspondent held the flicker of hope that Percy might still be alive somewhere:

> I am deeply sorry that you have not had news of Percy and feel much for you and Mrs Pope in the great anxiety which you have. I suppose it is not certain that he is not a Prisoner somewhere whose facility for communicating with relatives is not afforded. I have read of such cases, and hope this may be one.

Like Mr Clarke, this correspondent deplored what the German nation stood for: 'What fiends the Huns and their Allies are. Their acts would have been deemed impossible in the present day had they not been actually perpetrated.'

In August 1916, following the official confirmation of Percy's death, Robert King wrote from Highbury, lamenting the loss of 'an intimate and much valued friend of mine, of many years standing, and although I feel his loss keenly I am partly consoled with the thought of the noble way in which he went forth to do his duty, even until the end. My prayers go after him.' King had been 'hoping against hope that he was still in the body and that we should at some time hear news of him, but now alas, I fear that this is not to be'.

Walter Nowell, a dental surgeon, wrote from Deal, Kent, on 9 August, still hoping that Percy had been picked up by the enemy 'and is being treated humanely somewhere'. Nowell had been a good friend not only of Percy's, but of a wide circle of men who had been wiped from the earth. Sadly, Nowell reflected, 'I have lost nearly all my old friends, who were for the most part in the original expeditionary force & many many young friends too.'

War news could take months to cross the oceans. R.A. Courthope had studied at Oxford with Percy before entering the Anglican ministry, initially working in a deprived London parish. The devout Percy had assisted Courthope in this work, before the latter left for New South Wales in 1905 to serve with the Brotherhood of the Good Shepherd, an organisation that provided clergy to the Australian outback. Courthope had received news of Percy's demise and wrote to Alfred in January 1917, the letter not arriving at South Court until 5 May that year. He recalled that Percy was 'always a good friend to me and I shall sadly miss him when I return to England. I know that it was a real sense of duty that took him to the war and for which he has laid down his life.'

Dr W.A. Spooner had been Percy's warden during his studies at New College. Spooner was renowned for giving his name to the 'Spoonerism', a verbal error in which a speaker accidentally transposes the initial sounds or letters of two or more words, often to humorous effect. One of his more sombre duties was to organise a service in the college chapel in October 1916 in memory of those students and ex-students who had fallen in the war. For Spooner, who had nurtured so many promising young men like Percy, the war brought regular increments of grief:

> You know that I was fond of your boy whom I always thought an excellent fellow and I deeply lament his loss. Alas our list of those who have fallen this time is a very long one, the longest we have had since the beginning of the war. … It seems hard to see how we and indeed the country generally are to go on after the war is over with all the flower of our youth swept away.

A further memorial service was held in late 1916 at London's Temple Church to commemorate members who had fallen in the war since December 1915. As well as Percy, one other notable name amongst those being remembered was Raymond Asquith, son of the former Prime Minister. Two hymns were sung, 'When I Survey the Wondrous Cross' and 'No More to Sigh, No More to Weep', and Psalms 80 and 71 were read. The service ended with the hymn 'My Eyes Have Seen the Glory of the Coming of the Lord'.

Members of the Dorset Quarter Session Bar Mess passed a resolution on 16 July 1916: 'That Mr and Mrs Alfred Pope be asked to accept the sympathy of the members of the Dorset Quarter Sessions Bar Mess upon the death, in action at the Battle of Loos, of their son Lieutenant Percy Pope of the 1st Welsh Regt.'

The mess felt the loss of their fellow member 'very deeply'. During his short career at the bar, 'his professional ability showed great promise of success and his loveable character had endeared him to all his brother barristers who knew him'. Like so many of those who had given their lives for their country, Percy 'was one of a type of English gentleman who can ill be spared, and the members of the Mess desire to place on record their sorrow at the cruel cutting short of their friend's young life'.

Alfred Pope and his family would ensure that the sacrifices his entire brood had made during the war would forever be remembered. Percy Pope had for some years taken a great interest in the restoration and enlargement work his brother-in-law, the Reverend R.G. Bartelot, was undertaking at St George's Church in Fordington, Dorchester. He had already been an annual subscriber to its funds and had offered his professional skills in assisting Bartelot in overcoming various legal obstacles that had emerged. In his will, Percy left a 'munificent legacy' of £2,100, which enabled the enlargement of the chancel to take place. Reverend Bartelot wrote in the parish magazine of May 1917, with no small degree of poetic licence, that 'there is no greater comfort in the mystery of his passing, than to think that the eternal good of St. George's Church and Parishioners was doubtless foremost in his mind as he lay wounded and dying in the "no man's land" between the contending armies'.

St George's is one of three churches in the Dorchester district that commemorate Percy, along with a memorial tablet in the Holy Trinity Church, on the town's high street. A simple but most remarkable war memorial stands outside the parish church of St Mary in the village of Stratton, close to the Pope family's Wrackleford Estate. Of the eleven names listed from the First World War, four were the sons and son-in-law of Alfred and Elizabeth Pope. A memorial service was held in the church on 30 May 1918 in the honour of both Percy and his brother Charles, attended by a wide circle of family, friends and parishioners, during which a bronze tablet was dedicated. A couple of years later, another tablet was affixed to the opposite wall, commemorating Alfred and Elizabeth Pope's first son, Captain Alec Pope, and their son-in-law, Lieutenant Colonel A.R. Haig-Brown.

For Alfred Pope, the breadth of his family's war contribution and sacrifice warranted a further layer of commemoration beyond the community, church and IWGC pieces. He commissioned his son-in-law, the Reverend R.G.

Bartelot, to compile a book of remembrance, of which 200 copies were privately printed in 1919. Alfred was able to persuade his friend, Thomas Hardy, to write a foreword. Hardy reflected on the unique nature of the Great War, taking men who would in normal circumstances never have pursued a military or naval career. Recognising that the story of the war would need to maintain a focus on the lives of individuals in contrast to grand narratives, Hardy concluded, 'It often has happened that an account of what befell particular individuals in unusual circumstances has conveyed a more vivid picture of those circumstances than a comprehensive view of them has been able to raise.'

Memorials including Percy's name exist in at least six known locations in England, as well as on the Loos Memorial in France. The memorial, which forms two 15-foot high walls and four small circular courts of the Dud Corner Cemetery, contains the names of more than 20,000 men with no known grave. The memorial was designed by Sir Herbert Baker and was unveiled on 4 August 1930.

Percy's is one of 268 names listed on the New College War Memorial in Oxford, unveiled in 1921, whilst his old school, Winchester College, built a permanent reminder to the sacrifice of a generation of pupils and teachers. The Winchester College War Cloister, again designed by Sir Herbert Baker, consists of a roofed quadrangle. The Grade I listed building is the largest known private war memorial in Europe. The school's headmaster, Montague Rendall, was determined to provide a fitting commemoration to the 500 Wykehamists killed in the Great War and the 2,000 further former pupils and staff who had served in the armed forces. A foundation stone was laid on 15 July 1922 by Edward Grey, the former Foreign Secretary, and the monument was completed with knapped flint and Portland and Purbeck stone from Percy's native Dorset. The walls were decorated with the badges of the 120 regiments within which the Wykehamists had served. Symbolising the contribution of former pupils from the British Empire, an apse in each of the four corners of the cloister was dedicated to South Africa, Australia, Canada and India. Stone from each of those nations was transported across the seas to complete the apses, with the addition of four small stones from Ypres set into the floor near the Meads Gate.

Art master Reginald Gleadowe also designed the Lombardic script used for the rhetorically intense main inscription running around the outer wall of the cloister:

THANKS BE TO GOD FOR THE SERVICE OF THESE FIVE HUNDRED WYKEHAMISTS,WHO WERE FOUND FAITHFUL UNTO DEATH AMID THE MANIFOLD CHANCES OF THE GREAT WAR. IN THE DAY OF BATTLE THEY FORGAT NOT

GOD, WHO CREATED THEM TO DO HIS WILL, NOR THEIR COUNTRY, THE STRONGHOLD OF FREEDOM, NOR THEIR SCHOOL, THE MOTHER OF GODLINESS AND DISCIPLINE. STRONG IN THIS THREEFOLD FAITH THEY WENT FORTH FROM HOME AND KINDRED TO THE BATTLEFIELDS OF THE WORLD AND, TREADING THE PATH OF DUTY AND SACRIFICE, LAID DOWN THEIR LIVES FOR MANKIND. THOU, THEREFORE, FOR WHOM THEY DIED, SEEK NOT THINE OWN, BUT SERVE AS THEY SERVED, AND IN PEACE OR IN WAR BEAR THYSELF EVER AS CHRIST'S SOLDIER, GENTLE IN ALL THINGS, VALIANT IN ACTION, STEADFAST IN ADVERSITY

At the memorial's dedication on 31 May 1924, Prince Arthur, Duke of Connaught, declared: 'Five hundred, alas, paid the ultimate tribute and fell on the field of battle.' It is possible that Alfred Pope attended this ceremony alongside Mr H.A.L. Fisher, who had also been instrumental in the raising of the Sheffield City Battalion within which Arthur Greensmith had served, and Margot Asquith, stepmother of the late Raymond Asquith. Percy's sacrifice receives multiple acknowledgement on a daily basis as, to this day, it remains a school tradition for staff and pupils to raise their hats on entering the cloister, in recognition of the war dead.

Arthur Greensmith

'There is a yet unmarked and unknown shrine'

The 1 July In Memoriam section of the *Sheffield Daily Telegraph* from 1917 onwards makes for grim reading, with dozens of names of men who had joined together, trained together, fought together and been killed together filling the columns. The Greensmith family ensured that Arthur's name was included. The city also collectively mourned the hundreds of its youth who had been wiped from the face of the earth on that date in 1916, and in subsequent engagements, with the erection of collective memorials both in Sheffield and on the Somme.

The first opportunity for a collective act of commemoration in the city occurred on 1 July 1917, with a service held at Sheffield Cathedral. According to the *Sheffield Daily Telegraph*, the occasion would be held:

In memory of the lads of a Yorkshire Battalion who gave their lives for England just a year ago [and] will, I hope, become an annual event. Not merely as a Battalion Memorial Day, but as a Memorial Day for all the men of Sheffield who, choosing the brave man's part, have shed their blood that Britain may be great and free.

Apart from the city's recently consecrated cathedral, dozens of other places of worship held commemorations that day. The local press carried reports of the sermons of clergymen from all the main Protestant denominations as Sheffielders turned to the solemnity of religious observance as a means of marking the heartbreaking anniversary. The Reverend C.E. Shipley of Cemetery Road Baptist Church remarked on Sheffield's 'pride and grief':

> It was the day the young men of Sheffield, standing in the ranks of their battalions, faced the full fury of the foe. They had been brought up in Sheffield, had walked our Sheffield streets, had worshipped in our houses of prayer. They came from our University, or banks, offices, shops and factories. They had acquitted themselves like men. No man surrounded and the last that was seen of some of them was that they were pursuing the retreating foe.

A private memorial to Arthur's life was kept by his grieving sister, Cecilia Spittle, in the form of a scrapbook. The cuttings that Cecilia curated in her commemoration of her brother included newspaper reports announcing he had been reported missing, the confirmation of his death, extended accounts of the battle written by Richard Sparling from his hospital bed, an amusing piece about the quality of billets in France and mention of Arthur's disappearance in the Wesleyan Trinity church magazine. Cecilia's scrapbook and other papers relating to her dear brother have been treasured through succeeding generations of her family. Recently, descendants of Cecilia have visited the site where Arthur Greensmith perished, laying a commemorative poppy on the battlefield and paying their respects at the Thiepval Memorial.

Richard Sparling, who had served with the battalion from its inception right through to its eventual disbandment in February 1918, published his *History of the 12th Service Battalion York & Lancaster Regiment* in 1920. In his preface Starling emphasised that 'the heroism of those who fell deserves a lasting recognition', and intended his book to be such 'a memorial to old comrades'. As with the sacrifices of the Pope family, someone intimately connected with this tragic period would commemorate the loss of the fallen. A further book, the novel *Covenant with Death*, written by ex-*Sheffield Telegraph* reporter John Harris, was published in 1969. The book's launch took place in the city's Grand Hotel, with many survivors of the battalion present, and the work is widely considered a masterpiece of war fiction. One chilling line was created by a Leeds Pal, A.V. Pearson, in his 1961 memoirs to describe the fate of these battalions: 'Two years in the making. Ten minutes in the destroying.'

The awfulness of the loss continued to eat away at the soul of Sheffield. Survivors from the battalion formed a 'Twelfth Club', from an initial reunion dinner held in the Grand Hotel on 21 December 1918. The club would continue to meet, regularly at first then more intermittently as the years took their toll, before its eventual disbandment in July 1976 was agreed on by its twenty-six surviving members. The second reunion dinner of the Twelfth Club had been preceded by the dedication of the battalion's memorial in Sheffield Cathedral's St George's Chapel. The memorial tablet, which had been designed by former Sheffield Pal F. Ratcliffe, reads:

1914–1919. TO THE GLORY OF GOD, AND TO THE EVER GLORIOUS MEMORY OF OFFICERS, NCOs AND MEN OF THE 12TH BATTALION YORK AND LANCASTER REGIMENT (SHEFFIELD CITY BATTALION), WHO AT THE CALL OF DUTY AND IN THE CAUSE OF FREEDOM NOBLY MADE THE SUPREME SACRIFICE. THE TABLET IS ERECTED BY THE SURVIVING MEMBERS OF THE BATTALION AND DEDICATED ON 20TH DECEMBER 1920

The grateful villagers of Serre donated a piece of ground for the erection of a memorial to those who had died trying to recapture the area. It was designed by a former Sheffield Pal, Mr J.S. Brown, a pre-war architecture student at the University of Sheffield. Its unveiling, on 24 May 1923, was attended by a large contingent of mourners from Sheffield. Following the ceremony, former soldiers and relatives of the dead took the opportunity to walk the battlefield, some of them bringing back war debris to Yorkshire as souvenirs.

The delay in erecting a cenotaph in the centre of Sheffield caused some local frustration. The *Sheffield City Telegraph* of 15 May 1922 gave voice to the exasperation of bereaved Sheffielders at the sluggish progress towards a permanent public memorial in the city:

CENOTAPH WANTED. Appeal by Sheffield War Graves Association. The Sheffield and District Branch of the British War Graves Association: is doing a tremendous amount of work behind the scenes with the object of getting the Sheffield city authority to erect a Cenotaph in memory of the local men who laid down their lives in the Great War. So far, the response has been disappointing. Every member of the Association lost a near relative in the war, and they feel that if everyone in Sheffield who suffered similar bereavement would communicate with and be prepared to help the Association, the City Council would realise that there is really a big public feeling that a cenotaph should be erected. Proof of this was given in remarkable fashion on the last anniversary of Armistice Day.

The Sheffield and District Branch of the British War Graves Association placed a wreath on St. Paul's Church gates, and, of the hundreds who paused to view it, many made audible Comments on the failure of the city authority to provide a proper resting-place for such tributes.

The report, heavily influenced by the perspective of the Sheffield War Graves Association's members, bitterly concluded:

Eventually Surrey Street, or the bottom of Barker Pool were suggested, but, we understand, were not very favourably received by the civic powers. The contention of the Association is that a cenotaph should have prior claim over traffic, cab stands, or anything else. This matter has been taken up by those who have lost and suffered. Those who for various reasons stayed at home and were fortunate enough to escape bereavement should be amongst the keenest supporters of this scheme. It is at least a simple way of showing for all time their gratitude to those who lost their lives.

The cenotaph was eventually unveiled in October 1925, in a prominent location in front of Sheffield City Hall. It suffered shrapnel damage in the Second World War as more misery rained down on the people of Sheffield during the intense blitz the city endured. It was decided to leave the monument unrepaired as a mark of the wounds that Sheffield had faced twice within a generation. A War Memorial Hall was added to the rear of the Sheffield City Hall in 1932, with a roll of honour containing 5,000 names, including Arthur Greensmith's. Meanwhile, Weston Park, adjacent to the University of Sheffield, saw the erection, in 1923, of a memorial to all 8,814 men of the York and Lancaster Regiment who had been killed.

One posthumous piece of memorialisation of the men of the Sheffield Battalion was left to the world by one of its own men, Sergeant John William 'Will' Streets. Will, who hailed from Whitwell in Derbyshire, had grown up a talented and intelligent boy who played the piano and excelled at school. He also enjoyed painting, sketching and writing about the Derbyshire countryside. From the age of 14 he worked at the coal face of the local mine, helping to support his large family. Will continued his studies by night and served as a Sunday school teacher in the Whitwell Wesleyan chapel. Although a peaceful man at heart, he heeded the call to join up. During his war service, Will continued to write poetry. Will's body was recovered ten months after his disappearance on 1 July 1916 and buried in Euston Road Cemetery, a location which unnervingly echoes the thoughts of one of his poems, as if he had foreseen the fate of his mortal remains:

Behind that long and lonely trenchèd line
To which men come and go, where brave men die,
There is a yet unmarked and unknown shrine,
A broken plot, a soldiers' cemet'ry.

There lie the flower of Youth, the men who scorned
To live (so died) when languished liberty:
Across their graves, flowerless and unadorned,
Still scream the shells of each artillery.

When war shall cease this lonely, unknown spot
Of many a pilgrimage will be the end,
And flowers will bloom in this now barren plot
And fame upon it through the years descend-
But many a heart upon each simple cross
Will hang the grief, the memory of its loss.

To this day, Sheffield continues to honour the memory of its young men who joined up with such willing enthusiasm in the late summer of 1914. In 2018, haunting *There But Not There* silhouette was erected overlooking the site of the Redmires camp, on the ridge where trench digging and practice manoeuvres had been undertaken by Arthur and his comrades during the first months of 1914.

Although no identifiable physical trace of Private Arthur Greensmith exists, his memory is held dear by his family. Cecilia Spittle's granddaughter, Rosemary Gregory, grew up knowing there was always a sadness in her grandmother's life over the loss of her much-loved brother Arthur on the Somme. By the time Rosemary was born in 1948, the loss of Arthur received infrequent reference as the more recent exigencies of the Second World War were given prominence. However, Cecilia never gave up hope of finding more news of her brother. When the *World at War* series was broadcast to commemorate the fiftieth anniversary of the outbreak of the war, she watched every episode intently in the hope that Arthur's face might appear in the archival material displayed on screen. She also ensured that his name was recorded in the In Memoriam column of the local press for many years.

As with so many families it was the centenary of the outbreak of the First World War that caused further reflection on ancestors who had served and perished. In 2014, Rosemary's cousin Dorothy, granddaughter of Arthur Greensmith's sister Dora, suggested the pair visit the Somme to pay their respects to the memory of their Great-Uncle Arthur. Rosemary reflected, 'The fact Arthur has no known grave seems to make it all the more sad.' She and Dorothy were able to visit the Thiepval Memorial and Sheffield Park, walking the area that had contained the copses named Matthew, Mark, Luke and John some ninety-eight years previously. It was 'a dreadful thing to contemplate' the thought of Arthur standing in the same spot witnessing the destruction of the first two waves of his comrades, fearing he was about to meet the same fate. Rosemary and Dorothy symbolically placed poppies at the grave of an unknown soldier, 'a very poignant moment'.

On their return to England, the cousins, along with Dorothy's brother Malcolm, purchased one of the 888,246 ceramic poppies, each representing a British military fatality, which had formed the *Blood Swept Lands and Seas of Red* display within the Tower of London's moat in 2014. They also dedicated an oak sapling at the National Memorial Arboretum in Staffordshire, so Arthur's memory will continue to flourish for years to come. The creation of new commemorations of the sacrifice of Arthur Greensmith not only ensured the perpetuation of his remembrance, but 'has been an important thing to do on behalf of Grandma and the family who had mourned him for so long. I really felt I was doing something on their behalf they had never managed to do.'

Ernest Blackburn

'We are very glad that you have your dear children to live for & pray that they may grow up a very real comfort & blessing.'

Even before the death of Leeds schoolteacher Ernest Blackburn had been officially confirmed, Annie had begun to receive condolence letters. One came from Miss Mary Masters, the 40-year-old headmistress of Park Road School, Batley, where Annie had taught before her marriage. Mary assured Annie that she had been in the thoughts of the teaching staff 'a great deal lately', sympathising with her 'in this dreadful sorrow you have had to bear'. Not only was the sorrow dreadful, but so was the war, 'and it seems to take all we have'. Drawing on a shared Christian faith, Mary stated, 'You must feel it a great comfort that your Husband was so prepared to meet his God.' The existence of young Stanley and Ernest junior made the loss even more tragic, but there remained the 'hope they will be a great solace to you & grow up a blessing'.

Another to correspond was Albert Smith, a former colleague of Ernest's at the Ebenezer Congregational Church Sunday school. Writing on 9 October, he expressed his 'deepest sympathy in your very severe trial'. Albert had spoken at the Sunday school the previous day of Ernest's previous good work there, and it had been decided that Albert should 'convey to you our appreciation of his noble character & also their sympathy to you in your trouble'.

Another to express his sympathy and anxiety was Mr William Grassham, headmaster of the Upper Wortley Council School. Writing on 20 October, William told Annie that he had shown Ernest's 'confrères' a letter she had written, and that they were 'anxious to have any news of him'. Poignantly, the boys in Ernest's class were also beseeching their headmaster to elicit any news he could. The helplessness of Mr Grassham's position was evident: 'I know no way of getting information. We must wait in patience and hope.' William sent Annie his good wishes for her and the 'War Baby', and for her 'speedy return to full strength'. Referring to the huge loss of life amongst a generation of British men, William assumed that Annie had probably wanted to give birth to a girl, 'most mothers do', but 'as times are moving now, men will be wanted in twenty years' time'.

The mundane had to continue in the midst of the tragic, and William signed off by apologising for writing in red ink as 'my kiddies have grabbed the black for their home work'. He had written the letter from home as his school day had been taken up with 'such matters as paying out allowances to soldiers' dependants, celebrating Trafalgar Day & preparing for tomorrow's flag day etc.'

Ernest still appeared on a staff list compiled in January 1917 with a note 'missing since 15.9.1916'. However, on 14 March, Annie Blackburn 'called to inform me that she had received official intimation that her husband, Mr E. Blackburn, for 10 years assistant master here, was killed in action last September'. Upper Wortley School was eventually able to recover from the exigencies of war, but it would have to do so without the reliable rock that was Mr Ernest Blackburn.

Once Ernest's death had been formally declared, the *Dewsbury Reporter* carried a piece extolling the virtues of the 'promising Dewsbury man' who had met a 'sad end'. After highlighting the 'deep sympathy' that would be felt for his widow, two children and wider family, the newspaper commented:

> He had a whole host of friends in Dewsbury who admired him for his excellent qualities, his sound common-sense, his devotion to the work he undertook to do, and his interest in good causes. It is a tragedy that so many promising young men like Ernest Blackburn should be taken, and the country is greatly the poorer for this death.

Maurice T. Oldroyd, a member of the choir at the Ebenezer Congregational Church, in which Ernest had previously sung, expressed his condolences on 19 March 1917. Having heard that Ernest was 'now sadly reported killed', Oldroyd had been 'hoping up to now that his life had been spared'. On behalf of the choir, Maurice sent Annie 'our truest sympathy to you in this great sorrow &

pray that you may be comforted in the fact that he gave himself for his country & for his home & dear ones'. Already the desire to turn Ernest's sacrifice into a worthwhile act had begun, with that triumvirate of noble causes giving reason to suggest that Annie's loss was not in vain. Furthermore, there was a future to look forward to, albeit one without her dear husband. 'We are very glad that you have your dear children to live for & pray that they may grow up a very real comfort & blessing.' Whilst expressing regret that 'we shall see him no more', Maurice assured Annie of the 'great respect' in which he had been held, and utilised Christian symbolism to finish with the uplifting message that 'I always think of him in our choir at Ebenezer, but now he is raised to the Heavenly Choir, where they "praise unceasingly & never tire"'.

One year on from Ernest's disappearance, memorial messages appeared in the *Dewsbury Reporter*. One, from 'Walter, Kitty & Douglas' in Brighouse, remembered:

> One of the best that God could lend
> A loving brother, a faithful friend

Another, inserted by Ernest's parents and four of his siblings, attempted to give his death some higher collective meaning:

> A British hero to the heart
> His precious life he gave
> He died upon the battlefield
> The British flag to save.

The insertion ended with the widely used quote from John 15:13: 'Greater love hath no man than this, that a man lay down his life for his friends.' Finally, in order to cement the family's patriotic credentials, Harold was referred to as being a member of HM Forces.

As Ernest's body was never recovered, his sacrifice was formally recorded on the Thiepval Memorial to the Missing of the Somme. In addition, both Dewsbury and Armley wished to record the loss of their sons. The war memorial in Armley Park, situated a short distance from the house in which Annie Blackburn was left to bring up young Stanley and Ernest junior, would have acted as a frequent reminder for the trio of the aching hole in their family. Unveiled in 1921, it consists of a hexagonal base surmounted by four pillars supporting a cross, with the names of 361 men being listed on three panels on the side of the base. An inscription was chosen to give meaning to those hundreds of grieving families for their loss:

TRUE LOVE BY LIFE
TRUE LOVE BY DEATH IS TRIED
LIVE THOU FOR ENGLAND
WE FOR ENGLAND DIED

Dewsbury's War Memorial, unveiled in September 1924, was in a prominent position in Crow Nest Park. A hugely commanding sculpture, it consists of a round tower with an internal vault and piers supporting a capitol. In the centre is a tripod candle holder. A doorway is located on one side of the memorial, which stands on a large paved based with three steps leading up to it. A total of 1,070 names, including that of Ernest Blackburn, are commemorated as First World War casualties, on marble plaques set around the sides of the tower.

The recognition and remembrance of Ernest's death was to perpetuate. Stanley Blackburn, a mere 18 months old at the time he became fatherless, inherited Ernest's aptitude and interest in scientific subjects. Having passed through West Leeds High School, in 1937 he was awarded a Parkinson Research Scholarship by the University of Leeds to study Chemistry. Stanley continued to live at home with Annie, the family relocating just around the corner from Moorfield Avenue to Highthorne Street in Armley, still a short walk to Armley Park and it's solemn war memorial, which continued to remind the community of the

Dewsbury War Memorial, Crow Nest Park. (*Author's collection*)

shadows cast by the scale of the losses of 1914–18. By 1939, Stanley Blackburn was working as a research chemist, and after the Second World War pursued a successful career, working for the Wool Industries Research Association and having many articles published in the academic press. Stanley was also appointed a Fellow of the Royal Society of Chemistry. Family ties with his late father's extended relatives remained strong, as Stanley acted as executor of the wills of Ernest's siblings, Harold, Lily and May.

Sadly, Annie and Stanley were to suffer a further loss in 1946. Ernest Leslie Blackburn had been born on 17 October 1916, just days after the shattering blow of his father's disappearance had been notified to the family. Whilst his elder brother Stanley reflected Ernest senior's passion for science, Ernest junior followed his late father into the teaching profession. By 1939, he was a resident assistant master at Kibworth Beauchamp Grammar School in Oadby, Leicestershire. Meningitis cut short another promising Blackburn teaching career in 1946, leaving Annie to grieve deeply once again.

Stanley continued to carry the memories of his father into his old age. In 1996, the *Yorkshire Post* reported that a plaque, erected in the Leeds Education Authority building in Great George Street to commemorate the city's teachers who had been killed in the war, had been stored in a conference room for the past decade, following the authority's relocation to new premises in the 1980s. The plaque included Ernest's name, and over the following fifteen months, Stanley fought to persuade the authority to give the memorial a more prominent home. His persistence was rewarded when, in August 1996, the plaque was re-erected in its original position in Great George Street. Four years later, Stanley died, aged 85, having donated a wealth of information about his father to the University of Leeds. In doing so he ensured that Ernest's story would be kept alive for future generations.

Gilbert Donnelly

'He was lost, and is found'

On 29 July 1919, 4,000 people gathered in Belfast's Celtic Park Stadium where, eight years earlier, Gilbert Donnelly's elder brother Billy had challenged the Irish bantamweight champion. The attendees, including many war veterans, were there to 'honour … the Belfastmen of the 16th (Irish) Division' in 'a notable demonstration of the part played by Belfast nationalists'. Joseph Devlin, MP for Belfast Falls and one of the handful of moderate Nationalist MPs to survive the Sinn Féin advances in the 1918 General Election, declared that Gilbert and his comrades 'died not as cowards died, but as soldiers of freedom, with their faces toward the fire, and in the belief that their life-blood was poured out in defence of liberty for the world. Unfortunately,' he continued, 'the close of the war brought to Ireland no peace and freedom, but strife and repression.'

Later in 1919, on the first anniversary of the armistice, at 11.00 am Belfast offices, factories and shops fell silent. Traffic stood still. Guns fired in Belfast Lough to mark the beginning and end of the two-minute silence. However, in the city of Derry there was no public commemoration of the sacrifice of war. The collective memory of the Catholic Irish who went to war was quickly thrust to one side in the sectarian turmoil that engulfed Ireland in the 1920s. Whilst cities, towns and villages on the British mainland went to great lengths to ensure each community gave appropriate space to memorials, in public spaces, in churches, schools, workplaces and sporting societies, the honouring of the Catholic war dead was sporadic. What was worse was that many returning soldiers found their previous jobs were no longer available, and it proved particularly difficult to obtain a government position.

However, within the predominantly Protestant milieu of Queen's University Belfast, there was a determination that the sacrifice of former students and employees, of whatever religious denomination, would not be forgotten. In May 1919, a mass meeting of students was held in the examination hall to consider a scheme 'towards the raising of a memorial to those Queensmen who have fallen in the war'. Mr R.I. Poston, the Honorary Secretary of the Services Club, recalled the death of over one-third of his contemporaries who had been admitted to the university. Major Gregg Wilson, commander of the Queen's OTC, commented that there were few of the university's fallen whom he did not know intimately, 'and he hoped that the students would keep before them the noble example of these men'. The meeting unanimously passed a resolution to raise money for and to erect a memorial 'worthy of the self-sacrifice and inspiring example of those of our fellow-students who have fallen in the war'.

The War Memorial, situated in front of the main Lanyon Building in University Road, Belfast, and containing the names of 253 staff and students including Gilbert Donnelly and his former OTC colleague Hugo Bell Fisher, was first dedicated on 21 July 1924 by HRH the Duke of York. It is very likely that Gilbert and Hugo would have been friends, being so closely associated at the University Medical Faculty, in the OTC and in the regiment to which they were assigned. They remain companions today in the green fields of France and in name in front of the university they had entered in 1915 with such high hopes of a life of adult achievement, advancement and satisfaction. The memorial's inscription reads:

TO THE MEMORY OF THE MEMBERS OF THIS UNIVERSITY
AND ITS OFFICERS TRAINING CORPS WHO GAVE THEIR
LIVES IN THE GREAT WAR, LEAVING THEIR SUCCESSORS
A PERPETUAL EXAMPLE OF SELF-SACRIFICE AND LOYAL
SERVICE.

1914–1918

As Ireland divided into two separate countries, the memory of its war dead bifurcated. The year 1966 saw the fiftieth anniversary of both the Easter Rising and the Battle of the Somme. Whilst the sacrifices of the Ulster Division were commemorated in Northern Ireland, south of the border the Irish Roman Catholic community celebrated the emergence of an independent Irish state. The awkward story of Irish Roman Catholics, men like Gilbert Donnelly, who had fought in the British Army, was overlooked. Their legacy did not fit in with either of the two prevailing political narratives in a bitterly divided Ireland.

Individually, Irish families who had lost a relative in the war continued to publicly commemorate the sacrifice in the In Memoriam columns of local newspapers. Sometimes these contained a religious strain of Roman Catholic invocations. Less often there might be reference to the more Protestant ideal of sacrifice for King, Country and Empire.

By 1918, the Orange Order had fully incorporated memorialisation of the sacrifice of the Ulster Division at the Somme into its activities, thus driving out any hope of a united commemoration of the dead. Peace day, to commemorate the signing of the Treaty of Versailles in 1919, was celebrated on 19 July in Great Britain but not until 9 August in Belfast, to avoid clashing with the Orange Order marches. When the Belfast Cenotaph was unveiled in 1929, Catholic organisations were absent from the main ceremony, veterans of the 16th Division laying wreaths later in the day. This polarisation meant that the First World War became an untold and eventually forgotten story for nationalists and republicans.

Thus, for nationalists collectively, remembrance of the dead became problematic. Roman Catholic churches did not produce lists of the dead like their Protestant counterparts did, although there was a Requiem Mass at St Mary's Belfast for the souls of Belfast Catholic soldiers and sailors who had lost their lives in the war. Whilst many Catholics were not ashamed of their ancestors' service, their remembrance was increasingly expressed in private. Peace Day was seen to celebrate militarism. The *Irish News* opined in 1919 that 'there is absolutely no difference between the manner and temper of a Red Indian victory carnival and the gorgeous processions arranged to celebrate the triumph over Germany'. A separate INVA parade of Belfast's nationalist ex-soldiers took place on Sunday, 19 October, followed by a Requiem Mass at St Peter's Pro-Cathedral in the Falls Road area.

In contrast to the rest of the UK, memorials to specific divisions were a more resonant focus for remembrance for Belfast's population. An Ulster Tower was erected at Thiepval in France, an exact copy of Helen's Tower in the grounds of Clandeboye Estate in County Down in memory of the volunteers who had trained there before going to the front. The 16th (Irish) Division was commemorated with stone Celtic crosses at Guillemont and Wytschaete. In Dublin, the Islandbridge memorial gardens, a splendid parkland in a riverside meadow, designed by Edwin Lutyens, played host to a series of commemorations to those who had fallen fighting in the British and Irish armies in the first half of the twentieth century. By the mid-1980s, the gardens were run down and neglected. Two Irish Republican paramilitary attacks in 1956 and 1958 had caused some minor damage to the Stone of Remembrance, with the gardens having been frequently vandalised and also used as a rubbish dump by the Dublin Corporation.

By the late 1980s, the Irish public began to re-examine aspects of pre-Irish Revolution history and national identity, and the gardens and monument were restored. As a sign of the maturing of Ireland's relationship with a British imperial past, the considerable funding for the renovation of the gardens was raised and it was formally dedicated on 10 September 1988 by representatives of the four main churches of Ireland.

A decade later, as the Northern Irish Peace Process ground towards the breakthrough of the Good Friday Agreement, Mary McAleese, the President of Ireland, and Queen Elizabeth II together dedicated a memorial to all Irish people who had fallen in the First World War. The 'Island of Ireland Peace Tower', unveiled on 11 November 1998, acted as a symbol of political reconciliation via shared commemoration of the war dead. A beautiful replica of an ancient Irish round tower, made from stone from an old workhouse in Ireland, it is sited on Messines Ridge in Belgium, close to the spot where Gilbert Donnelly had experienced the horror of war seventy-one years previously.

It would be a further two decades before a public memorial to the 16th (Irish) Division was erected in Ireland. In November 2016, the French-Irish memorial was unveiled jointly by French and Irish government ministers. It was a gift to the Irish people from France, given in recognition of the solidarity and the sacrifice made by those on the island of Ireland in the defence and freedom of France, particularly during the First World War. The memorial is adorned with a replica of the Ginchy Cross, itself a monument built by the men of the 16th (Irish) Division in a French churchyard in honour of their comrades who had fallen during the Battle of the Somme. Containing at its base words written by Field Marshal Foch ten years after the signing of the Armistice, commending the Irish for their 'unconquerable spirit', it is significant that Ireland was willing to accept a French tribute to the war dead on their soil, rather than a British one.

Although the collective commemoration of the Irish war dead has been controversial and contested for more than a century, taking place against the backdrop of ongoing turmoil and efforts to bring peace and reconciliation to the island, the individual memorialisation of Lieutenant Gilbert Donnelly suffered from no such strife.

On 21 March 2018, members of his family attended two separate venues to commemorate the centenary of his death. Phil Donnelly, who had compiled a history of the family, visited St Emilie Valley Cemetery in France and there was also a wreath laid at the grave by RMFA members the following day. Meanwhile, Dan Donnelly travelled to Belfast with his wife to meet up with his extended family for a ceremony at the QUB memorial. This commemoration had been organised by Mark Doherty, Hugh Donnelly's grandson. For over thirty years he had walked past the memorial without realising his close family connection to one of the men remembered on it. The war dead had not been mentioned much in his broadly Roman Catholic nationalist family during his formative years, as the Protestant loyalist community had taken strong ownership of war commemoration, using it, in Mark's view, 'as a political badge of honour showing their loyalty to Britain and the Crown'. His interest pricked by the war's centenary commemoration, he had come across the forum thread on which Dan and James were posting. Mark's research also discovered Gilbert's name on the memorial plaque in the old OTC Training Hall in Belfast, and his inclusion in the Irish Memorial Books, copies of which reside in the Linen Hall Library in Belfast and St Anne's Cathedral, as well as in a reading room at the National War Memorial Gardens in Dublin.

Descendants of five of Gilbert's brothers were present at the centenary ceremony, in addition to representatives from the Somme Association and the university's Officers' Training Corps. Dan Donnelly gave a short oration about Gilbert's life and death before Mark Doherty performed 'Irish Boy', a whistle lament. Séan Donnelly, grandson of Gilbert's brother John, sang 'Danny Boy'. Dr Stanley Hawkins, representing the university, read Wilfred Owen's tender poem 'Futility', in which a dying man's comrades attempt to effect the sun into breathing fresh life into him:

> Move him into the sun—
> Gently its touch awoke him once,
> At home, whispering of fields half-sown.

Always it woke him, even in France,
Until this morning and this snow.
If anything might rouse him now
The kind old sun will know.

Think how it wakes the seeds—
Woke once the clays of a cold star.
Are limbs, so dear-achieved, are sides
Full-nerved, still warm, too hard to stir?
Was it for this the clay grew tall?
—O what made fatuous sunbeams toil
To break earth's sleep at all?

An aficionado of Wilfred Owen's work, Mark had selected this poem as it had greater resonance given the facts that both Gilbert and Wilfred signed up in the same week, both reached lieutenant status and both died in 1918, in Owen's case, a few weeks before an armistice was declared.

In keeping with the religious milieu within which the First World War generation was raised, prayers were said. Dan wrote: 'The message we wanted to convey to Gilbert was clear – your descendants, your Regiment's Association, your University, have gathered, to let you, your parents, your brothers and your sisters know that we did not forget.'

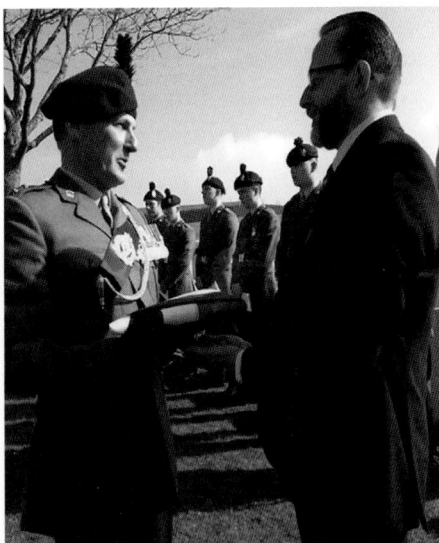

Dan Donnelly receives a Union Flag on behalf of his great-grandfather from Brigadier Mike Murdoch. (*Courtesy the Donnelly family*)

On 21 March 2019, precisely 101 years after Gilbert's death, a rededication ceremony, organised by the Ministry of Defence's Joint Casualty and Compassionate Centre, took place at St Emilie Cemetery. It was attended by more than sixty people, all of whom felt a connection to the long-dead soldier. James Uzzell, whose expertise had initially raised the possibility that the grave might belong to Gilbert, was present. James started visiting the Western Front, and notably St Emilie, after discovering that many servicemen's graves and memorials there have never been visited by their families, due to the cost and difficulty of travelling to Europe in the decades immediately after the First

World War, and so he felt obliged to do so for his own relatives lost in the conflict. James said, 'Contributing to Gilbert being found and the Donnelly family at last being able to visit his grave after waiting for over 100 years has been both an amazing privilege and experience.' Dan Donnelly, representing his great-grandfather, John, was presented with a Union flag by Brigadier Mike Murdoch MBE, Deputy Colonel of the Royal Irish Regiment. 'It was a very intense and poignant experience,' recalled Dan. The fact that Gilbert had fought as an Irishman within the British Army was signified by the dual attendance of Colonel Chris Borneman, Military Attaché to the British Embassy in Paris, and Colonel Bergin, Military Attaché from the Republic of Ireland to the French Republic. Representatives of other organisations, including Liam Nolan, chair of the Royal Munster Fusiliers Association, Emma Worrall of the National Army Museum's War Graves Adjudication Unit, Julian Blake of the Commonwealth War Graves Commission and Carol Walker of the Somme Association, laid wreaths at Gilbert's grave.

More than a century after Captain Tom Duggan CF, chaplain to 1st Battalion Royal Munster Fusiliers, had been unable to provide Gilbert with a full Christian burial due to his own capture by the Germans, it fell to the Reverend Nathan King CF, chaplain to 1st Battalion The Royal Irish Regiment, to conduct the service that would finally honour his death.

In his sermon, the Reverend King declared:

> By such acts of rededication, we remember again and renew our thoughts about those who have passed and are known not only to God but also to family members past and present. We are reminded again of the great sacrifices made and recognise in them the courageousness of the human spirit. There is an important spiritual element to such remembrance with a sense held in the Christian faith that the souls of the faithful rest in the presence of God and that peace has been found.

Ten members of the Royal Irish Regiment, the successor to the many Irish regiments that fought in the First World War, were in attendance.

Twenty-five members of Gilbert's family attended the service. Dan Donnelly spoke on their behalf: 'We know Gilbert's father and siblings were left bereft at news of his loss and that they had tried to find out the details and whereabouts of his death. We are therefore delighted to gather on their behalf and remember this brave young man who voluntarily left the comfort of home for the horror of war.'

Gilbert, the godson of a prominent Irish musician, had his memory honoured in melodic fashion by other relations. 'Danny Boy' was again sung by Séan Donnelly. 'Amazing Grace' was played on the bagpipes by Sean McLaughlin,

The rededication party for Lieutenant Gilbert Donnelly, silhouetted against the skies under which he fell a century previously. (*Courtesy the Donnelly family*)

a descendent of Gilbert's younger brother Samuel, and Mark Doherty and his son Barra also played a mellow duet on the low whistle.

In a radio interview, Dan emphasised the impact of the finding of Gilbert's grave and the rededication ceremony on the wider family:

> It's important for us to give our respect and pay our dues to the sacrifice that he went through all those years ago. Most of Gilbert's brothers and sisters have family and the Donnellys have blossomed into a huge family. Gilbert didn't have that opportunity, his life was cut short at the age of 20, he didn't have children or great-grandchildren to remember him. We are Gilbert's descendants, we are his family and it's very important for us to recognise the loss felt by my great-grandfather, my great-uncles and aunts who did know Gilbert and would've felt his loss very greatly at the time.

Mark Doherty was keenly aware of the wider implications of the closing of the chapter of the search for his great-uncle:

> As well as the closure of standing by his grave, there is also the closure within his Irish family of fully and publicly recognising the noble sacrifice that he had made. Unfortunately, there are many others from Ireland who remain forgotten due to their families never talking about their stories and refusing war medals.
>
> It was a great tragedy in Irish Society that to take part in the Great War was afterwards culturally entrenched as a show of loyalty to the British

Crown. Hence participation in any show of commemoration had been claimed by those of a Protestant/Pro-Union persuasion and was generally spurned by the opposing Catholic/Irish Nationalist group.

For a century, the Donnelly family had not known where the body of their precious young relative had lain. A collective effort had ensured that the gravestone in St Emilie Valley Cemetery that had for nearly a century read 'An Unknown Lieutenant of the Great War' now read:

> SON OF JOHN AND JEMIMA
> GLASTONBURY AVE, BELFAST.
> HE WAS LOST AND IS FOUND

Alan Stirling

'We shall find our missing loved one, in the father's mansion fair.'

Religious tropes were to the fore in the public commemoration of the life of Alan Stirling. Although the Stirlings were Anglicans, Alan may have had some association with his local Methodism, as his is one of twenty names listed on the Trinity Methodist Church Memorial in Wolverhampton, situated less than a mile from the Stirling abode. A three-stepped base surmounted by a tapering plinth, shaft and 20-foot-high Gothic cross today sits somewhat incongruously outside a block of flats, the church itself having been demolished in 1976. The cross was made of red granite due to, according to one newspaper report, 'red being the colour of sacrifice'.

The inscription reads:

> TO THE GLORY OF GOD
> AND IN MEMORY OF THE FOLLOWING
> WHO GAVE THEIR LIVES IN
> DEFENCE OF THEIR COUNTRY
> 1914–1918
> FAITHFUL UNTO DEATH

The memorial was unveiled and dedicated on Sunday, 31 October 1920 at 10.45 am by Lieutenant Colonel T.F. Waterhouse, DSO, DL.

Alan's family also received a commemorative card upon the erection of the memorial statue in the grounds of Winchester Cathedral, dedicated to the men of the King's Royal Rifle Corps who had fallen in the war. It is a bronze statue of a rifleman in full fighting kit by sculptor John Tweed, erected near the west entrance of the cathedral. Annie Blackburn received the same card in respect of her husband Ernest. A roll of honour was compiled comprising the names of the officers, warrant officers, non-commissioned officers and Riflemen of the regiment, who fell in the Great War, 1914–1919, engrossed on vellum, in alphabetical order and stating in each case the date of death. Bound in a large volume, it lies in an oaken case resting upon a stone plinth between two of the columns of the nave of the cathedral.

The Winchester memorials were unveiled on Empire Day 1922 by HRH Prince Henry, a former member of the KRRC, and by HRH Princess Beatrix, whose son, Prince Maurice of Battenberg, had served as a lieutenant in the 1st Battalion, and had been killed while leading his platoon on 27 October 1914.

Along with hundreds of thousands of other families, the Stirlings commemorated their son's death in the classified section of the local press:

STIRLING – In loving memory of our dear son, Rifleman Alan Stirling, reported missing in action March 21st 1918, now presumed dead.

> Far beyond this land of changes,
> Far beyond this world of care,
> We shall find our missing loved one
> in the father's mansion fair.

Although Alan Stirling was not originally listed on the Aldridge War Memorial, he did feature in the town's Great War Centenary commemorations. Station Road, where he had been living in about 1911, was informally renamed 'Poppy Road'. Almost a hundred of the street's neat red-brick terraced houses were transformed with displays of 24,000 red poppies, and each of the sixteen men who had lived on Station Road were represented by a black silhouette statue bearing their name. Alan's niece, Rosemary Phillips, proudly stood next to the representation of the man she never knew, but whose precious letters she had lovingly cherished for decades. The houses where another forty soldiers had lived, whose families were able to welcome them home from war, each displayed a poster to mark that man's contribution.

Rosemary was also able to undertake an emotional pilgrimage to France, along with her sister Christine, the pair becoming the first relatives of Alan Stirling's to visit the area where he fell and pay their respects at the Pozières Memorial. Finally, a connection between Alan's roots and the land of his demise had been established, with memories to cherish for evermore.

John Butt

'I thank God for every remembrance of him'

As official confirmation of Lieutenant John Gillis 'Jack' Butt's death became public news, many who knew him and his family were keen to record their admiration. Sir Alfred Keogh, Director General of Army Medical Services, the most senior officer in the Royal Army Medical Corps, wrote personally to Jack's mother, Mrs Helen Butt:

> There is alas! no further doubt. The letter [written by Lieutenant Colonel Earle, Jack's commanding officer] is a splendid testimony to your gallant son. He gave his life doing his duty. He knew no doubt the chances of his being killed were very great, but he could not have reckoned on being assassinated by these ruffians. ... Let the remembrance of his noble and devoted conduct be a great consolation to you.

Helen responded on 17 July 1916, her letter trimmed with the black border of mourning, thanking Keogh for this letter: 'it is one which any mother would be proud to receive and I shall treasure it for the kind things you have written of my dear son.' It was a great consolation to Helen to know that Jack did his duty 'in this struggle and I also think I am fortunate to be able to say that I can thank God for every remembrance of him'.

Helen also entered into correspondence with Jack's former tutor at Trinity College Dublin, Francis Dixon, sending him copies of letters which the latter felt to be 'a splendid testimony of your son's courage and good work'. Dixon had previously shared his admiration of Jack with her on 29 January 1916, when his death was still unconfirmed, joining Helen in her hope that her son was a prisoner in Belgium. Dixon related how well Jack had been thought of by his university peers:

> I wish you could realise how many friends your son has here in Dublin. I know of no one more beloved than he was as a student in T.C.D. Indeed he was regarded as the ideal type of Trinity College Medical Student, and among Arts Men he has almost as many admirers as among Medicals. ... I am very glad to have his photograph, which I hope you intend me to keep.

In all, the college lost 471 students, staff and alumni during the war and a Hall of Honour was dedicated in 1928. In 2015, a stone, quarried from the Isle of Portland, was placed outside the hall with inscriptions in both Gaelic and English. Its unveiling was observed with a minute's silence. The revival of memorialisation that accompanied the Great War centenary commemorations saw further acknowledgement of Jack's sacrifice. His college photograph, along with those of ninety-five other students of the Medical School of Trinity College Dublin, were resurrected from the archives and curated on a website in honour of those ex-students who had been killed in the conflict. Out of the 3,000 students or alumni of the college who served in the armed forces, nearly a third had graduated from the School of Medicine.

Jack's alma mater, Marlborough College, opened a war memorial hall in 1925 to commemorate the 749 Old Marlburians who were killed in the conflict. A 'J.W. Butt' is recorded on one of two large marble panels that name the fallen, and as no soldier of that name appears on the Commonwealth War Graves Commission website, it may be surmised that this is a recording or transcription error of Jack's middle initial.

Mrs Helen Butt had conducted her relentless search for Jack's whereabouts from Crumlin Lodge, on the outskirts of the Buckinghamshire village of Datchet. The village's official war memorial was unveiled on 8 May 1920, but, as was the case with many towns and villages up and down the country, there had previously been temporary memorials erected. A wayside shrine had been raised on the London Road, and a Celtic cross was built just inside the boundary wall of the churchyard. The London Road crucifix showing Christ's death at Calvary was paid for by a Mrs and Miss Curling in thanksgiving to the safe return of their loved one, Richard Curling, and in memory of the sacrifice of so many of his contemporaries. It was unveiled in May 1919 and became the focus of an Empire Day congregation, which included many soldiers recently returned from the war. A procession went from the parish church to the memorial, to be addressed by the Bishop of Buckinghamshire, whose address commented that the memorial was intended as a wayside shrine, a feature that would be a familiar sight to those who had served in France but of which there were few examples in England. The memorial was adorned with an inscription from the Nicene Creed:

I LOOK FOR THE RESURRECTION OF THE DEAD AND THE LIFE OF THE WORLD TO COME. AMEN

The shrine also became the focal point of the first Armistice Day commemoration later that year, during which a floral tribute was placed at the foot of the shrine by the women of Datchet.

An unknown group of women also paid for a 9-foot-high Celtic cross made from Cornish granite in the churchyard, in memory of those who had fallen in the war. The words from the Book of Revelation, 'Faithful Unto Death' adorned its south face.

The *Windsor and Eton Express* discussed the range of options available to a specially appointed committee of the Parish Council from which they could choose the most appropriate official war memorial for Datchet. The possibilities included a recreation ground with a monument, endowed beds at the Edward VII Hospital, a prominent clock, accommodation for disabled ex-servicemen or almshouses for pensioners. By November 1919, £600 had been raised via a special war memorial fund and a design agreed by the subscribers. The memorial was to be sited in a prominent location on the village green. It was unveiled by the Lord Lieutenant of Buckinghamshire, the Marquis of Lincolnshire, on 8 May 1920, with most village inhabitants attending the ceremony. The handsome obelisk was designed by Lionel Cust of Datchet House, who had previously held the posts of Director of the National Portrait Gallery and Keeper of the King's Pictures. Children from the village school, some of whose fathers' names were on the memorial, were given a post of honour near the memorial and demobilised soldiers were drawn up in line along the main path. The Marquis noted in his speech that it was fitting that memorials were being erected in communities across the county, rather than there being, as some had advised, one large memorial in the county town. 'How much better it was that loving hearts had decided to set up memorials in every township and village of England.' A parchment roll of honour containing the names of fifty-four men killed in the war was placed in the parish church of St Mary the Virgin.

Unusually, the memorial's lengthy inscription was explicit about the nations that had been vanquished due to the efforts of Datchet men and women, giving the impression of having been written by committee:

THIS MONUMENT IS ERECTED BY INHABITANTS OF DATCHET
TO COMMEMORATE THE GREAT WAR OF 1914 – 1919
AND THE GLORIOUS VICTORY OF THE BRITISH FORCES AND THEIR ALLIES BY SEA, ON LAND, AND IN THE AIR OVER THE COMBINED FORCES OF GERMANY, AUSTRIA, TURKEY AND BULGARIA

ALSO TO RECORD THE SHARE TAKEN BY THIS VILLAGE IN PROMOTING THIS VICTORY AND TO PAY GRATEFUL AND REVERENT TRIBUTE TO THOSE WHO LAID DOWN THEIR LIVES
FOR THEIR KING AND COUNTRY IN THE CAUSE OF JUSTICE AND FREEDOM THE NAMES HERE RECORDED ARE OF THOSE INHABITANTS OF DATCHET WHO AT THE CALL OF DUTY LAID DOWN THEIR LIVES FOR THEIR COUNTRY

MOURN NOT FOR THEM FOR THEY CAN NEVER DIE

The inscription went on to record the numbers of Datchet inhabitants who performed military service at home or abroad, or who worked for the Red Cross, the Volunteer Defence Corps, the Voluntary Aid Detachment, the Hospital Supply Depot and those who served as Special Constables.

Sadly, Helen Butt was never to see these collective and public monuments to her son's sacrifice, or even the Allied victory in the war, which had yielded four further years of devastation since her son had laid down his life to save that of his commanding officer. After experiencing further heartache in May 1917, when her 83-year-old father, James Garraty, died while residing with her at Crumlin Lodge, Helen died, aged 51, on 15 January 1918, of complications following an ovarian operation five months previously and associated heart failure. She was buried in Datchet Cemetery, with her husband, Colonel Edward Butt, being interred in the same plot following his death in 1935. Jack's name was also added to the base of this personal family monument.

Helen had already kept her own private memorial to her son, in the form of a cutting of Rudyard Kipling's poem 'My Boy Jack', written in honour of 16-year-old Jack Cornwell. Helen kept the clipping amongst her personal correspondence. Cornwell had won the Victoria Cross after staying by his post during the Battle of Jutland, and Kipling had, like Helen, to endure months of painstaking but futile enquiries as to the fate of his own son following his loss at the Battle of Loos:

'Have you news of my boy Jack?'
Not this tide.
'When d'you think that he'll come back?'
Not with this wind blowing, and this tide.

'Has any one else had word of him?'
Not this tide.
For what is sunk will hardly swim,
Not with this wind blowing, and this tide.

'Oh, dear, what comfort can I find?'
None this tide,
Nor any tide,
Except he did not shame his kind —
Not even with that wind blowing, and that tide.

Then hold your head up all the more, This tide,
And every tide;
Because he was the son you bore,
And gave to that wind blowing and that tide!

Whilst commemoration of Jack's sacrifice was recorded in the places he had lived and studied, the Imperial War Graves Commission began the huge task of gathering the identifiable and unidentifiable corpses that were scattered across France and Flanders. As the front line had moved westwards in the days following Jack's death, it is presumed that both he and the unknown corporal were buried by the Germans, close to the spot where they had been slain. It is probable the graves were marked with crosses as when ground was retaken by the British in 1918, both bodies were exhumed and moved to the Hooge Crater Cemetery and interred beneath Imperial War Graves Commission headstones. Jack was identified as a lieutenant of the RAMC due to a badge on his tunic. His comrade was identified as a corporal, from the presence of stripes on the shoulder of his uniform. They lay side by side in Plot XXI, Row J, Graves 6 and 7. As it was impossible to identify his remains beyond his rank and corps, J.G. Butt was one of nearly 55,000 names of men with no known grave included on the sublime Menin Gate in the city of Ypres.

Edward Butt was sent a bronze plaque, popularly known as the 'death penny' due to its resemblance to the coin then in circulation. Along with this came a message from King George V: 'I join with my grateful people in sending you this memorial of a brave life given for others in the Great War.' For nearly a century, the unknown lieutenant lay in a Flanders field, as generations of visitors from around the world passed through the Great War battlefields to pay their respects and reflect on the sacrifice of Jack's generation.

Remarkably, the story did not end with the erection of the 'Known unto God' gravestone above Jack's body. In April 2016, a submission, prepared by Australian war researcher Michael Michael concerning Lieutenant J.G. Butt and the grave in the Hooge Crater Cemetery dedicated to an RAMC lieutenant, was accepted by the CWGC as sufficient evidence for the case to be reviewed by the Ministry of Defence. The MoD's Joint Casualty and Compassionate Centre (JCCC) acted as the final adjudicator on the case. The submission was based on two areas of evidence: the position of the Grenadier Guards at the Kruiseik crossroads and the statements made by Lieutenant Colonel Earle, Private Venton and the unidentified German doctor. The crossroads were under British control from 18–29 October 1914 and then from 28 September 1918 onwards. Seven RAMC lieutenants who were killed during that period had no known burial place. Of these men, only three died in Belgium. Lieutenant Rintoul was killed near St Julien on 21 October 1914, with Lieutenant Shields dying just to the east of Polygon Wood on 26 October. The positions in which these officers were killed were several miles from the crossroads so they could be excluded as possible candidates. The JCCC accepted this piece of historical detective work as satisfactory proof that Lieutenant Butt had lain in Hooge Crater Cemetery for the past century. On 26 June 2018, staff from the JCCC contacted a descendant of Edward and Helen Butt, having managed to trace him through a genealogy website, to inform the family of their conclusion and

Rededication ceremony of the grave of Lieutenant John Gillis Butt. Left to right: Captain Benedict Griffiths, The Mercian Regiment; Captain Terence Twining MBE, Adjutant General's Corps; Nicholas Previté, great-nephew; Lance Corporal Liam Brewster, 16 Medical Regiment, RAMC; Sub Lieutenant Harry Lewis, Royal Navy, representing the British Embassy; Alderman Jef Verschoore; Lizzie Brawley, Royal British Legion; Christine Connerty CWGC; Jeanette Page JCCC; The Reverend Tim Flowers CF Chaplain 4th Battalion The Mercian Regiment (back to camera); Rosie Barron JCCC; Sergeant David Pickles, Bugler, Volunteer Reserves. (*Courtesy Nick Previté*)

to extend an invitation to a rededication service to be held at the graveside on 9 October.

That close family member, Nick Previté, a grandson of Jack's twin sister Gladys, was asked to submit an inscription for the new gravestone. He chose the family motto, *Pax et Amor* (Peace and Love), a composition that was readily accepted by the Commonwealth War Graves Commission. The rededication service, conducted by the Reverend Tim Flowers CF, chaplain to the 4th Battalion of the Mercian Regiment, began with a call to worship followed by a bidding prayer. Mr Previté then read out 'My Boy Jack', the poem his great-grandmother had treasured during the grieving process for her son. The Reverend Flowers reflected on the significance of the ceremony:

As we approach the 100th anniversary of the end of the Great War, it is a great testament to the work that continues to be done to identify and honour those who fell all those years ago. For the family of Lt John Gillis Butt, it brings to an end a story that began at the very beginning of the war. Although the family have known that he had fallen, it is fitting that they now know his final resting place and that we are able to give him the service that his service so richly deserved. Now known to the family as well as known unto God.

With members of 16 Medical Regiment, Royal Army Medical Corps in attendance, the service concluded with a reading of the Lord's Prayer followed by a blessing. A hundred years on from the end of the war, the Christian faith proved central to the commemoration of a long dead soldier. A wreath laid at the grave by the family read: 'You gave your life for others and now your final resting place is recognized. Never forgotten by your family. God Bless You.' Jack was also commemorated in the Remembrance Sunday service at St Mary the Virgin, Datchet, on 11 November 2018, at which the popular hymn of the First World War, 'O God our Help in Ages Past', was sung.

The rededication of the grave at Hooge Crater Cemetery meant a great deal to the family. The uncertainty that Edward, Helen and Gladys Butt had endured throughout the search for news of John Gillis Butt, and for Edward and his daughter for decades subsequently, had finally received a definitive resolution. Documents relating to their missing relative had been treasured by generations of the family, in the hope that one day there would be a place at which they could pay their respects to Jack's memory in person. Mr Previté commented: 'It was a wonderful service and I am thrilled to know that John has finally been put to rest. The service was made extra special by the presence of so many people. It has brought closure to all the family.' A wreath laid by the family at the Menin Gate read: ' In memory of John Gillis Butt, Lieutenant RAMC. 12 July 1890– 29 October 1914. From your family with grateful thanks. You inspired others who carry on your good works.' Jack's death had not been in vain. He had saved the life of another man, and his sacrifice had stirred others to live by the fine values of devotion to duty and the care of others.

Charles Attwood

> We are the Dead. Short days ago
> We lived, felt dawn, saw sunset glow

The anniversary of Charles's death would continue to be a sorrowful occasion in the Attwood household. Superintendent Henry Attwood inserted a tribute to his son in the *Western Gazette*'s In Memoriam section of 20 April 1917, maintaining the date of death to be 23 April:

Attwood – IN loving memory of Charles, the eldest son of Supt and Mrs Attwood, Somerton, late 90th Winnipeg Rifles, Canada, who was killed in action April 23rd 1915, in France. Gone, but not forgotten.

In contrast, the Commonwealth War Graves Commission records state that Charles died on 25 April, whilst the information Henry had received from the adjutant of 90th Winnipeg Rifles correctly gave the time of death as the early morning of 24 April.

As with the memorialisation of Arthur Greensmith and his comrades in the Sheffield City Battalion, the war experience of the Canadian Division was honoured in verse. In the aftermath of the Second Battle of Ypres, Major John McCrae, a medical officer who had treated many of the men blighted by the German chlorine gas attack within the confines of his primitive dirt-floored dressing station at Essex Farm, wrote his iconic poem 'In Flanders Fields':

> In Flanders fields the poppies blow
> Between the crosses, row on row,
> That mark our place; and in the sky
> The larks, still bravely singing, fly
> Scarce heard amid the guns below.
> We are the Dead. Short days ago
> We lived, felt dawn, saw sunset glow,
> Loved and were loved, and now we lie
> In Flanders fields.
> Take up our quarrel with the foe:
> To you from failing hands we throw
> The torch; be yours to hold it high.
> If ye break faith with us who die
> We shall not sleep, though poppies grow
> In Flanders fields.

Sadly, there would be no cross to mark Charles Attwood's place beneath the Flanders poppies.

In 1920, the Canadian Battlefields Monument Commission organised a competition to design a series of memorials to mark the country's sacrifice during the Great War. Frederick Chapman Clemesha's sculpture *The Brooding Soldier* was selected to commemorate the men lost during the first gas attack of the war at the Second Battle of Ypres between 22 and 24 April 1915. Today the sculpture stands in the village of St Julien, Langemark. Clemesha, a native of Lancashire, had served in the South Saskatchewan Regiment during the war. His design, also known as the St Julien Memorial, comprised a single tower of stone surmounted by the head and shoulders of a soldier wearing a steel helmet, his head bowed in contemplation or prayer. His hands rested on his rifle butt in the reversed arms position, the barrel pointing downwards. The memorial was erected at a height of 11 metres, crafted from a single shaft of granite quarried from the Vosges mountains.

The memorial was inscribed:

THIS COLUMN MARKS THE BATTLEFIELD WHERE 18,000 CANADIANS ON THE BRITISH LEFT WITHSTOOD THE FIRST GERMAN GAS ATTACKS THE 22ND–24TH OF APRIL 1915. 2,000 FELL AND HERE LIE BURIED

Charles Attwood was one of tens of thousands of Canadian soldiers whose bodies were never identified, remaining to this day at the spot where he fell, or in an anonymous grave in a nearby cemetery. The St Julien Memorial was unveiled by HRH the Duke of Connaught on 8 July 1923, with the former Commander-in-Chief of the Allied Armies, Marshal Ferdinand Foch, in attendance. Charles's name was also one of the 55,000 inscribed on the Menin Gate Memorial to the Missing in Ypres.

As in most cities, towns and villages, the people of Somerton saw fit to mark the loss of so many of its men who never came home from war. Fifty-five names, including that of Charles Attwood, were initially inscribed on the memorial, which

Somerton War Memorial. (*Author's collection*)

was situated in a prominent position in the town, in the Market Place directly in front of the path to the Church of St Michael and All Angels. This meant the solemn reminder of sacrifice was also in full view of the police station, although by the date of its dedication by the Reverend Jackson, vicar of Somerton, 21 May 1921, Henry had retired from the force and he and Emma had moved away from the town. However, Charles's sister, Edith, continued to live in Somerton, and would have had a near daily reminder of the loss of her brother.

The memorial consists of a Portland stone statue of a helmeted soldier, the head not dissimilar to that one adorning the St Julien Canadian memorial, with the additional resonance of him resting at arms his rifle. The figure is in full service dress, and the inscription on the pedestal reads:

LEST WE
FORGET

IN GRATEFUL
AND
EVERLASTING

MEMORY OF
THE SOMERTON
MEN/ WHO LAID
DOWN THEIR
LIVES FOR/
THEIR KING
AND COUNTRY
IN THE/ GREAT
WAR/ 1914–1919/

The memorial was paid for from a private subscription campaign which had raised £208 2s 0d. The young man who had left Somerton full of hope of exploring new horizons would remain in the hearts and minds of the citizens of his home town in perpetuity.

Frank Mead

'MY MOTHER MY FATHER, MY BROTHER REMEMBERED … NEVER LOST'

Frank Mead's sacrifice was initially recorded on the Cambrai Memorial to the Missing in the Louverval Military Cemetery, along with more than 7,000 British and South African soldiers whose remains were never identified following the Battle of Cambrai. 'F. Mead' was one of 167 names of alumni of Wilson's School, situated a short distance from the Mead residence, recorded on their memorial, unveiled on 21 October 1921 by Sir John French. In May 1922, Thomas Mead acknowledged receipt of his son's British War and Victory medals.

By the time Thomas Mead died in January 1938, he was a relatively wealthy man, leaving an estate worth £13,734 – over £900,000 in 2020 money – to his wife Elizabeth. Financial wealth, however, could not buy the peace of mind and closure that would have been provided by the opportunity to visit their son's grave to pay their respects and mourn. Meanwhile, Reg Mead kept his dear brother's precious letters, sketchbook and autograph book for sixty-one years until his own death in 1978, before ensuring they were passed down through the Mead family. Still there was no battlefield grave for the family to visit to pay their respects to the remains of their beloved Frank.

Then, in February 2016, the owner of a farm in Anneux was digging a trench in his back garden in order to lay a drainpipe when he came across a shocking discovery. Three bodies were found, with a military shoulder tie attached to one of them. This allowed expert researchers to conclude that the three unidentified soldiers had been members of the 1/23rd London Regiment. This was not an uncommon occurrence, as each year around forty bodies are discovered by French or Belgian landowners whose properties extend across the former battlefields of the First World War.

DNA samples were taken from each of the uncovered corpses, and the Ministry of Defence's Joint Casualty and Compassion Centre set about tracing family members who might be able to provide a matching sample. Consulting the battalion war diary and the records of the Commonwealth War Graves Commission, the identity of the three soldiers was narrowed down to nine possible individuals. DNA matches were found for two of the bodies; Private Henry Wallington of 1/23rd (County of London) Battalion and his comrade Frank Mead, whose great-nephew, Paul Mead, was traced to California.

On 12 June 2019, a funeral with full military honours took place at Hermies Hill British Cemetery, near the town of Albert, for Frank, Henry, and the third, as yet unidentified, soldier. Readings were given by relatives, a firing salute was sounded and the Last Post played. The coffins of the three men were draped in Union flags with wreaths of poppies and the service was led by the Reverend Martin Wainwright, the reserve chaplain to the 4th Battalion of the Princess of Wales's Royal Regiment. The inscription chosen for Frank, whose family were finally able to assign a personal epitaph for him, was:

FROM THE FIELD OF HEROES I EMBRACE, MY MOTHER MY FATHER, MY BROTHER REMEMBERED ... NEVER LOST

Frank's great-nephew, Chris Mead, had been stunned by the news that the aching pain that had been felt in the family for nearly a century could be addressed. 'We couldn't believe it when we heard. It's been an emotional time and we never dreamt of anything like this.' Chris's own father, Frank's nephew, had passed away in 2015, but had ensured that Frank's memory and archive be preserved. 'We had the letters from the trenches but did not know where he [Frank] was. We are just grateful for the opportunity for his story to be told.'

Epilogue

At Westminster Abbey, on 11 November 1920, 'The Funeral Service of a British Warrior' took place, timed to coincide with the second anniversary of the signing of the Armistice. The warrior's coffin had rested at Victoria station overnight, having been transported from Boulogne the previous day. It was placed by a bearer party from the 3rd Battalion Coldstream Guards onto a gun carriage drawn by six black horses of the Royal Horse Artillery. Crowds lined the streets as the coffin made its way across Westminster, stopping first in Whitehall. Here, King George V unveiled the Cenotaph before placing a wreath of red roses and bay leaves on the coffin. The wreath contained a card on which the monarch had expressed the collective esteem and gratitude of the nation of those whose remains would forever be Known unto God:

> In proud memory of those Warriors who died unknown in the Great War.
> Unknown, and yet well-known; as dying, and behold they live.

From the Cenotaph, the carriage made its way down Whitehall to the north door of Westminster Abbey, resting place of kings and queens, of statesmen and poets. While the Cenotaph unveiling was taking place, the congregation inside the abbey sung the hymn 'O God Our Help in Ages Past'. This was followed by prayers and two minutes silence at 11.00 am. The coffin was then met by the abbey's choir, singing 'Brief Life is Here Our Portion'. The coffin was then borne to the west end of the nave through the 1,000-strong congregation, flanked by a guard of honour of 100 Victoria Cross holders from all three branches of the services. The choir sang Psalm 23 before the mourners sang 'Lead Kindly Light'.

The King stepped forward and dropped a handful of French soil onto the coffin as it was lowered into the grave. The traditional funeral hymn 'Abide With Me' was sung, a personal favourite of King George, before Rudyard Kipling's recessional 'God of Our Fathers' was intoned. A silk funeral pall, presented by the Actors' Church Union in memory of their fallen comrades, was placed over the grave. Servicemen kept watch at each corner of the grave as mourners filed past. When the abbey had closed for the night, the living warriors remained on watch, their heads bowed and rifles reversed, over their unknown dead comrade. The scene was illuminated by just four candles.

A hundred sandbags of earth from across the battlefields were used to fill the grace and on 18 November it was covered by a stone inscribed:

A BRITISH WARRIOR WHO FELL IN THE GREAT WAR 1914–1918 FOR KING AND COUNTRY. GREATER LOVE HATH NO MAN THIS.

The concept of the Grave of the Unknown Warrior in Westminster Abbey had been inspired by the Reverend David Railton MC. The Folkestone curate had served as a chaplain with 2nd Battalion Honourable Artillery Company for the duration of the war. Returning to Margate upon relinquishing his commission, Railton pondered on the memory of seeing a grave of an 'unknown comrade' in 1916. Railton recalled the process by which the Tomb of the Unknown Soldier came into being in *Our Empire* magazine in November 1931. The inspiration for the idea of a national monument to the missing 'came to me. It was somehow sent to me – I know not how – in the early part of the year 1916.'

Railton had just returned from the line at dusk after laying to rest the mortal remains of a comrade. He went to a billet in front of Erkingham, near Armentières, at the back of which was a small garden containing a grave. At the head of the grave there stood a rough cross of white wood on which was written in deep black-pencilled letters, 'An unknown British Soldier', and in brackets underneath, 'of the Black Watch'. Railton recalled: 'It was dusk and no one was near except some officers in the billet playing cards. I remember how still it was. Even the guns seemed to be resting, as if to give the gunners a chance to have their tea.'

This incident gave the Scottish cleric Railton cause for reflection:

I love every inch of Scotland. I had served in the earlier days as a private soldier in the ranks of a Scottish Territorial battalion. How I wondered! How I longed to see his folk! But, who was he, and who were they? From which of the lonely mystic glens of old Scotia did he come? Was he a citizen of 'Auld Reekie'? Was he one of the grand old 'Contemptibles'? Was he just a laddie – newly joined – aged eighteen, the only son of a shepherd from the far away Highlands? There was no answer to those questions nor has there ever been yet.

Railton pondered on what could be done to ease the pain of the dead man's loved ones. His clear answer was, 'Let this body – this symbol of him – be carried reverently over the sea to his native land.' This answer proved satisfactory for about five minutes until Railton reminded himself of the fact 'There is a war on', and thought such an aspiration impossible.

Still, in his conversations with other army chaplains, the theme of 'broken' relatives wanting to know the exact locations where they had carried out burials shone through. The beseeching from people who had received the 'missing' telegram was particularly strong. All a padre was allowed to do in response was to provide a map reference.

Returning to his parish in Folkestone in 1919, Railton noted a: '[D]readful year of reaction? Men and nations stumbled back like badly wounded and "gassed" warriors to their homes. The endless shedding of blood ceased but there was no real peace in the souls of men or nations. The mind of the world was in a fever.'

Railton agonised as to the best person to approach with his idea of the repatriation of an unknown soldier, whose tomb could represent the hundreds of thousands of men with unidentified resting places. He was unsure whether Prime Minister David Lloyd George would approve of the idea. Earl Haig might prove more sympathetic but did not enjoy a good relationship with politicians. The Archbishop of Canterbury, Randall Davidson, might not possess the political clout to force Railton's idea to the top of the agenda. He had few doubts that King George V would applaud the idea: 'After all, there had been no nobler or wiser King in this land. I knew the King would hear any citizen. He would, I felt somehow sure, agree, because he understands the hearts of the people.'

But Railton feared the King's advisers would suggest an open space for the memorial, which would be subjected to the creative whims of artists. He was adamant the body of the 'Unknown Comrade' should rest in Westminster Abbey, 'the Parish Church of the Empire'.

Eventually, once 'the rush and noise of "Peace" quarrels seemed to be dying down', Railton wrote to the Right Reverend Bishop Herbert Ryle, then Dean of Westminster, asking 'if he would consider the possibility of burying in the Abbey the body of one of our unknown comrades'. Furthermore, Railton suggested that a flag that had been taken to the battlefields be used to adorn the tomb.

Ryle responded positively, agreeing to carry out the interment within the abbey, but would need War Office permission in order to repatriate one of the many unknown. After political deliberations, which took place in the succeeding few months, Railton was delighted to receive an affirmative response from Ryle:

Dear Mr Railton,

The idea which you suggested to me in August I have kept steadily in view ever since. I have been occupied actively upon it for the last two or three weeks. It has necessitated communication with the War Office, Prime Minister, Cabinet and Buckingham Palace. The announcement which the Prime Minister will, or intends to, make this afternoon, will show how far the Government is ready to co-operate. Once more I express my warm acknowledgement and thanks for your letter.

Yours sincerely Herbert E. Ryle, Bp. October 19, 1920

A careful process was then undertaken to ensure that families whose loved ones had gone missing on the Western Front could subscribe to the notion that the grave in Westminster Abbey might contain their son, husband or father. The body was chosen from unknown British servicemen exhumed from four battle areas: the Aisne, the Somme, Arras and Ypres.

The remains were brought to a corrugated iron hut, which had served as a chapel, at St Pol on the night of 7 November 1920. The General Officer in charge of troops in France and Flanders, Brigadier General L.J. Wyatt, with Colonel Gell, entered the chapel alone, where the four bodies lay on stretchers covered by Union flags. The pair had no idea from which area each of the bodies had come. General Wyatt selected one and the two officers placed it in a plain coffin and sealed it. The other three bodies were reburied.

The following morning, three members of the Royal Army Chaplains' Department, each representing one of the three principal denominational groups within the department – the Church of England, the Roman Catholic Church and the Nonconformist churches – held a service in the chapel before the body was escorted to Boulogne to rest overnight. On 9 November, the coffin was placed inside another, which had been sent over specially from England, made of 2-inch thick oak from a tree that had grown in Hampton Court Palace garden, and was lined with zinc. Within the wrought iron bands of this coffin had been placed a sixteenth-century crusader's sword from the Tower of London collection. The destroyer HMS *Verdun* carried the coffin across the English Channel to Dover, from where it was taken by train to Victoria station, London.

Bishop Ryle suggested that 100 sandbags' worth of French soil be brought to London to fill the grave, and accepted Railton's 'Padre's flag' for its adornment. The only wish of Railton's that did not come to pass was the designation of the tomb as the 'Unknown Comrade' rather than the 'Unknown Warrior', him thinking the latter tending more towards representing solely the army, rather than being inclusive of all the armed services; 'also, it seemed more homely and friendly'. The use of his 'Padre's flag' was of especial symbolic importance to Railton due to its presence at sacramental, ceremonial and committal ceremonies:

> The flag which is now in the Abbey was used during the War at Holy Communion, as a covering for the rough box, or table, altars. It was used at Church Parades and Ceremonial Parades. It was the covering – often the only covering – of the slain, as their bodies were laid to rest. For all I know it may have been used in Belgium or France when the actual 'Unknown Warrior' was slain. For the 'unknown' received exactly the same attention as the 'known'. It is not a new 'bit of bunting' bought for the occasion but a real symbol of every Briton's life. Indeed, it is literally tinged with the life-blood of fellow Britons.

The grave was capped with a black Belgian marble stone, upon which it is still forbidden to walk. Brass from wartime ammunition was melted down with which to engrave the stone with words composed by Bishop Ryle:

BENEATH THIS STONE RESTS THE BODY

OF A BRITISH WARRIOR

UNKNOWN BY NAME OR RANK

BROUGHT FROM FRANCE TO LIE AMONG

THE MOST ILLUSTRIOUS OF THE LAND

AND BURIED HERE ON ARMISTICE DAY

11 NOV: 1920, IN THE PRESENCE OF

HIS MAJESTY KING GEORGE V

HIS MINISTERS OF STATE

THE CHIEFS OF HIS FORCES

AND A VAST CONCOURSE OF THE NATION

THUS ARE COMMEMORATED THE MANY

MULTITUDES WHO DURING THE GREAT

WAR OF 1914 – 1918 GAVE THE MOST THAT

MAN CAN GIVE LIFE ITSELF

FOR GOD

FOR KING AND COUNTRY

FOR LOVED ONES HOME AND EMPIRE

FOR THE SACRED CAUSE OF JUSTICE AND

THE FREEDOM OF THE WORLD

THEY BURIED HIM AMONG THE KINGS BECAUSE HE

HAD DONE GOOD TOWARD GOD AND TOWARD

HIS HOUSE

Around the main inscription, four quotations from the New Testament were included:

The Lord knoweth them that are his (2 Timothy 2:19)
Unknown and yet well known, dying and behold we live (2 Corinthians 6:9)
Greater love hath no man than this (John 15:13)
In Christ shall all be made alive (1 Corinthians 15:22)

In the decade following the tomb's dedication, Railton received numerous letters of thanks and spoke to many relatives of missing men. These people had 'all grasped something of the true meaning':

Those whose loved ones were amongst the 'unknown' know that in this Tomb there may be – there is – resting the body of their beloved. They know also that he is not there himself, though he may often be near. They have, moreover, learnt the unity of all types of men at that grave. They see that in the long run, all men of goodwill are comrades in life, death and the hereafter.

The Unknown Warrior was of anonymous rank, wealth, education or history. From a wealthy home or a slum, education at public school 'or a gypsy', from any corner of the dominions or colonies, or even a sailor from the Royal Naval Division units that served in France. From a generation who grew up in a country with strong religious traditions, Railton noted the man might 'quite likely' be an Anglican communicant, 'or a Roman Catholic, a Jew, a Salvationist, a Wesleyan, a Presbyterian, or a member of any other, or of no religious denomination'. He was representative of all faiths and none.

The wording on the grave declared: 'Thus are commemorated the many multitudes who gave the most that man can give.'

Railton's final reflection was on what the Unknown Warrior might have become had he lived:

Who can say whether or no the War killed in the person of the 'Unknown Warrior' the man who would have been the great 'Genius' – to lead the rising generation in its gigantic tasks? If so, and as Christ saw him fall, it is not hard to think of Him praying again, over a world gone mad, 'Father, forgive them, for they know not what they do.'

For years the families of Lieutenant Gilbert Donnelly, Lieutenant John Gillis Butt and Private Frank Mead could believe that the Unknown Warrior might be their missing loved one. Today they can console themselves with the closure of a final known resting place. It remains the case that enclosed in the tomb could lie the remains of Private William Waller or Lieutenant Willie Lott, Private James William Longden, Private Percy Buck, Private Alfred Pittaway, Lieutenant Angus Macnaghten, Private Arthur Greensmith, Private Charles Attwood, Rifleman Alan Stirling, Rifleman Ernest Blackburn or Second Lieutenant Percy Pope. To the memory of those men and the hundreds of thousands of others who have no known resting place on earth, I dedicate this book.

Bibliography

NEWSPAPERS AND PERIODICALS
Belfast and Irish News
Belfast News-Letter
Belfast Telegraph
Birmingham Daily Gazette
Bournemouth Guardian
Central Somerset Gazette
Daily Sketch
Dewsbury Reporter
Flintshire Observer
Irish News
Larne Times
Leeds Mercury
London Gazette
Middlesex Chronicle
Morning Albertan
Northern Whig
Nottingham Journal
Our Empire
Salisbury and Winchester Journal
Scarborough Mercury
Sheffield Daily Telegraph
Sheffield Independent
Taunton Courier and Somerset Advertiser
Tavistock Gazette
The Globe
The Malburian
The Schoolmaster
The Sphere
The Times
Walsall Advertiser
Western Chronicle
Western Daily Press
Western Gazette
Western Mail
Windsor and Eton Express

Worksop Guardian
Trinity Wesleyan
Yorkshire Evening News
Yorkshire Post

ARCHIVAL SOURCES

Australian War Memorial
W.F. Macbeath, Diaries, AWM PR00675

Imperial War Museum
Department of Documents
W.E. Southgate, IWM DOCS Misc 136(2118)
J. McCauley, IWM DOCS 97/10/1
A.C.L.D Lees, IWM DOCS 91/22/1

Library and Archives of Canada
8th Canadian Infantry Battalion (90th Winnipeg Rifles) War Diary, RG9-III-C-3, R611-78-4-E. Item ID number: 182387
Interview with Lester Stevens, https://www.collectionscanada.gc.ca/first-world-war/interviews/025015-1130-e.html, accessed 3 May 2019
Interview with John Uprichard, https://www.collectionscanada.gc.ca/first-world-war/interviews/025015-1120-e.html, accessed 5 May 2019
Charles Attwood, RG 150, Accession 1992–93/166, Box 296–44, Item Number: 16726

West Yorkshire Archive Service
Upper Wortley Primary School Records, LC/ED93

THE NATIONAL ARCHIVES

War Office: Officers' Services
Lieutenant Gilbert Donnelly, Royal Munster Fusiliers, WO 339/47043 Captain John Butt, Royal Army Medical Corps, WO 339/9823
Lieutenant James Arnold Brewster, The Royal Fusiliers (City of London Regiment), WO 339/17037

British Army war diaries 1914–1922
1 Battalion Royal Minster Fusilier's War Diary. WO 95/1971
1st Battalion Welsh Regiment War Diary, WO 95/2277
9th Battalion King's Royal Rifle Corps, WO 95/1900
12th Battalion King's Royal Rifle Corps, WO 95/2120
12th Battalion York and Lancaster Regiment, WO 95/2365
1/23rd Battalion, The London Regiment, WO 95/2744
94th Infantry Brigade, WO 95/2363

University of Leeds Special Collections
Liddle Collection
Brewster, J.A., LIDDLE/WW1/GS/0196
Blackburn, Ernest, LIDDLE/WW1/GS/0145

FAMILY ARCHIVES
Charles Attwood
John Gillis Butt
Gilbert Donnelly
Arthur Greensmith
Frank Mead
Percy Pope
Alan Stirling

BOOKS AND ARTICLES
Barker, Granville, *The Red Cross in France* (London: Hodder & Stoughton, 1916)
Bartelot, Rev. R.G., *'Lest we forget': a book of remembrance: being a short summary of the service and sacrifice rendered to the Empire during the Great War by one of the many patriotic families of Wessex: the Popes of Wrackleford, co. Dorset* (London: Chiswick Press, 1919)
Bostridge, Mark & Berry, Paul, *Vera Brittain: A Life* (London: Virago, 2008)
Brittain, Vera, *Testament of Youth* (London: Victor Gollancz, 1933)
Cassar, George H., *Hell in Flanders: Canadians at the Second Battle of Ypres* (Toronto: Dundern Press, 2010)
Cook, Tim, *The Secret History of Soldiers: How Canadians Survived the Great War* (New Jersey: Prentice Hall Press, 2018)
Crane, David, *Empires of the Dead: How One Man's Vision led to the Creation of WW1's War Graves* (London: Harper Collins, 2013)
Denman, Terence, *Ireland's Unknown Soldiers: the 16th (Irish) Division in the Great War* (Newbridge: Irish Academic Press, 1992)
Donnelly, Phil, *The Donnellys – the Story of a Belfast Family* (privately published, 2020)
Dunn, J.C., *The War The Infantry Knew*, (London: Abacus, 1994)
Earle, Lionel, *Turn Over the Page* (London: Hutchinson & Company, 1935)
Finnan, Joseph, *John Redmond and Irish Unity: 1912–1918* (New York: Syracuse University Press, 2004)
Fitzpatrick, David, *Politics and Irish Life* (Dublin: Gill & Macmillan, 1977)
Garrod, Lt A. Noel RAMC, 'Notes on the Existence of a Regimental M.O. – At the Front', *St Bartholomew's Hospital Journal*, Vol. XXIII, p.66 January 1916 (London: Adlard & Son, 1916)
Gibson, Ralph & Oldfield, Peter, *Sheffield City Battalion: The 12th (Service) Battalion York & Lancaster Regiment* (Barnsley: Pen & Sword, 2016)
Gladstone, Viscount, *William G.C. Gladstone: A Memoir* (London: Nisbet & Co. Ltd., 1918)

Gosse, Capt Philip RAMC, *Memoirs of a Camp-Follower* (London: Longmans, Green & Co., 1934)

Graham, Stephen, *The Challenge of the Dead* (London: Cassell, 1921)

Grayson, Richard, *Belfast Boys: How Unionists and Nationalists Fought and Died Together in the First War* (London: Continuum, 2009)

Hanson, Neil, *The Unknown Soldier: The Story of the Missing of the Great War* (London: Corgi Books, 2007)

Hodgkinson, Peter, 'Clearing the Dead', Birmingham University Centre for First World War Studies, *Online publication*, Sept 2007, Vol. 3:1

Jeffrey, Keith, *Ireland and the Great War* (Cambridge University Press, 2000)

Johnstone, Tom, *Orange, Green and Khaki: the Story of the Irish Regiments in the Great War, 1914–18* (Dublin: Gill & Macmillan, 1992)

Joint War Committee of the British Red Cross Society and Order of St John of Jerusalem, *Reports by the Joint War Committee and the Joint War Finance Committee of the British Red Cross Society and Order of St John of Jerusalem in England* (London: HMSO, 1921)

Knowles, Valerie, *Forging Our Legacy: Canadian Citizenship and Immigration, 1900–1977. Citizenship and Immigration Canada* (Ottawa: Citizenship and Immigration Canada, 2000)

Lago, M., & Furbank P.N. (eds), *Selected Letters of E.M. Forster, v, 1879–1920* (London: Collins, 1983)

MacCarthy, Carthach, *Archdeacon Tom Duggan: In peace and in war* (Dublin: Blackwater Press, 1994)

Macnaghten, Angus, *Missing: An Account of the Efforts Made to Find an Officer of the Black Watch Reported 'Missing' on 29th October, 1914, During the First Battle of Ypres* (Bala: Dragon Press, 1970)

McCance, Captain S., *History of the Royal Munster Fusiliers* (Aldershot: Gale & Polden, 1927)

Orr, Philip, *The Road to the Somme: Men of the Ulster Division Tell Their Story* (Newtownards: Blackstaff Press, 1987)

Ponsonby, Sir Frederick, *The Grenadier Guards in the Great War of 1914–1918* (London: MacMillan, 1920)

Reed, Paul, *Great War Lives: A Guide for Family Historians* (Barnsley: Pen & Sword, 2010)

Reed, Paul, *Walking Ypres* (Barnsley: Pen & Sword, 2017)

Reed, Paul, *Walking the Somme* (Barnsley: Pen & Sword, 2018)

Richardson, Mike, *Keeping The Old Flag Flying: The World War 1 Memoir of Kenneth Basil Foyster Canadian Soldier, Prisoner and Internee* (Peterborough: Book Printing UK, 2019)

Rooney, Kevin & Heartfield, James, *The Blood-Stained Poppy: A Critique of the Politics of Commemoration* (Zero Books, 2019)

Schneider, Eric F., 'The British Red Cross Wounded and Missing Enquiry Bureau: A Case of Truth-Telling in the Great War': *War in History*, 1997 4(3), 295–315

Steel, Nigel & Hart, Peter, *Passchendaele: The Sacrificial Ground* (London: Cassell, 2001)

Sparling, Richard A., *History of the 12th Service Battalion, York and Lancaster Regiment* (Sheffield: J.W. Northend, 1920)

Van Emden, Richard, *The Quick and the Dead: Fallen Soldiers and Their Families in the Great War* (London: Bloomsbury, 2012)

Van Emden, Richard, *Meeting the Enemy: The Human Face of the Great War* (London: Bloomsbury, 2013)

Van Emden, Richard, *Missing: The Need for Closure after the Great War* (Barnsley: Pen & Sword, 2019)

Wadsworth, Jacqueline, *Letters from the Trenches: The First World War by Those Who Were There* (Barnsley: Pen & Sword, 2014)

Wadsworth, Jacqueline, *Weymouth, Dorchester & Portland in the Great War* (Barnsley: Pen & Sword, 2015)

Warr, Peter, *Sheffield in the Great War* (Barnsley: Pen & Sword, 2014)

Wickham, E.R., *Church and People in an Industrial City* (Cambridge: Lutterworth Press, 1962)

WEBSITES

www.danhillhistory.com (Percy Buck)

http://datchethistory.org.uk (John Gillis Butt)

www.dewsburysacrifices.org (Ernest Blackburn)

www.ww1hull.com (Sharp Street, Hull Street Memorial)

Index